The
BOARD OF DIRECTORS
and
EFFECTIVE MANAGEMENT

The

BOARD OF DIRECTORS
and
EFFECTIVE MANAGEMENT

Harold Koontz

Mead Johnson Professor of Management
University of California
Los Angeles

McGRAW-HILL BOOK COMPANY
New York   Toronto   London   Sydney

THE BOARD OF DIRECTORS AND EFFECTIVE MANAGEMENT

35314

1234567890VB72106987

To

Judge Chester Pendleton

able scholar, astute judge and businessman,
and appreciated benefactor

PREFACE

This book has been primarily inspired by my long interest in management as an executive, university professor, and corporation director. The need for it was first brought to my attention when I was leading seminars in management theory and practice for top managers in this country and overseas. Many top executives told me that one of their major obstacles to making management effective was that many members of their boards of directors understood neither modern management nor their appropriate role in managing. Moreover, my own observation of board operations, first as a subordinate to presidents in two companies and later as a private and public business director, convinced me that their criticism was justified.

As a result, I have attempted in this book to define the role of boards of directors in top management and in assuring that a company is, in fact, well managed. Over the past six years I have not only tried out these concepts in practice, but tested them against some 1,500 top executives and directors in this country and abroad. In Australia over the past five years, in response to the specific demand of many chief executive officers, I have led a series of special conferences limited to company directors. As might be suspected, I did not find, in this test market of ideas and operations, unanimous agreement with the concepts advanced here. But these concepts do seem to fit fairly well the kinds of things a board can and must do to fulfill its responsibilities.

It is my belief that boards of directors are far from being an historic legal anachronism. On the contrary, I am convinced that they are an important and permanent part of the managerial hierarchy in all enterprises. Moreover, I discern clear signs that boards will become an increasingly effective force and will more fully realize the nature and importance of the position in which they have been placed by law and the demands of society. In addition, there is every reason to expect that boards must take a significant place in the scheme of modern management, an area of practice where underlying science and technology are growing fast.

As this book attempts to show, boards of directors become effective not only by what decisions they render and how they make them. Their effectiveness also depends upon how well they understand and discharge their responsibilities and legal liabilities. It is also determined by factors in board composition, board leadership, and the way in which the directors coordinate their activities and cooperate with operating executives.

My primary debt for assistance in writing this book is owed to the large numbers of executives with whom I have worked, whose interest in the growing knowledge of management I have been privileged to share, and who have thoughtfully criticized the ideas I have advanced. These intelligent leaders, whom I have found so devoted to their enterprises, are too numerous to mention by name. However, I wish to acknowledge a special debt to John A. Calfas, Esq. who gave unstintingly of his time and that of his staff in helping me untangle in a brief chapter the legal complexity of directors' liabilities.

In gathering certain basic material, I have also enjoyed the able research assistance of Howard J. Schwab of the University of California (Los Angeles) Law School. I also wish to express my appreciation for the enthusiastic, intelligent, and competent assistance of Miss Judy Finer, who patiently prepared several drafts of this manuscript and aided me in some of the research.

But, as can be easily understood, my appreciation to those who helped me so much cannot extend to making them responsible for any shortcomings in this book.

Harold Koontz

CONTENTS

CONTENTS

chapter *1*

DIRECTORS AND
MANAGEMENT

In the United States, over three-fourths of the state laws under which corporations are established require that the corporation be "managed" by a board of directors, usually comprised of at least three members. The logic behind this requirement is that the corporation is an artificial entity "existing only in contemplation of the law," established by a sovereign power through contract with a group of members (in business, the shareholders). As such, this fictitious person must have real persons who are responsible for management. Historically, this responsibility has been placed in a plural executive, the board of directors.

A board of directors charged with such responsibility is common not only in the United States. Boards, commissions, or committees in similar positions of responsibility exist in virtually every part of the world. It is an interesting commentary on human affairs that, except for relatively rare instances of monarchy or dictatorship, power over enterprises of all sorts has tended to rest in groups. Even in authoritarian societies, one finds groups holding considerable power over individual enterprises or segments of enterprises. This should not be surprising. It attests to the fact that people have historically distrusted placing too much power in the hands of any individual.

The origin of the corporation itself goes far back into antiquity. The Code of Hammurabi in 2083 B.C. gave Babylonians a type of special partnership with long life through which business could be carried on for years. The ancient Romans, probably borrowing from the Greeks, used a corporate form, the *societates,* considered as an individual person in place of others with limited liability and a board of directors required at its formation. In the thirteenth cen-

1

tury, Pope Innocent IV developed the concept of the corporation as an artificial entity created by papal authority. And in the late Middle Ages, with the rise of towns, guilds, and merchants, the chartered company came to be widely used.

The modern business board of directors owes its immediate ancestry to the board of proprietors of the early English joint stock company. This form of business, developed from the earlier use of corporations and the common law partnership, provided for joint ownership of a business by a number of persons, some or all of whom often had limited liability. As the numbers of joint owners increased, and opportunities for major owners or insiders to manipulate funds likewise grew, principles of common law as well as the demands of investors required establishment of a board to stand in the place of the joint owners. This device was carried over into English practice and law and subsequently into the corporation statutes of American states.

Both historically and practically, whenever power or funds have been entrusted by a group to individual managers or entrepreneurs, the practice has been to establish a board to see that the resources given to an enterprise are well managed. It is, therefore, both logical and practical that the board of directors be placed in the position of *managing* a company, or more accurately of *seeing to it* that the company is well managed. This means simply that a board should undertake certain managerial functions itself and regularly pursue other activities to assure itself that the entire company is so managed as to achieve appropriate goals set by the board.

THE PRESENT MANAGEMENT REVOLUTION

The role of the board of directors should become more prominent as the importance of managing is increasingly recognized. Yet, despite broad acceptance, particularly since World War II, of management's importance as an intellectually based art, with great obligations to and opportunities for society, boards of directors have not yet come to be generally regarded as a key organizational factor in this revolution.

The organization of human beings for the attainment of common objectives is a phenomenon as old as organized society itself; but the scientific approach to management is primarily a product of the twentieth century. In terms of a widespread realization that scientific knowledge applicable to management practice is available, this approach has received its primary impetus only in the past quarter-century. To bring the role of the board of directors into focus in the light of the present management epoch is the purpose of this book.

First, however, it is desirable to look at the nature of the present emphasis on managing. The effective company director, while he may not be able to manage a company day by day, must take some part in managing and must assure himself that the company is well managed. To do this he must understand not only when it is well managed, but also what he can do to make sure that he, as a director, is contributing effectively to adequate management. This is his major responsibility. But to meet this obligation, he must understand the nature of management.

WHAT IS MANAGEMENT?

The task of the manager, regardless of his level in an enterprise or the type of enterprise, is to establish an internal enterprise environment for effective and efficient operation of individuals working together in groups. Such an environment is characterized by a commonality of understood purpose, an intentional structure of roles, the removal of obstructions to performance, and the motivation of individuals for performance. The manager, then, is in a very real sense an environment creator. His job is to design and operate an environment where people, working together in groups, contribute as individuals to the attainment of group purposes.

It is only in the sense of environment creation that the manager gets things done through people. The manager is not a manipulator, a practicing psychiatrist. He is rather a person who recognizes that people of all kinds respond to an environment, that most people want to accomplish something and that, in the long run, rewards of any kind come only to those who do.

To see the manager's task as one of designing an environment for performance is to see it as an electronic engineer, an architect, or a physician sees his task. Such persons are in a very real sense artists who use underlying science—organized knowledge—to create a product that yields optimum results, usually applying compromises, or "blends," of knowledge and reality to accomplish the desired end result. It should not be forgotten that mere knowledge in the form of science does not in itself create; only knowledge applied to solve a problem or to accomplish a desired result is truly creative.

The Goal of Managing. A manager's task, like that of other artists, involves an economic goal. His work must be effective, in the sense of reaching some desired goal, and it must also be efficient. In this sense it is the manager's task to accomplish as much of a desired goal as possible with the least input of resources—human time and effort, materials, and money. In non-business enterprises, as well as in business, inputs are always essentially economic. It is therefore understandable that managers are regarded as trustees of human and material resources.

The only problem in comparing managers in business and non-business enterprises is that of distinguishing between enterprise objectives or goals. Every manager, it would appear, should seek to obtain the optimum surplus of outputs in terms of enterprise goals with the minimum of inputs. In business this is measured by profits. In most other kinds of enterprises, where goals or objectives are not objectively verifiable (or at least have not been made so), there is no demonstrated measure of outputs. Efficiency, as well as effectiveness, is therefore difficult or impossible to measure.

The Major Environmental Elements. It is widely agreed that any managed situation, any formally organized group, must have clearly understood common purposes, with means of determining priority where purposes are multiple and may conflict. But while commonality of purpose is easy to perceive as the major requisite for organized life, it is not so easy to make operative. As many top managers in all kinds of enterprise have found, it is often extremely difficult to spell out the overall objectives of the enterprise in quantitatively or qualitatively verifiable terms. It is likewise extremely difficult to break basic objectives into derivative goals suitable for subunits of an enterprise. In addition, one of the most formidable tasks of any top manager is establishing meaningful policies that will give subordinate managers needed discretion to be imaginative and creative in their decision making and yet channel their thinking so that their decisions contribute effectively to company goals. There are further difficulties in communicating purpose, goals, and policies. It sometimes appears to top managers, including directors, that no matter how clearly an objective or policy is framed, if it can possibly be misunderstood, it will!

Another essential to managed enterprise is the existence of an intentional structure of roles. As Lord Wilfred Brown has wisely pointed out:

Formalization of organization delineates authority or roles, and prescribed policies make clear to people the area in which they have freedom to act. Without a clearly defined area of freedom there is no freedom. This, in fact, is a very old story reaching down through the history of mankind: there is no real freedom without laws.[1]

Or, put another way, people must always operate in some kind of role. Unless these are properly defined and integrated, there can be no teamwork. In emphasizing this, this does not imply, of course, that roles must be spelled out in such detail that there is no room for imagination, creativity, and job enlargement. A role may be clear without being detailed. Far from making people organizational automatons, an intentional structure of roles can and should make them effective team members with adequate room for creativeness and imagination where these are desired.

A major segment of a manager's task in establishing an environment for performance is to see that obstructions to performance are removed if at all possible. Because team roles often cannot be made clear, cannot easily adapt to changed conditions as fast as necessary, may be misunderstood by group participants, or cannot be performed as planned—and because these and other factors may cause impediments beyond an individual's control—performance

---

[1] "What Is Work?", *Harvard Business Review*, Vol. 40, No. 5, p. 127, September–October, 1962.

may suffer. In this case, the responsible manager should remove the obstructions if he can. If, as is often the case, the removal of obstructions is beyond his control, he should be given the opportunity, indeed the obligation, to press upwards in the organization structure to accomplish their removal.

The importance of this aspect of the manager's task rests on the obvious fact that a superior cannot expect performance if obstructions exist. As a general rule, where obstructions are removed, various motivating factors, including the natural desire for accomplishment, will tend to assure performance by those qualified. It is strange that too few managers see this duty as an essential part of their task. But in the clinical situations where this author has seen this element earnestly worked upon, the results in performance and morale have been spectacular. To be sure, this requires of the manager an attitude of service to subordinates, patient leadership, and an ability to analyze problems and design solutions.

To design an environment which conduces to a desired performance, a manager hardly needs to be reminded that people do things because they want to, because they find it worth their while to, or because they must. As can be seen, these motivations for performance are primarily resultants of the environment in which people operate. Compensation and managerial authority (which normally carries with it the power to grant or withhold rewards or impose sanctions) are two important kinds of environmental factors to which people respond. Other factors are status, personal power, peer approval, or the simple satisfaction of achievement.

For example, one of the most effective techniques, not immediately (if at all) related to pay or power, is a systematic, formal, and regular review of an individual's performance and plans. Experience in a large number of companies that have used this technique for divisional manager review, and in a smaller number of companies that have employed it beyond the general division level to the lowest level of supervision, has attested to the efficacy of this environmental device. There appears to be adequate evidence that such reviews strongly motivate people to performance. This motivation seems to arise partly from desire for peer approval, partly from desire to participate in solving enterprise problems, partly from the satisfaction of obtaining approval of courses of action (and thereby more meaningful delegation of authority), and partly from the opportunity to take advantage of the presence of superiors to get impediments to performance removed. Other techniques might be mentioned, but the scarcity of such techniques and the demonstrated motivational powers of the technique of review strongly suggest the need for more research to find additional methods of this kind.

THE MANAGEMENT PROCESS

In analyzing the task of the manager, there is no better way to look at managing than as a process—a series of actions definitely conducing to an end. In classifying the operations of an enterprise, one should differentiate between those which are *enterprise* functions, such as marketing and manufacturing, and those that are managerial. One of the most useful methods of classifying managerial functions and seeing the managerial job as a process is to group *managerial* activities under the categories of planning, organizing, staffing, directing, and controlling.[2] This classification reflects the way perceptive practitioners see their tasks and gives a clear, completely operational concept of what managers, as managers, do. Yet even as we break the managerial task into these five functions, it is apparent that they are not mutually exclusive. Nor should they be. On the contrary, one would expect the managerial job and the process of managing to represent a reasonably closed system of interrelated functions.

Planning. Planning is the fundamental function of managers. It involves a selection from among alternative goals, policies, procedures, and programs. In other words, planning comprises deciding what objectives or goals are desired and determining means of reaching them. Planning is, of course, decision making since it in-

[2] For a more thorough analysis of these functions see H. Koontz and C. O'Donnell, *Principles of Management*, 3d ed., McGraw-Hill Book Company, Inc., New York, 1964.

volves selecting among alternatives. To aid in accomplishing objectives, there are, for example, policies relating to prices, competition, and financing; programs of production, management training, and new product development; procedures requiring a specific method of handling paper, people, or products. The essential element of planning, then, is choosing a course of action for the future in the light of desired objectives, and determining the most effective and efficient way of accomplishing such goals.

Organizing. Organizing involves a determination and enumeration of activities required to achieve objectives, the grouping of these activities, the assignment of such groups to a department headed by a manager, the delegation of authority and exaction of responsibility to carry them out, and provision for coordination of authority and informational relationships horizontally and vertically in the organization structure. Organizing, therefore, is the means by which an intentional structure of roles is established so that individuals, acting within them, contribute to the accomplishment of group objectives. Thus, organization structure is not an end in itself but a tool for accomplishing objectives.

Staffing. Staffing entails manning, and keeping manned, the positions provided for by the organization structure. This function of a manager necessitates defining requirements for the jobs to be done, selecting candidates for positions, and training or otherwise developing candidates and incumbents to accomplish their tasks effectively. This function also includes necessary inventory and appraising of individuals for role requirements of the organization. In other words, the objectives of an enterprise or a department and the means of reaching them are a function of planning; the structuring of roles and role relationships for people to fill is a function of organizing; and the placing of qualified people in these roles is a function of staffing.

Directing. Directing embraces guiding, supervising, and teaching subordinates, to ensure that they understand the objectives they are to accomplish, the means by which they are to accomplish them, and their individual roles in accomplishing these objectives. Directing largely comprises interpersonal relationships and communication; it imposes a continuous responsibility on the superior to make sure that subordinates understand their tasks.

Likewise, primarily through teaching and example, the manager who directs well will make his subordinates see how their self-interests and personal goals may be satisfied by accomplishing enterprise goals, particularly if proper motivating factors are built into the job role of each person. Communication is the essence of directing, but it is wasteful unless a superior has something to communicate and knows to whom he should communicate it. Moreover, communication is not a one-way process. It also implies receiving information and suggestions from subordinates.

Control. Control is the measurement and correction of activities of those for whom a manager is responsible to make sure that goals are accomplished. It thus involves measuring performance, correcting negative deviations, and assuring accomplishment of plans. Although planning must precede control, plans are not usually self-achieving. The emphasis on control is measuring activities, not people—but the measurement must, of course, be done through people, since they are the means by which activities are accomplished. Likewise, control does not necessarily imply pressure, but rather measuring and assisting in correcting for deviations. Obviously, the best kind of control is self-control, where an individual understands what is expected of him, knows his position, knows how well he is doing, and takes steps on his own to correct his actions or to redraw his own plans so as to meet objectives.

The managerial function of control involves "closing the loop" of managerial functions. If performance against plans is off course, correcting the deviation may require new plans, restructuring roles (reorganization), better teaching or supervision (directing), or revised staffing through such means as better training or selection. It may be argued that this makes the managerial function of control overlap other managerial functions; but to conceive of control as stopping short of correction is to imply that a manager is controlling only when he is measuring. Certainly, no company would think it had adequate quality control if all it did was to measure the quality specification of its product and throw the rejects in a trash can. Control must imply action, and the action taken will necessarily involve other managerial functions. Moreover, closing the loop emphasizes that managerial functions comprise an interrelated system of activities.

What of Other Functions? It may be argued that the manager undertakes other functions, such as coordinating, motivating, integrating, or communicating. It is true that all of these are important to the management process. However, it does not seem that they can be separated as operationally as can the five functions outlined above.

In the first place, to say that a manager's function is to coordinate is essentially to say that a manager's function is to manage. Coordination of effort is obtained through establishing clear and verifiable goals or plans; designing clear-cut roles and role relationships; properly appraising, selecting, and training people; patiently teaching and guiding individuals; and exercising control.

Furthermore, even though motivation is obviously important, it is certainly best evoked in an environment where people have a commonality of understood purpose, where their role and role relationships are clear, where they are well appraised, selected and trained, where the superior gives them patient guidance and teaching, and where they know how well they are doing. Motivation, like coordination, is largely the result of all the manager's functions. Moreover, proper development of role and role relationships implies building motivational factors into the position itself.

One may speak of integrating in the same way. Moreover, since communication pervades all the functions of managers and lies at the core of the directing function, it would be redundant to distinguish it as a separate function.

The Board of Directors and the Management Process. If the board of directors is to discharge its managerial responsibilities, every board member should understand the management process and the principles underlying it. Otherwise, they may overlook certain basic elements of managing and thereby fail to meet their responsibilities.

Putting this another way, effective boards of directors must:

1. Comprehend what management is if they expect to be responsible for the managing of a company

2. Understand the elements and fundamental principles of management if they are to have some guidelines as to what *effective* management in their various companies implies

3. Clearly appreciate their managerial role as well as the role of the top officers to whom they will necessarily entrust most of the actual operating management of the company

Without this minimum knowledge it is hard to see how a board of directors can competently discharge its responsibility. In fact, a common complaint of top operating managers has been that board members do not understand the task of managing and their position in it.

BASIC CHALLENGES TO MODERN MANAGERS

To put the task of the modern manager in perspective and thereby see some of the fundamental problems facing boards of directors, let us summarize some of the most important challenges facing managers today. There are doubtless many not outlined here, and certainly many others can be derived from each of those we shall consider. Moreover, these challenges face managers at all levels and in all enterprises.

As one might expect, the challenges facing managers are related to the unprecedented quickening of change brought about during the past half-century by two world wars, a long cold war, and a space race. They are likewise related to a vigorous period of worldwide super-competition, a world-wide rivalry for ideas, men, resources, markets, and progress. These challenges, along with the inherent importance and complexity of managing, must be dealt with by every enterprise if it is to survive and succeed in the years ahead.

Ensuring Needed Flexibility in Management. A major challenge to managers is that of needed flexibility in the face of change. Change in the external environment of an enterprise implies that those responsible for the internal environment must not only be aware of the external, not only be able to move with it, but, in order to have time to plan, be able to forecast it. It means that effective managment is flexible management. It requires that a manager understand resistances to change, especially those rooted in human nature. As the scientist Edward Teller has so aptly said, "The most inert material I have found in my scientific explorations is the human mind, with one exception: a group of human minds."

Related to this challenge are inflexibilities imposed on managers. These are of many types. They include the stubbornly inert network of government regulations and labor rules and practices; the tendency for companies to regard their policies as inscribed on stone instead of designed to structure future action in the light of changed environments; the extensive procedures, found in all enterprise, which stultify thinking and tie up action; the fear or inability to depart from precedents; and the already mentioned natural resistance of human beings to change.

The alert company is faced with a need for flexibility to meet change in the face of many built-in inflexibilities in both the internal and external environments. To meet this problem requires a high order of imagination and innovativeness, careful study of environmental factors, analysis of strengths and weaknesses, and programs for deciding upon wise courses of change and of instituting change.

Providing a Balanced Environment for Creativity. One of the major problems facing all managers is how to create an environment for innovation in roles where this is needed, recognizing at the same time that all social existence involves a high degree of conformity, beginning with language. Any group operation implies some conformity, and any efficient group activity implies the exercise of authority. What is needed is balanced design of roles, allowing each individual to be creative and imaginative where we wish him to be, yet requiring him to conform where he must if the group operation is to succeed.

The question is not conformity, but how much conformity. The question of formalized management is not a matter of dividing practitioners into a category of "Theory X" or "Theory Y"[3] but rather

---

[3] Made famous by Douglas McGregor in *The Human Side of Enterprise,* McGraw-Hill Book Company, Inc., New York, 1960, pp. 33–57.

one of whether a manager is establishing by his formal organization structure, his formal plans, or his formal controls, an internal environment that removes obstacles to and supports desired individual and group performance.

Balancing the Carrot and the Stick. As the British *Economist* said in an editorial some twenty years ago, "the human donkey requires either a carrot in front or a stick behind it to goad it into activity." Perhaps in pursuing our social and managerial goals we have tended to lose sight of this. Our pressing for equality—through seniority, level pay, guaranteed wages, executive bonuses not based on individual performance—may have removed much of the stick. Through taxation, social security from womb to tomb, and other programs, we may have taken away much of the carrot. Likewise, through government limitations on proprietary interests, such as in patents, and increased government control over private decisions through regulation and informal "guidelines," both the carrot and the stick may have been somewhat whittled away.

This is a matter for real concern. How can managers maintain incentives (either through the carrot or the stick) without abandoning desirable aims of social security and economic equality? How can we still have worthwhile social goals and still preserve an interest in accomplishment? Or, as the *Economist* put it, "How can the carrot and the stick be combined with a pleasant life for the donkey?"

Coping with Increased Sophistication in Management. A fourth challenge facing all managers is the increasing sophistication in all aspects of management, particularly planning and control. As the

---

Theory X managers (defined as "traditional") are described as those who regard people as disliking work, needing therefore to be coerced, controlled, and threatened, and preferring to be led. Theory Y managers are those who find expenditure of human effort in work as natural as play or rest, who see that man will exercise self-direction and self-control in the service of objectives to which he is committed, who see the human being as one who seeks responsibility, who recognize that imagination and creativity are widely distributed in the population, and who see the intellectual potentialities of the average human being as only partially utilized in modern industrial life.

techniques of the physical sciences in particular and of the behavioral sciences to a far lesser extent have been introduced into management, the task of the manager has become increasingly complex. Although practice has been slow in adopting the newer techniques such as operations research, the use of models and systems, and the new information technologies, there is no doubt that the company of the future will increasingly rely upon these scientific and systematic approaches to solve business problems. In addition, companies who use these new tools—along with many of the less sophisticated tools such as variable budgeting, network analyses (e.g., PERT), and formalized product planning—will certainly have a tremendous advantage over those companies who do not. Through sharper planning and better control, managing is certain to become more efficient.

Some of the lag in actual practical use of these newer techniques borrowed from the physical sciences has occurred because too many managers do not understand them and too many experts have invested them with a mystic mumbo-jumbo that makes understanding difficult. There is too much insistence on pure mathematics as a means of appreciating the use of these techniques, where there should be emphasis on the key importance of conceptualizing problem relationships. The manager needs to know the principles behind these tools, and a working knowledge of mathematics may be desirable. But requiring the practicing manager to know all the mathematics is like asking him to know how to design a typewriter before he has his secretary type a letter.

Achieving Better and More Useful End Product Development. Important as it is to expand the frontiers of knowledge in the new techniques and adopt the newer approaches, it is even more important for creative minds to develop better ways of making this knowledge operational. This applies, of course, to the new techniques and approaches of the physical sciences, but it applies as much if not more to findings of the behavioral sciences, which to date appear to have had little real influence on managers and their operations.

Taking Advantage of New Vistas of Information. Still another major challenge facing all managers—and one which promises to change their roles materially—relates to new vistas of information and new ways of systematizing information. It has been well said that "the reach of the executive is determined by the information system at his command" or that "to manage is to manage information."

This means, however, that the manager must receive information, preferably of a forecast nature, that is material to the task at hand, that is weighed against time limits, that measures performance against goals, and that indicates why and where actions are missing goals.

Our problem today appears not to be data processing, storage, or retrieval, but rather data indigestion. The challenge lies in information design, both of needed information inputs and of information outputs. It is one of solving the problem of data indigestion while keeping abreast of a broadening spectrum of data and looking deep into its levels. It is dangerous for a manager to rely wholly on averages; it is meaningless, for example, for a program to be on time "on the average" when one little part three months late will delay an entire program.

In some respects, the present so-called "information revolution" is simply a deluge of data on an increasing scale of complexity, volume, and kind, with greater reliance on data not traditionally provided by conventional accounting systems. But this deluge of data has too often not led to more or better *information*—i.e., data that inform someone. In fact, looking at the situation today, one is reminded of an automated factory in the form of data-processing equipment, where we pick up what materials are lying around on the data floors of our company, and then wonder why the "product" coming from this factory is inadequate for the customer's needs. Clearly, what is required here is the same thing that is required in the development of new products. First, the manager must determine what he needs by way of information; then, backing his requirements through the "factory," he must determine what is needed by way of information inputs. This calls for special design, an art not yet very far developed.

Assuring the Quality of Management. Perhaps the most formidable challenge before managers today is that of assuring the quality of management. It has been well said that the most direct of all control is controlling the quality of managers, simply because well qualified managers make fewer mistakes and require fewer controls. Despite tremendous advances in both management appraisal and training, needs appear to be greater than ever before.

To be sure, some progress is being made. In recent years businesses and other enterprises have been moving toward the sensible system of appraising managerial performance by comparing actual results against verifiable quantitative and qualitative goals. If these are properly developed and structured consistently with other goals of an enterprise, this system has the great merit of tying performance tightly into the operations of an enterprise. Likewise, as this system has developed, it has shown the way toward information needs. And by helping in information design, it has aided in getting the right information to the right person, thereby hastening the day of control through self-control.

But good as such performance appraisals are, they are not good enough. To remove elements of doubt or luck, and to get a better picture of probable future results, steps must be taken to audit or appraise the quality of managing itself. How well does a person plan, organize, staff, direct, and control? By addressing ourselves to the principles of management, we may soon be able to frame and ask fairly objective questions which can cast useful light on these subjects. But this cannot be done without considerable thought and experimentation, or without understanding the essence of the managerial task.

SOCIAL RESPONSIBILITIES OF BOARDS OF DIRECTORS

A popular subject of reflection and discussion in recent years has been the social responsibilities of managers, particularly business managers. It is frequently assumed or implied that there is some inconsistency between good management or good business and the requirements of society. Actually, nothing could be further from the truth.

In the first place, an effective manager is one who designs and maintains an environment so as to utilize material and human resources in the most efficient way. This does not mean that the manager regards human beings as inert instruments, such as material resources. Rather, it means that effective management takes into account human beings, their feelings and desires, their cultures and relationships. To do otherwise is to operate neither effectively nor efficiently.

In the second place, every type of enterprise has a practical and unavoidable obligation to be responsive to its social, political, ethical, economic, and technological environment. Not to recognize this obligation is to manage unrealistically, since no enterprise can expect to succeed over any period of time unless it is responsive to its environment. Basically, therefore, social responsibility is a matter of recognizing and reacting to the social environment in which the executive finds himself.

To put this in more realistic terms, a business enterprise exists as an economic instrument of society. Those who manage it fulfill their social obligations only if they obtain results (in terms of products or services) which society wants, at the least cost in terms of material and human resources. Operating as it must in an external environment with considerable social, political, ethical, economic, and technical elements, the successful business will—as history shows—be one that recognizes its weaknesses and strengths and responds to the opportunities offered by this environment.

If a company is well managed, therefore, it will attempt both to optimize its use of resources for results desired and to be responsive to its external environment. However, as we shall see, one of the major problems of managers absorbed in their jobs is to recognize the impact of a changing external environment. And one of the main functions of any board of directors is to make sure that they do so.

chapter 2

BASIC AUTHORITY AND
FUNCTIONS OF BOARDS

In the business corporation, board members legally stand in the place of the real owners of the corporation, the stockholders. In this position, they are not legal agents in the sense that they must do the individual shareholder's bidding, but are rather representatives of the stockholders as a group. They are in much the same position as government legislators. While these are elected by voters, they are expected to represent them as a group and to use their own judgment in decisions, acting in what they believe to be the best interests of those they represent. The position of corporate boards is quite similar to that of other boards and commissions. In the typical university, the board of trustees or regents are expected to represent the public, alumni, faculty, and students in governing the university and seeing that it is well managed. In government agencies, the typical commission is appointed or elected to represent the public interest.

As representatives of the stockholders, therefore, the directors have the authority to exercise the powers of the corporation—subject only to restrictions imposed by the laws of the state and the Federal government—as such powers are conferred upon it by shareholders through the articles of incorporation (charter) or company by-laws.

In other words, the stockholders own the corporation and the corporation owns the assets of the business. Although this distinction may appear tenuous, it has tremendously important legal implications. Among these are the separation of the liabilities of the corporation from those of the stockholders, thereby limiting the liability of the latter; a legal immortality apart from the transient nature of real persons; and an ability to enter into contracts and to own property quite distinct from the legal powers of individual stockholders.

AUTHORITY OF BOARDS OF DIRECTORS

The corporation is established by contract with a sovereign power—in the United States, normally a state—and its authority is conferred by this contract. Some corporations have been established by special legislative acts, but most are created by the various states under general incorporation acts that set forth procedures by which the privilege of incorporation can be obtained, the powers of corporations so created, and limitations on their authority. Since it is a settled principle of law that a sovereign power cannot contract away its sovereignty, all corporation charters are issued in contemplation of existing law and of all future legislation that may be necessary for the protection of the health, morals, safety, and welfare of the people, or for effective prosecution of any other essential incidents of sovereignty. A state may thus charter a corporation to manufacture and sell alcoholic beverages, but this contract must give way to any later legislation outlawing any such activity.

As indicated above, the board of directors, as managing head of the corporation, has authority to exercise the corporate powers, subject to any limitations placed by stockholders in the charter or by-laws. However, except where power to do so is reserved to the stockholders, by-laws usually may be changed by the board. In addition to repeating many of the powers outlined in the articles of incorporation or the charter, typical by-laws include matters having to do with the internal government of the corporation. Thus they will usually contain rules governing rights of stockholders, the power and qualifications of directors, issue and transfer of stock, sale of assets, annual stockholders meetings, directors meetings, methods of making contracts, and rules empowering directors to authorize proper officers to handle funds, sign checks and contracts, and undertake other corporate activities.

The authority of the directors is such as may be necessary to conduct the ordinary business activities of the corporation. Except in matters reserved for the shareholders by the by-laws or by corporate law, directors are free to exercise their judgment without interference by the stockholders. Apart from these limitations, the directors are in somewhat the same position as individuals who must comply with the law but otherwise may exercise their judgment in making decisions on behalf of the corporation.

However, like any possessor of organization authority, directors have responsibility to use their powers lawfully and in the best interests of the stockholders. Also, as will be seen in Chapter 5, they are subject to certain enforceable liabilities.

BOARD OF DIRECTORS: LEGAL ANACHRONISM OR IMPORTANT FORCE?

Observation of boards of directors in typical corporations supports the belief that many boards actually do not manage the operations of the corporation. Understandably, managing, in its usual sense, is largely the job of the president and other corporate officers of the typical corporate enterprise. Indeed, corporate boards have often been criticized for not even directing the affairs of the business.[1]

Peter Drucker has referred to the "gradual erosion of the board of directors as a functioning organ of the enterprise."[2] This author and management specialist goes on to say:

In reality the board as conceived by the lawmaker is at best a tired fiction. It is perhaps not too much to say that it has become a shadow king. In most of the large companies, it has in effect been deposed and its place taken by executive management. This may have been achieved in the form of the "inside" board, that is, one composed exclusively of executive management men who meet the first Monday in every month to supervise and to approve what they themselves have been doing the other twenty-nine days of the month. Or the board may have become a mere showcase, a place to inject distinguished names, without information, influence, or desire for power. Or—a typical pattern in the smaller

[1] W. O. Douglas, "Directors Who Do Not Direct," *Harvard Law Review*, Vol. 47, pp. 1305–1334, June, 1934.

[2] *The Practice of Management*, Harper & Row, New York, 1954, p. 178.

company—the board may be simply another name for the meeting of the family members, usually the ones that actively engage in the business, plus a few widows of former partners.[3]

Separation in the large corporation of ownership and management has sometimes tended to make the inside managerial group all-powerful and the board of directors a legal sham. Prominent stockholders, often controlling with only a minority interest, have occasionally made boards of directors willing approvers of their wishes. In addition, the boards of many small companies and family-owned companies exist only to meet the requirements of the law and to supplement the ability of the company attorney to write and file minutes fulfilling these requirements.

Boards may be usefully classified into seven general types:

1. *Dummy Boards.* These are boards established usually to meet incorporation requirements, particularly when a new corporation is formed and the incorporators have not had time to select permanent members. They are characterized by a list of names with no significance as board members, and the incorporators normally hold automatic resignations of these persons. This is obviously not an operating board of directors.

2. *Family Boards.* In many family-owned corporations, the board of directors is comprised of family members who meet the requirements of the law but do not operate as a board. However, even in family-owned companies, one sometimes finds an effective operating board of directors including outside members and paying important attention to board duties and responsibilities.

3. *Owner-controlled Boards.* There are many boards where one or more prominent owners, who may hold a majority or even a minority of the stock, control the corporation, select the board members, and submit their nominations to routine stockholder vote. In these cases, the board may be a group of subordinates doing the bidding of a superior, or it may be one composed of truly independent and able directors which operates as an effective and representative board of directors.

[3] *Ibid.*

4. *Insider-controlled Boards with Outside Members.* Probably most typical of large publicly owned corporations are boards where no prominent owner controls enough votes to elect the members but where an inside group, through the use of proxy machinery, has effective control of the votes. In other words, established inside officers may or may not have a considerable stake in the company's stock, but they do have control in selecting the board of directors. As in the case of boards controlled by a prominent owner or owners, these boards may or may not be effective operating groups, depending upon the philosophy, actions, and desires of the insiders in the selection of members and in their operation of boards.

5. *Outside-controlled but Insider-led Boards.* Some boards are controlled neither by a prominent owner nor by insiders, and the members of the board are selected either by the shareholders generally or by such outside interests as outside board members. In many if not most of these cases, however, the inside officers tend to lead the board. This is because it is the natural task of the insiders to make proposals for board approval and the insider group is in possession of better information by which they can exercise effective leadership. Here again, whether the board is truly effective will depend largely upon the insistence upon control by the outside members and the actions of the insiders who have so strong a leadership position.

6. *Inside Boards.* A large number of closely held corporations and a few publicly owned corporations have boards comprised completely of officers or employees. As will be seen below,[4] public and investor groups have increasingly charged these boards with built-in ineffectiveness on the ground that insiders cannot reasonably be expected to operate the company and yet be their own superiors. Nonetheless, there are instances, as we shall see, where these boards have been effective.

7. *Outside Boards.* There are boards whose membership is predominantly or wholly comprised of directors who are not active officers of the corporation and who, therefore, presumably have complete detachment from the inside management.

[4] See page 126.

Although outside boards are common in public enterprises, state incorporation laws generally require that the president of a business corporation be a member of the board of directors, and the chief executive in other types of enterprise is normally a member of the board. The essential point is, however, whether the board has a truly "outside" flavor—neither insider-led nor insider-controlled.

It is the thesis of this book that boards of directors do have an important social and economic function: to see that the enterprise is well managed and that the interests of those it represents are faithfully followed. Thus a board should not be regarded as a legal anachronism coming down to modern times from the government committees of antiquity and the board of proprietors of the early English joint stock company. Nor should the board be allowed to become a "shadow king" or showcase.

Indeed, there are important social and practical reasons for an effective board of directors. There is always the danger of abuse of power by insiders who may forget their fiduciary relationship to those who have contributed the original capital of the corporation. In addition, executives, necessarily embroiled in the immediate problems of operations, can benefit, as can the corporation, by an impartial superior authority approving their proposals and actions, goading them into looking at problems from a broader point of view, and taking responsibility for major decisions affecting the successful growth and continuity of the company. Even in small, privately held corporations, there are tremendous advantages to be found in this same kind of practical "outside" guidance, even though the social importance of protecting the assets of investors may be very slight.

BASIC RESPONSIBILITIES OF BOARDS

Both by legal requirement and by the necessity of seeing that a company is well managed for successful growth and continuity, a number of basic responsibilities appear to be common to all boards of directors. These may be summarized under a number of headings. From these the various requirements for board action to assure effective management, discussed in succeeding sections of this book, are derived.

Trusteeship. Perhaps the most important single function of the board of directors may be summed up in the term "trusteeship"—the safeguarding and husbanding of the company's assets in the long-term interests of the shareholders. Even the most ineffectual board cannot escape this obligation.

In most effective boards, and especially in large, publicly held corporations, the concept of trusteeship extends beyond a feeling of immediate obligation to the stockholders. It includes responsibility to the public, without whose support a business or a corporation as a social institution could not endure; to employees of the company, whose efforts are necessary for its success; and to customers, who buy its products.

It may be argued that a director has only the duty to operate exclusively for the benefit of the stockholders. It is their funds that he manages. To manage them for the benefit of others might be interpreted as misappropriation of private property. At the same time, a true sense of social responsibility and responsiveness to the external environment of the corporation *is* in the interests of the shareholders. Directors who remember that their first obligation is to the owners of the corporation whose funds they manage, and regard their obligations to society as consistent with this primary duty, are in fact living up to their primary obligation.

Determination of Enterprise Objectives. Another major function of the board of directors is to determine enterprise objectives. It is not enough to say that a business exists to make a profit. Although this must be a basic goal of any business, it must be translated into enterprise goals supportive of profit. These, to be meaningful, must be verifiable and understandable, and the decision making involved must be channeled through formulation of major policies designed to assure goal achievement.

While there can be no doubt that the board of directors has this responsibility for determining enterprise objectives and major policies, it must be recognized that these seldom develop merely by discussion among a group of individuals. The operating management of a company must be regarded as a staff group to suggest, clarify, and sharpen enterprise objectives and major policies. But the board has the responsibility of insisting that this staff work be done, of considering carefully the adequacy of such goals and policies, and of approving them as the controlling expression of the corporation.

Selection of Executives. Incorporation laws universally require that the board of directors elect company officers. Many directors, however, regard their primary function as one of selecting the chief executive officer or president of the corporation and approving the chief executive's nomination of other officers.

In order to allow the chief executive officer a real hand in selecting his lieutenants who carry responsibility for major functions, so that he can be held responsible for the successful operation of the corporation as a whole, most corporation boards of directors feel that they should have only a ratifying power over selection of these key subordinates. This understandable feeling arises for two reasons.

In the first place, these executives are presumably in charge of major functions or divisions of the company's operation and are therefore of importance to the board. Many a chief executive has taken the attitude that the board should look only to him and have no say whatsoever concerning other executives of the corporation. They reason that, if the chief executive officer is to be responsible, he must not have interference, and the board should only retain the power and obligation to discharge him if he fails in his task. However, as in so many matters in management, a higher authority cannot fully meet its responsibilities by the power to discharge. A considerable corporate error or great loss is not made good by replacing the person responsible.

In the second place, most boards feel that they should know the competence and personalities of key line subordinates under the chief executive officer. They reason that the chief executive's successor will probably come from this rank, and since the choice of a new chief executive should be made by the board of directors, any conscientious board would wish to know the potential of individuals at this level and have the power to approve their appointment.

Securing Long-range Business Stability and Growth. An often overlooked function of the board of directors is that of securing long-range business stability and growth in a changing physical, social, and biological environment. Barnard has remarked that, although formal organization is "omnipresent and inescapable," it is a fact that "successful cooperation in or by formal organizations is the abnormal, not the normal condition." [5] In other words, even though people have a natural propensity to organize, history shows that few of the many organizations existing at any one time survive, since most fail to keep their objectives, policies, and programs in tune with the changing environment. From the standpoint of business, these environmental forces include such critical factors as changes in technology, changing markets, new and different tastes, varying political and economic conditions, and the growth of new business institutions, such as the discount house which has so influenced department store operation.

An alert outside director, with his detachment from everyday operations of a company and with wide experience, can often call attention to the need for changes in objectives and programs. As Copeland and Towl have pointed out, a competent board, operating as a group, has "a vitality which transcends the membership of the individual directors." [6]

There are those who feel that securing long-range stability is the fundamental function of the board of directors. As one writer has said, "Board and management alike are in the business of avoiding calamity, of preserving the company, maintaining its personality, ensuring its continuity." [7] In other words, as the corporation form is designed as a legal entity separate from its owners in order to furnish immortality, so it is the duty of the board of directors to accept responsibility for survival.

[5] Chester I. Barnard, *The Functions of the Executive*, Harvard University Press, Cambridge, Mass., 1938, pp. 4–5.

[6] M. G. Copeland and A. R. Towl, *The Board of Directors and Business Management*, Division of Research, Graduate School of Business Administration, Harvard University, Boston, 1947, p. 32.

[7] H. B. Maurer, "Boards of Directors," *Fortune*, Vol. 41, No. 5, p. 130, May, 1950.

Assuring that Major Plans Are Designed to Meet Objectives. In order to discharge its responsibility for securing long-range stability and growth and its obligation for objectives, every effective board must take steps to assure itself that major plans are, in fact, designed to meet objectives. This involves selecting certain areas of primary importance to the attainment of objectives and requiring that the basic programs be submitted to the board for review and, perhaps, approval.

Approval of Major Company Decisions. There are a number of areas in which the board is required by law to make company decisions. There are also a number of areas where, in the interest of assuring effective management, the board *should* make decisions, though typically not required to do so by law. These areas will be dealt with more thoroughly in Chapter 4. Suffice it to say that there are a number of major decisions, involving long-term stability and growth of the company and effectiveness of management, that the board must make if it is to carry out its responsibilities. These areas, of course, should be spelled out very carefully lest the board get itself involved in decisions that should be, and in most cases are, delegated to operating managers.

Checking on Results. One of the unavoidable functions of the manager is control: ascertaining that events are conforming to plans. Directors, by establishing corporate objectives and formulating major policies, are doing basic planning. And to meet their function of trusteeship for successful operation of the company, they must discharge their responsibility to stockholders by checking on the results of their planning.

Such evaluation involves more than a review of financial statements and the receipt of an audit from an independent accounting firm responsible to the board. From the financial side, it means a careful review of forecasts of cash availability, operating revenues and expenses, and capital expenditures, as well as performance against budgets. Although an audited statement may disclose whether funds have been honestly received and dispersed and accounts kept in accordance with accepted accounting principles, it does a director little good to find, when all the statements for the prior year are in, that the company became insolvent some months before.

If the board is to control, it should check on results while they are occurring and, ideally, *before* they occur. Indeed, one of the basic tenets of successful managerial control is to correct deviations from plans before they occur, wherever possible. Even quickly furnished information on past events is not good enough. A year, or even a week, after the event may be too late to implement a change in direction. Control based entirely on past data is often no more than a frustrating post-mortem.

The breadth of this control should extend into the entire area of policy formulation. For example, if a board has decided that authority should be decentralized and that the organization should proceed along product-division lines, it should have some means for determining from time to time whether the developing structure actually reflects board policy. If a board establishes a product development policy, it should check on current and anticipated results. If certain basic personnel policies have been established by a board, its area of control should extend to them. Too often, boards of directors approve policies and planning programs and then forget them.

Disposition of Company Profits and Assets. Another major function that must be exercised by directors, at least to meet the requirements of corporation law and obligation to stockholders, is disposition of company profits and assets. Directors must decide whether earnings should be distributed to owners as dividends, returned to the business for expansion, or utilized to eliminate outstanding indebtedness. Likewise, because a board is charged with safeguarding and husbanding the assets of the company, and laws generally give shareholders certain powers in the disposal of assets, a board of directors has a virtually undelegatable interest in the disposition of important company assets.

When a director decides the policy to be followed in the distribution of earnings, he is making a decision of exceptional importance. If he decides that earnings should be distributed to owners, he is taking the position that the owner would rather have immediate earnings in hand than invest in future earnings of the company or in capital gains. Should he decide to keep earnings for expansion, he is, to some extent, forcing owners to reinvest funds in the corporation. Likewise, if earnings are to be used to retire debt, the director is once more exercising his trusteeship of the investors' funds. Disposition of earnings is, to the stockholder, second in importance only to the actual making of earnings through efficient utilization of his capital investment. Yet all too often directors regard the distribution of earnings as a financial planning matter without the serious implications of trusteeship that this function necessarily implies.

In most corporate statutes and charters, restrictions are placed upon the power of the directors to sell corporation assets. Courts have uniformly held that directors must have the consent of stockholders to dispose of the entire assets of a corporation or any substantial portion large enough to materially affect its activities. On the other hand, if the corporation is insolvent or if its assets must be sold to pay corporate debts, courts have held that directors must sell the property without stockholder consent.

But even where disposition of assets is not large enough to warrant shareholder approval, a board of directors, it would appear, should carefully watch piecemeal disposal of assets. This does not mean that sale of assets in the ordinary course of business or retirement of assets no longer required for business operations, unless relatively large, should be subject to board approval, but that a board should set appropriate limits above which operating management cannot go. To do otherwise is to take unwarranted chances with a fundamental duty toward the owners of the corporation.

Mergers and Acquisitions. Another unavoidable responsibility of boards is approval of mergers and acquisitions. So far as mergers are concerned, the major distinction between these and the sale of assets is essentially a legal one and incorporation laws uniformly require stockholder approval for mergers. This, in turn, would require the board of directors to take a part in any such activities.

On the other hand, stockholder approval is not ordinarily required for acquisitions of companies unless a corporation must go to the stockholders for additional authorization to issue stock, for a new security issue, or reclassification of a security. In some states, stockholder approval is required to mortgage corporate assets, although normally this power is vested in the board of directors and may seldom be delegated, except by express provision in particular instances. However, the major point is that in acquiring another company, either through purchase of assets, merger, or otherwise, a board of directors should hardly consider delegating its power of approval to operating officers. These acquisitions are normally major actions which shape the nature and future of a company, and they are almost universally regarded as subjects for board decision.

chapter 3

HOW THE BOARD MANAGES

Since it is obvious that a board cannot in a complete sense manage a corporation, it may well be asked how the board can fulfill its responsibility for management. Even referring to its task as seeing that a corporation is well managed appears inadequate. It implies that the board is an observer of the scene—an auditor who has no specific operational management responsibilities.

As the top rung on the management ladder of a company, a board should do far more than hire a chief executive and watch him manage the corporation, rewarding him if he is right and discharging him or otherwise penalizing him if he is wrong. No one responsible for managing in any enterprise can do so little. He must exercise authority commensurate with the responsibility he assumes for the function given him. In the case of a board of directors this is, of course, responsibility for the enterprise as a whole. Therefore, it is reasonable to expect that an effective board will actually enter into company management and will make decisions in a number of specific areas.

The decision areas recommended for a board are discussed in the succeeding chapter. At this point, let us examine the ways that a board manages. As will be seen, these involve more than actual decision making. Since a board cannot manage the enterprise in detail, it must not only make decisions itself but also adopt techniques of seeing that others manage the enterprise well.

ASSURING EFFECTIVE PLANNING AND DECISION MAKING

There are a number of special techniques and conditions for assuring effective planning and decision making. It should be remembered that decision making implies rational action—that is, action that leads most effectively and efficiently toward some preselected goal. Decision making entails, therefore, selecting what appears on the basis of the best possible information to be the best way of attaining a given objective. There can be no rational action without (1) a clear goal, (2) a clear understanding of alternatives for reaching this goal, (3) an adequate analysis of alternatives in terms of the goal, and (4) a desire to optimize the use of resources in reaching the goal.

To assure that effective plans and decisions are made, one need not make them oneself; other techniques are available. These techniques are useful to any manager, and they are useful to a board of directors that naturally makes a relatively small proportion of the decisions made in the typical enterprise.

Insisting on Complete Planning Proposals. In most cases where a board does make decisions, or where it ratifies or reviews the decisions of operating management, it must insist upon adequate analyses, studies, and recommendations. The board, as a group, cannot well initiate planning proposals or do the necessary research for them. But it can insist that proposals in areas important to it be submitted by operating managers. It can demand that these proposals be adequately documented and the recommended action sharply defined, with its major advantages and disadvantages outlined. It may also ask that closely competitive alternatives be noted. This is, of course, saying that the board wishing to operate effectively must insist on completed staff work on the part of operating managers.

In observing and participating in the operation of many company boards of directors and their operating management, the author has found that people responsible for operations often tend to wait for the board to hand down major decisions in areas the board has properly reserved to itself. Indeed, much managerial inertia at all levels arises from the tendency of subordinates to wait for guidance from their superiors. Superiors, on the other hand—and this is particularly true of boards of directors—may not know what guidance to give since they may not have the knowledge or the means of doing the staff work required to analyze proposals and directions.

Like any other superior manager, therefore, a board must insist on receiving from its subordinates well analyzed and weighed planning proposals. It should expect from the top executives of a company their best judgment in the light of the information available and their analysis of variables involved. In asking for this, however, a board, like any other superior, must ever be wary of receiving a one-sided point of view and must continually attempt to find out whether or not the disadvantages of a proposed course of action have been weighed as carefully as its advantages.

In doing this, a board must necessarily appreciate the problems of limited time and information and realize that there are decision areas where conclusions unavoidably must depend largely upon judgment. At the same time, to make decisions on important matters without adequate analysis of available facts and expectations is foolish. A wildcatter operating on little more than hunch may discover oil, but use of scientific knowledge and analysis has certainly proved to be far more fruitful.

Insisting upon Review of Performance and Plans. For those areas of operations that are important to the board for adequate discharge of its responsibilities, but in which it does not choose to make decisions, members should insist on reviewing the major plans the operating managers intend to pursue, and reviewing company performance against previous plans. This is simply an application of the technique of insisting on completed proposals for board decisions. As a matter of fact, the very act of insisting upon review of performance and major plans will in itself tend to encourage better planning and performance by operating managers.

Watching for Decision Approaches. Members of a board, being relatively detached from the operating details of the company, are in an ideal position to watch carefully for approaches to decisions made by operating executives. A decision may be made exclusively on the basis of past experience. This can be dangerous. Unless experience is distilled and underlying causes identified, reliance upon experience may lead individuals to assume wrongly that the future will repeat the pattern of the past. There is nothing deader than a fact, because what makes anything a fact is that it is past. Decisions made today take effect in the future. Rarely if ever will a past situation, with all its environmental elements, be precisely duplicated in the future.

Yet experience can be an extremely valuable asset if it leads to true wisdom and judgment. However, it will probably not do so unless coupled to an understanding of underlying forces and influences and an appreciation that problems represent opportunities that can yield to solution. In fact, it is sometimes thought that judgment is basically a kind of panic resistance, an ability to recognize that to act hastily in the face of pressing problems is to overlook fundamental elements and precipitously reach conclusions without analysis or thought. A director will do well to watch for this very natural tendency on the part of operating executives and make sure that experience is used only where and how it is most valuable.

The impact of experience on profitable growth is illustrated by a company whose management problems the author analyzed several years ago. The three founders and major stockholders of the company naturally occupied influential positions on the board of directors. They were highly intelligent and interested in the growth of the company. During an analysis of divisional and functional management thinking in an attempt to discover why new products were so rarely suggested and so slowly developed, several executives referred to what they called "a screwdriver complex" on the part of the company founders. This turned out to refer to a situation some years before, when the company had come up with an unusual new screwdriver. The product was well market-researched and tested, and mechanics found it very desirable. After extensive promotion and large production, the company was surprised to find that the new screwdriver would not sell. The reason was simple: although it was demonstrably superior, mechanics were unwilling to pay the additional price, small as it was, for this superior instrument. As a result, the product line was abandoned.

Apparently, at least for a time, this simple product failure had led the founders to exercise extreme caution on new product proposals. Transmitted in turn to operating managers, this caution led people to feel that it was not worth taking a chance to offer new product ideas unless there was virtually a 100 percent certainty of success.

The interesting thing is that the aftereffects of this experience lasted for many years after the company's founders had long forgotten it, still persisting at a time when they were pressing vigorously for more new product ideas and development.

Another way of approaching decisions is to experiment. In other words, try it. If it works, it was the right decision; if it doesn't, it was wrong. In some cases, experimentation is the cheapest way of determining the rightness or wrongness of decisions, particularly where the decision is not very important in terms of consequences. Again, experimentation may be the only way of finding out whether a course of action is correct where information on the problem adequate to rationally reach a correct decision is not available. Generally, however, experimentation is the most costly approach to decision making, especially if a better answer can be found more cheaply through research and analysis.

Through lack of information or sheer unwillingness to analyze available data thoroughly and take normal risks, operating managers may sometimes overdo experimentation. The author has seen this in a number of instances of market testing, normally a very desirable way of determining whether a new product or product idea will actually be accepted by customers. Some individuals, however, become so committed to market testing that they will test ideas when the underlying research indicates a high degree of certainty, where market testing is expensive, and where it tips the hand of the innovator to his competitors, giving them time to duplicate what might have been a very profitable innovation. On the other hand, there have been cases where a management group, so certain of their analysis as to be blind to disadvantages and pitfalls, failed to experiment enough before committing the company to an expensive and inflexible course of action. In both instances, the board member can make a material contribution to effective management by weighing the adequacy of the experimentation.

In general, the most effective approach to decision making is through research and analysis. This is an approach by which the problem to be solved is conceptualized in terms of the major variables and constraints involved and the goal to be attained. It requires, therefore, an ability to see relationships in a problem as an interrelated system. Then, once the problem is conceptualized in its relationship to a goal, it requires studying variables and constraints and their impact on a desirable solution, with a view to reaching the optimum course of action in light of the goal.

The obvious advantage of the research-and-analysis approach is that it forces a decision maker to conceptualize a problem and to select the most important elements affecting its solution. It likewise has the advantage of limiting most of the cost of a decision to time and pencil and paper (or, today, to data and computer) before an expensive commitment is made.

With the introduction of the system approaches and mathematical techniques of the physical sciences into business and other social problems, and the availability of rapid data storage, retrieval, and processing, it is only natural that this approach to decision making should increasingly become more practicable and fruitful. While it is not nearly so expensive as experimentation where important planning decisions are involved, nor so dangerous as relying on experience, it can be both costly and time-consuming. A company should certainly not spend $50,000 worth of research time for a decision involving a $1,000 risk. On the other hand, what concerns most observers of the management scene is the tendency to spend less than $1,000 of thinking time for a $5,000,000 risk.

Obviously, through his position of power and his ability to ask questions, probe reasoning, and insist upon completed research, a director can do much to create an environment in which the management group will undertake adequate research and analysis before submitting planning proposals to the board, or before making planning programs, not requiring board decisions, that are reported as a matter of information to the board. The most effective managers in any enterprise welcome this. No board of directors is assuring effective management unless it makes certain that decisions amenable to the research-and-analysis approach are indeed attacked in this manner.

Forcing Consideration of the Limiting Factor. Because variables and constraints involved in most important top management decisions are virtually numberless and there is almost never the time or resources to study them all, the secret of effective decision making is the search and solution for the limiting (or critical, or strategic) factor. In choosing among alternatives in a problem situation, primary attention should be given to those factors which are limiting or strategic to the solution of the problem. In every problem situation, if we are astute enough to discover it, there is a factor or a small number of factors which make the most difference. Thus, in a new product program, the limiting factor may be the company's ability to develop a service organization to service the product once it is in the field. Or, in an acquisition program, the limiting factor might be the relatively low price-earnings ratio of a company's stock, which makes it difficult for the company to acquire another enterprise without diluting its own earnings per share through being forced to give too many shares of stock.

Through probing, as well as analysis from his own experience and knowledge of company affairs, a director can contribute a great deal to effective management by making certain that the limiting factors in a program have been discovered and considered and a solution for them found. This ability to search and solve for the limiting factor is one of the most creative and important of the managerial arts. A director can make a major contribution to effective management both by practicing it himself and by ensuring that it is practiced by his fellow directors and the management group of his company.

Asking the Discerning Question. Closely related to searching and solving for the limiting factor, is the long recognized but sometimes forgotten technique of the discerning question. An individual not intimately familiar with a problem nor intimately embroiled in it can often ask searching questions which will soon show whether a problem has been adequately thought through and researched. It does not take long to ascertain, by asking a few questions at critical points and seeing whether credible answers are readily available, the adequacy of preparation in a planning proposal.

The most effective corporate directors, as well as the effective managerial superiors, develop great skill in asking the searching or discerning question. Indeed, this is one of the major reasons why certain individuals can serve effectively on a board of directors without intimate knowledge and contact with the company.

In a large company where the author was once responsible for preparing planning proposals for the president to submit to the board of directors, a certain outside board member in an entirely different business had an unusual ability to ask what was then referred to as the "embarrassing question." If he discovered an area where an important question had not been considered, the result was, naturally, embarrassment to the president and, it goes without saying, much greater embarrassment to the president's assistant. But the important thing was that the staff's anxiety that such questions might be raised led to more thorough preparation of board proposals than probably otherwise would have been the case.

A chief executive concerned with making the best possible decisions should welcome the contribution which the discerning question can make. And a director would fail in his duties if he did not feel that he could and should ask such questions. This is unquestionably one of the great weaknesses of the "rubber stamp" board, and it subjects the company to the same danger as the manager who is satisfied to be surrounded with a group of "yes-men."

In analyzing the board of directors and its relationship to business management, Copeland and Towl stated many years ago that "the discerning question is a director's principal tool and one of his major contributions to the management process." [1] Moreover, as these authors pointed out in their study, asking discerning questions is not only important from a management point of view but also has special significance from a legal standpoint. Courts have repeatedly taken the position that if a board of directors is to discharge its responsibilities in conformity with its office, its members have the right and obligation to express their individual viewpoints for the purpose of obtaining an exchange and for arriving at conclusions after deliberate consideration of an issue. [2]

Maintaining a Tradition of Individual Independence. Experience teaches us that any group, whether board, commission, committee,

[1] M. T. Copeland and A. R. Towl, *The Board of Directors and Business Management,* Harvard University, Graduate School of Business Administration, Boston, 1947, p. 95.

[2] *Ibid.,* pp. 96–97.

or panel, tends to develop a tradition of unanimity. As is well known, in many instances where a group attempts to find a decision on which all can agree, the result is compromise at the least common denominator and therefore a relatively weak decision. Sometimes the compromise decision is worse than any of the different decision possibilities through which it was reached. In addition, a desire for unanimity often leads to "back scratching," rather than free discussion and independent arrival at conclusions, as well as the possibility that an individual with strong opinions may become a board tyrant forcing others to his will.

Since board members are or should be organization equals, reluctance to force a conclusion on a dissident minority is understandable. However, a board of directors is truly a plural executive in which every individual bears equal authority and responsibility, even though the board makes its decisions as a group. Provisions always exist for majority rule. If this responsibility is to be discharged and the best possible deliberation of complex problems obtained, the board must, it would seem, develop a certain tradition of individual independence. In other words, individual board members should not hesitate to take positions their own intelligence and analysis judge to be correct, nor should a majority group who may think otherwise hesitate to make the decision despite dissenting votes.

Obviously, emotional overtones through differences of position can actually harm effective deliberation. But board decisions are made by a majority of individual decisions, and pressure for complete agreement can lead to ineffectual deliberation and decision.

MAJOR VARIATIONS IN WAYS BOARDS MANAGE

In those areas of company operation of concern to it, there are many ways a board of directors may manage. Some imply making decisions; others, influencing decisions.

Making Original Decisions. Original decisions made by the board include those it cannot delegate to the operating executives by statute, charter, or by-laws, such as officer selection and pay, dividends, and by-law changes. They may also include decisions the board will not delegate, even though it could lawfully do so, such as major program commitments, certain capital expenditures, and budget approvals. The elaboration of these areas is the subject of the following chapter.

Confirming Executive Decisions. Practically speaking, there are often matters in which the board should make the original decision but cannot easily do so because certain elements of the decision or of the program may be missing or must be negotiated by operating management. This is likely to be the case with important contracts, such as major sales contracts or leases, where the board cannot feasibly take part in the final negotiation or approval of terms. In these cases, it is customary for the board to approve the program in principle with certain boundaries for executive guidance. Then, later, the board ratifies the contract as made by an operating executive.

Again, there are instances when operating executives find it necessary and desirable to go beyond the limits of their authority and make decisions which would normally be made by the board. There are occasions when a decision must be made quickly without waiting for board action. While most boards are and should be properly wary of executives going beyond their limits and into the board's domain of authority, and this should be done only in rare circumstances, there are few companies where it never occurs.

Obviously, in this case, the chief executive or other company officer is taking a personal risk. He should understand quite clearly the thinking of the board on cases of this kind and have a full appreciation of the principles upon which the board has operated. In other words, it should be an exceptional circumstance. If it is a normal circumstance, either a board should review its authority delegations to see whether or not it would be desirable to delegate authority, with policy guidance, to the executive to make decisions in this area, or else steps should be taken to limit what might become flouting of board power by operating executives.

Counseling Executives. One of the major contributions of board members is to act, either individually or as a group, as advisers to the chief executive in particular and, with his knowledge and concurrence, to other top executives of the firm who need help and counsel on major problems within their jurisdictions.

This is particularly true of the chief executive of a company, who almost invariably suffers from what has been called "the loneliness of the summit." Surrounded by subordinate executives with either specialized functional or operating interests, the chief executive usually has no one but the board to turn to for counsel and advice on decisions that comprehend the company as a whole. While outside consultants are often very useful in assisting the chief executive in such matters, and a general staff assistant can be invaluable in making sure that his superior has a balanced and objective analysis of company-wide issues, access to wide experience and company knowledge on the part of outside board members in particular can be extremely useful to the chief executive.

In addition, executives may counsel with the board on matters which will later come to it for action. The complexity of company problems at the top level, and the fact that they often involve departures into new areas where no policy precedents exist, make it particularly wise for top executives to determine a board's thinking and attitudes in advance before spending much time and effort in preparing major planning proposals. In addition, the mere preparation of a major planning proposal may entail a certain amount of commitment of direction, both to subordinates and outsiders, that could embarrass top management if its planning recommendations were to be reversed by an unsympathetic board. In fact, in reviewing experienced and observed board operation, the author has found this aspect of board managing often to be the most fruitful (and time-consuming) of all.

Reviewing Performance and Plans. As has already been indicated, perhaps the most effective way of forcing adequate planning and exercising the fundamental function of checking on results is the regular, formal, and rigorous review of performance and plans. This has long been done by the chief executives of divisionalized companies with respect to the division manager. It has not been done as often with subordinate managers. And board operation often leaves much to be desired in effectually utilizing this approach.

If a board is to make sure that a company is well managed, both from the standpoint of its own information and from the point of view of creating an environment for effective management, it should regularly, formally, and rigorously review the performance and future plans of the company for which it is responsible. This means selecting the right areas to review. It also means avoiding unnecessary involvement with detail, which could interfere unduly with the normal operations of line managers in a company.

CLARIFYING BOARD AUTHORITY

One of the common complaints of both board members and operating executives is that the board, the chief executive, and other executives do not understand clearly in what areas they have final authority to make decisions. This is also a common complaint at all executive levels. But the result at the board level is to cause unnecessary friction or misunderstanding between the board and the chief executive and other executives of the company. This lack of understanding often leads board members to raise questions and attempt to decide matters in which operating executives properly feel the board should not be involved. It likewise leads presidents and vice presidents to make decisions that rightly should be referred to the board.

This problem can be greatly clarified and simplified by means of a chart of executive approval authorizations, a tool which every company, large or small, with any significant delegation of authority, should utilize. The chart of executive approval authorizations is simply a technique by which, normally on a single sheet of paper or chart, the various authority delegations of a company are outlined and clarified. Since most of these delegations have to do with the right to commit the company for money, most of the chart has to do with expenditure limits. However, there are other matters, such as policies and programs, which can and should be shown on such a chart.

An example of a chart of approval authorizations for a medium-sized company is shown in Figure 1. It will be noted that a list of major decision areas appears on the left-hand side of the chart. It has been found useful to group these decision areas under the classifications of personnel, capital expenditures and commitments, operating expenses, prices and sales commitments, major programs, and general. Across the top of the chart may be listed those various managerial levels which have approval authority, along with certain staff personnel who have either functional authority in a decision matter or whose consultation is necessary for advice or information.

In developing a chart, it will be apparent that a division must be made between those decisions which are in the province of the president or chairman of the board and those belonging to the board of directors. When this is done—and approved by the board of directors, since it does have primary power to delegate its authority to the various officers of the corporation—both the executives and the board members should then be clear as to those areas where decisions must be made. A board of directors should know what it wants to approve, and the chief executive and other operating executives should know what they must bring to the board and what they need not bring. Not only will this knowledge improve board operation by forcing board consultation in the right decision areas, but it can remove many causes of irritation to operating executives and reduce waste of directors' time.

DETERMINING DECISION-MAKING IMPORTANCE

A board of directors must determine those areas where it wishes to make decisions and those which it is willing to delegate to operating management. It also appears reasonable that a board of directors should approve delegation of authority below the chief-executive level. This is necessary to make effective a policy of proper centralization-decentralization, and a board should be apprised of those decision areas where appropriate delegation is or is not made. It is also in the board's interest to know where the decision-making

Chart of Approval Authorization

Nature of Transaction		Department Manager	Staff Manager	Division Director	President (Corporate and Domestic) Chairman of the Board (International)	Board of Directors
1. Personnel						
Employment of new personnel	Hourly	All	Personnel Manager to process and review for consistency with company policy	All exceptions to company policy		
	Salaried	All	Personnel Manager to process	All over $800 per month	All over $1,200 per month	All over $2,000 per month
Wage and salary increases	Hourly	All	Personnel Manager to process and review for consistency with company policy	All exceptions to company policy		
	Salaried	All	Personnel Manager to process	All	All resulting in salary over $1,200 per month	All resulting in salary over $2,000 per month
Moving expenses			To be processed by Controller	All	All over $2,000 in cost	
Leaves of absences		All	To be processed by Personnel Manager	All	All over 30 days	All over 90 days
2. Operating Expenses						
Procurement of materials and services (Approval of manufacturing and engineering schedule by Vice President Manufacturing and Engineering)	In accordance with approved schedules	Manager of Purchasing on all				
	Not in accordance with approved schedules		Vice President of Manufacturing and Engineering on all. Controller on all exceeding $5,000.	All		
	Consultation Services			All	All corporate services	All contracts or retainers over $2,500

2. Operating Expenses (continued)

Supplies and maintenance materials and services		All		All over $5,000	All over $5,000	
Travel and entertainment requests and reports		All those reporting to him		All those reporting to him	All those reporting to him and all over $1,000	President and Chairman of the Board approved by Board of Directors
Advertising and public relations	In accordance with approved program	Manager of Advertising and Sales Promotion on all		General Sales Manager on all		
	Not in accordance with approved program				All outside total budget	
Contributions	Budgeted	Controller				
	Non budgeted				Chairman of the Board	
Memberships and Subscriptions		All			Chairman of the Board on all except technical magazines and books	
Research and development projects		All		Director of Research and Development on all	All involving new product lines	
Miscellaneous expenses		All	Controller on all	All over $1,000	All over $5,000	
Tax payments and adjustments					President and Secretary where law requires	Tax adjustments over $15,000
Guarantees and replacements			General Sales Manager and Controller on all		All over $1,000	All over $5,000
Contract cancellations			General Sales Manager and Controller on all		All involving more than $2,500	
Leases	Temporary leases not to exceed $1,000 in total commitment	All	Controller on all	All		
	Other leases		Controller and Secretary-Treasurer on all		All	
Operating expense budgets: basic variable budget			Secretary-Treasurer on all		All	

47

Nature of Transaction		Department Manager	Staff Manager	Division Director	President (Corporate and Domestic) Chairman of the Board (International)	Board of Directors
3. Capital Expenditures and Commitments						
Capital Expenditures	In accordance with approved budget		Controller to check for budgetary accuracy	All	All individual items exceeding $5,000	All items exceeding $25,000
	Not in accordance with approved budget		Secretary–Treasurer on all		All items over $1,000	All items exceeding $5,000
Capital expenditure budgets		All	Secretary–Treasurer on all	All	All	All
Disposal of capital assets			Secretary–Treasurer and Controller on all	All	All over $5,000	All over $100,000
Patent applications, licensing and patent agreements			Secretary–Treasurer on all	All	All	All basic policy
4. Prices and Sales Commitments						
Sales price formulas			Secretary–Treasurer on all		All	
Sales commitments	Catalog standard items	Manager of Sales Service on all	Controller on all acceptance of credit	General Sales Manager on all orders exceeding $100,000		
	Nonstandard items	Manager of Sales Service on all	Controller on all acceptance of credit	General Sales Manager on all exceeding $10,000	All exceeding commitment of $20,000	All exceeding commitment of $100,000
Variations from standard prices		Manager of Sales Service on all		General Sales Manager on all over $5,000, Vice President of Manufacturing and Engineering on all over $15,000	Inform President of variations in excess of 10% on orders exceeding $10,000	
New product lines				General Sales Manager on all	All	All
Contracts with sales representatives			Form approved by legal counsel	General Sales Manager on all	All nonstandard contracts	Basic items of commitment in standard form

5. General

Bank loans for company operations	Line of Credit	Secretary–Treasurer on all	All	All
	Loans Within Line	Secretary–Treasurer on all	All	
Loans for buildings and land		Secretary–Treasurer on all	All	All
Acquisition of financial interest in or loan to any company		Secretary–Treasurer on all	All	All

FIGURE 1 Chart of Approval Authorization. A person required to approve transactions as outlined in this chart may authorize another person to sign for him in his absence. The person so authorized must affix the proper signature showing his initials under such signature.

49

authority lies in a company, so that it can be aware of some of the requirements for quality of executives.

The exact degree of delegation is always a difficult question, both to determine what it should be and to make it effective in practice. In fact, analyses of management failure in business place poor delegation of authority at the top of the list of causes.

Delegation of authority is a matter of subjects which may be delegated or held for top management decision as well as the degree of commitment involved in each subject. For example, a board of directors would probably have no interest in the employment of new personnel in factories and offices, but would have a very great interest in the employment of personnel at the top-executive level and, perhaps, in all key top positions of the company. Likewise, directors would not wish to approve a capital expenditure for a few filing cabinets, but they would usually wish to approve one for a new factory building.

While the degree of authority delegated will vary between companies, and there are no generally applicable limits which can be established for all types of companies and operations, there do seem to be some useful criteria for determining decision-making importance. As these are applied to various companies, one might find a board of directors approving a relatively small dollar amount of capital expenditure in a small and new company with inexperienced managers and inadequate capital, but being concerned only with fairly large capital expenditures in a much larger and more seasoned company.

The criteria which the author has found useful in determining decision-making importance are the following:

1. *Size of Commitment.* Since all decisions involve some commitment, one of the important criteria is the size of the commitment involved in a decision, either in terms of money or impact on the company. Size is a relative thing and must be determined by each company in accordance with its desires and the practical exigencies of the situation.

2. *Length of Commitment.* The commitment involved in some decisions may be fulfilled in a short period of time or may not be

met for months or years ahead. Short-term commitments tend to involve a much higher degree of certainty than long-term commitments. Moreover, short-term commitments have less effect on future company operations than those which cannot be discharged for a period of time in the future. Therefore, because of their impact and importance to the company, commitments that require a long time for their fulfillment should be determined at a higher level than short-term ones.

3. *Inflexibility of a Course of Action.* Some commitments entail a high degree of flexibility, that is, ability to change direction without undue cost or embarrassment to the company. For example, a commitment to rent a typewriter on a month-to-month basis is one where both little risk is taken and change may be easily accomplished. On the other hand, certain types of commitments are intrinsically highly inflexible. One of the best examples is the commitment to build a petroleum refinery. Since this huge investment in specialized equipment has no other practical use than the refining of petroleum products, this decision should be given a high level of attention. Obviously, when high inflexibility, large size, and long-term commitment are all involved, the decision area is one of utmost importance to a company.

4. *Extent of Certainty.* Another consideration in determining the importance of decisions for management attention is the extent to which the variables and goals in a situation are known. If a high degree of certainty exists, little judgment is usually required, since the decision can be made practically on the basis of mathematical analysis. Therefore, such decisions, other things being equal, can be safely delegated to lower levels of an organization. On the other hand, more importance should be attached to decisions that entail a high degree of uncertainty. For example, the top-level executives of a company would seldom think of approving the detailed production plan of a factory, since this ordinarily embraces a high degree of known factors and factor relationships. On the other hand, a major marketing program would tend to command a high level of attention and consideration because of the number of unknowns typically involved.

5. *Quantifiability.* Another significant factor in determining

decision-making importance is the extent to which variables, limits, and goals in a situation may be quantified. If they can be quantified, the solution yields to mathematical and computing approaches and requires little or no judgment. While this criterion is closely related to that of certainty of goals and variables, it does have a somewhat different connotation. Situations may have a high degree of certainty and yet not be quantifiable.

Even though a high degree of certainty would tend to reduce an area's decision-making importance, it would not lower it as much as if the elements of certainty were also quantifiable. Moreover, even where elements with a low degree of certainty may be credibly quantifiable, management may feel that it can safely delegate the actual decision, particularly if the underlying premises have been quantified and it has examined and approved them. Thus, appropriate numerical weights may be given to a program of evaluating a factory location, such as weights given to tax, labor, freight, and other factors. These weights are ordinarily based upon judgment and may therefore be scrutinized by top management, but the actual application of them in a quantitative way can be safely delegated downward.

6. *Human Impact of Decisions.* The greater the human impact of a decision, the more management time and attention should be given to it. It is possible for a decision to have a high degree of certainty and quantifiability and at the same time a great probability of dangerous human impact.

For example, a certain large company in the defense industry had embarked a few years ago on the development of an electronic business computer program, largely because the engineers and scientists in the company believed that the company should be engaging their talents not only in destructive materials for war but also in products for peace. As the program had moved along and the company had spent over $10 million in it, top management discovered that, even if the program should be a technical success, establishing an effective marketing and service organization would be prohibitively expensive and risky. Analysis of the program indicated unequivocally that the company should abandon this program. However, with the emotional attachment of the scientific leaders of the company to this program, this was a dangerous decision. Needless to say, this was given considerable attention and analysis by the top management of the company and various means were used to sell the abandonment to key scientific leaders before the decision was actually made.

STRENGTHS AND WEAKNESSES OF BOARDS AS MANAGERS

As a group of persons to whom power to make decisions and undertake one or more of the managerial functions has been given, the board of directors has certain strengths and weaknesses. Most of these are applicable to any type of committee, but some are especially characteristic of a committee given authority to make decisions, in contrast to one whose function is advisory or for the exchange of information only.

Strengths of Boards. Perhaps the most important reason for the use of a decision-making group is the fear of delegating too much authority to a single person. This fear is especially noticeable in government, where there are many instances of such groups, ranging from legislatures and courts to administrative commissions. As we noted in discussing the history of boards of directors, this factor played an important part in the establishment of the original English board of proprietors of the joint stock company.

Another important reason for use of groups to make decisions is the presumed advantage of group deliberation and judgment. A group of people can usually bring to bear on a problem a greater variety of experience, opinion, and specialized knowledge, as well as a more thorough probing of facts, than can a single individual. Moreover, thorough discussion of ideas will tend to clarify the problems and stimulate the development of new ideas.

Other basic reasons include the desire to obtain representation of interested groups. This may be seen with boards in the desire to have shareholder interests represented, as well as certain public, marketing, financial and other special business interests.

Other reasons for the use of committees have had rather little influence in the establishment of decision-making groups. These include coordinating plans and policies through exchange of information, consolidation of authority of individual members, and motivation of people by participation. Also, it should not be overlooked that committees may be used when a person does not want any immediate action to ensue. It is well known that committees with the "right" kind of membership can deliberate indefinitely on almost any problem.

Weaknesses of Boards. The principal weakness of a board is the danger of compromise at the least common denominator which results from the tendency of groups to develop a tradition of unanimity. It should also be remembered that when a board attempts to seek unanimous or near-unanimous decisions, rather than abiding by majority rule, minority members may be placed in an exceptionally strong position where, if they are vociferous enough, they can tyrannize the majority.

Another weakness of a board is its high cost in money and time—not only the normal cost of travel to meetings but the cost of members' time at meetings and preparing for them. If each member is expected to express himself on issues, and some individuals do too much of their thinking aloud, time expenditure can be considerable. One of the major problems boards of directors face is that the members are too often called upon to make major decisions with too little time to discuss the implications of the problem. If, in addition, staff work to support the proposals is inadequate, time demands are understandably increased. There is perhaps nothing more fruitless than a group attempting to find facts, undertake research, or do staff work in a meeting. Yet, unless the meeting is very well organized and operated, this is likely to happen.

Another weakness is the fact that it is difficult for the individual person to feel the same degree of responsibility for a group decision as he would feel if he were personally charged with the same task. Because no individual can practically or logically be held accountable for the actions of the group, this tends to make no one feel responsible. This built-in tendency can be partially avoided, however, by keeping careful minutes of positions taken and matters discussed and by following up board decisions with reports on the results. By so doing and by continually impressing upon individual board members their individual responsibilities, some of the loss of personal responsibility involved in group decision making may be avoided.

Making Groups Effective. In view of the advantages of group operation and the fact that a board or committee is a desirable managerial form in certain circumstances—and in light of the weaknesses normally encountered—it is important that steps be taken to make them as effective as possible.

In the first place, the authority and areas of responsibility for decision should be clearly defined. The members should know whether they are operating in an area where it is their responsibility to make decisions, or whether it is their responsibility to review or counsel those responsible for administering its decisions. The way subjects are presented is also important. As indicated in the discussions above, proposals made before a board should be clearly presented with definite recommendations and adequate staff work to support them. Furthermore, so that members may have some notice of what is to be discussed, it is imperative that a well-prepared agenda be circulated in advance, preferably with enough information on the matters to be considered that the time of a group need not be used to educate its individual members.

With any decision-making group, also, the number of members should be large enough to promote deliberation and incorporate the breadth of knowledge required for its task but not so large as to waste time or encourage indecision. Although no precise ideal number can be stated, a group as large as five or six members but no larger than fifteen or sixteen is generally thought to be best.[3] If rep-

[3] See discussion of this point in Koontz and O'Donnell, *op. cit.*, p. 362. See also, E. Dale, *Planning and Developing the Company Organization Structure*, American Management Association, New York, 1952, p. 90. There are others, however, who believe that a workable committee should be much smaller. See *e.g.*, W. H. Newman, *Administrative Action*, Prentice-Hall, Inc., Englewood Cliffs, N.J., 1951, who states (p. 234) that a committee should be held down to three or four members. Like-

resentation requirements or other considerations necessitate a larger group, general experience indicates that it is better to have one or more subcommittees to whom problems may be assigned for adequate deliberation and action.

Of importance, also, is the compatibility of members and their ability to perform well as a group. This does not mean a group of individuals who are fearful of stating their positions on matters and always desirous of compromising, or a group reaching conclusions through political or organizational strength. It means rather a group in which the participants are at the same level of intelligence and organizational status and sufficiently independent of one another not to fear reprisal. In other words, boards are more likely to reach agreement without weak compromise or power politics if the members are aware of their individual responsibilities, friendly, and mutually respectful of one another's positions.

Importance of the Chairman. In any group success will depend a great deal upon the skill and ability of the chairman. Through planning the meeting, preparing the agenda and seeing that proposals are well researched before presentation, and by recognizing the strengths and drawbacks of the board, the chairman is probably more responsible than anyone else for its effective operation. His position and functions will be discussed more thoroughly in Chapter 8.

---

wise, J. Berwitz in his article "The Work Committee—An Administrative Technique," *Harvard Business Review,* Vol. 30, No. 1, pp. 110–124, January, 1952, suggests a maximum of seven members.

chapter 4

BOARD DECISION AND CONTROL AREAS

On the basis of legal requirements, decision importance, the basic responsibility of boards of directors, and empirical study of company operations, there appear to be ten major areas in which any board should actually make decisions. These are the following:

1. Determination of company objectives
2. Approval of major policies
3. Approval of company organization
4. Appointment of officers and major managers
5. Top-management compensation
6. Approval of company budgets
7. Approval of major plans and commitments
8. Approval of outside auditors and legal counsel
9. Company representatives
10. Matters where stockholders' action is required

In addition, in smaller companies the board is likely to be called upon to involve itself in certain areas which in larger companies would be delegated to operating managers. Likewise, in these same areas, the board being responsible for planning decisions, it should also exercise appropriate control techniques to assure itself that the plans are, in fact, being accomplished.

The author has clinically tested these decision areas with a number of company boards of directors, has presented them for analysis to more than 1,500 top executives and board members, and has received general agreement on their validity. A minority of operating executives, however, have disagreed on some of them. This is hardly surprising. Operating executives, particularly those at the very top

57

of an enterprise, often prefer to have the least possible interference by a superior in the form of a board of directors.

Some of this concern reflects misunderstanding of the board's role in determining policy versus its role in making more specific decisions under established policy. Some of it has resulted from a desire to be left alone and to be judged completely on the merits of the total operation. As pointed out above, no responsible executive, and this includes the board of directors, can expect to abdicate its responsibility in this way. Just as no parent should allow a child to bankrupt him, no board of directors, responsible as it is for the total operation of an enterprise, should give to a chief executive and his subordinates, freely and without strings, the authority to bankrupt a company.

In outlining these decision areas, it is natural that they would be elaborations on the basic functions and responsibilities of the board discussed in Chapter 2. However, they serve to give specific meaning to these functions and responsibilities.

DETERMINATION OF COMPANY OBJECTIVES

If the board of directors is responsible for anything in the management of a company, it must be the determination of company objectives. As pointed out above in the discussion of basic functions and responsibilities of the board, the determination of end-points of a company's operations should be made by the board of directors, although they should look to the chief executive and the operating management of the company for recommendation and guidance. But a board member can make certain that meaningful, actionable, and verifiable objectives are established. He can likewise take steps to assure himself that these objectives are translated into contributory objectives suitable for each subordinate level in the company.

In looking at the problem of objectives, a board must ask such questions as: What business are we in? What are our opportunities, particularly in the light of our strengths and weaknesses and the expected future environment of the company? Where are we going and how do we measure whether we are getting there? If a board answers these questions, or sees that information is presented so that answers may be agreed upon by the board, it will be going far toward determining useful company objectives.

The question of what business a company is in is not so easy as one might suspect. The apparent failure of most railroads to recognize early enough that they were in the transportation business rather than the railroad business, and the oversight for some time of the major steel companies that they were in the structural materials business rather than steel making, are cases in point. Again, many of the large glass container companies were late in getting on the plastic bottle bandwagon, seemingly because they forgot that they were in the container business, not the glass bottle business. This is a decision which every company must make. It obviously has great meaning in terms of giving substance to future plans and awareness that technology or marketing changes may modify the product and the market to be served.

In determining the kind of business a firm is in and wishes to be in, it must deal with the question of what its opportunities are. Opportunities are always a combination of company strengths and weaknesses on one hand, and the changing social, technical, economic and political environment on the other.

In asking the question of where a company is going, most objectives can and should be refined in numerical terms. One can expect to have growth objectives in sales, expressed in specific amounts or percentages, and profit objectives measured in total amount, percent of sales, or return on investment. In addition, fairly specific but not necessarily quantitative goals or objectives can be formulated with respect to product-line changes and expansion, marketing channels and approaches, and personnel.

In addition, since directors should be called upon to make major decisions dealing with such long-term and large commitments as capital expenditures for plant facilities, they should be aware of the time span of the commitments being made in order to see more clearly the probability of recovering cost through future operations. In other words, directors should be involved in long-range planning, both through setting goals and through relating current decisions to them. This does not mean that they need to be involved in the details of forecasting and analysis of long-range implications of programs, but rather they must be able to see how present decisions fit the pattern of long-range goals and plans. Effective long-range planning is not planning future decisions, but rather seeing the future implications of today's decisions.

Perhaps it is true, as Peter Drucker has pointed out, that any company's objectives must fall into several categories. He has asserted, for example, that:

There are eight areas in which objectives of performance and results have to be set: market standing; innovation; productivity; physical and financial resources; profitability; management performance and development; worker performance and attitude; and public responsibility.[1]

It is probable, however, that most people in operating management would think of the overall company goal areas as sales and markets, new products or services, and profits. While objectives in the area of human and material resources, productivity, managerial and worker performance, and public responsibility are important, they seem primarily to be supporting objectives or environmental factors which any alert management would consider in attaining the more primary economic goals of the firm.

APPROVAL OF MAJOR POLICIES

Another important area in which board decision should be required is approval of major company policies. Policies, it should be noted, are guides to thinking in decision making. They imply the existence of discretion, not the making of specific decision in individual cases. They give structure to operating decision making within the enterprise. By giving shape and general direction to plans, policies do much to influence the success, stability, and soundness of a company.

It must be emphasized that determination or approval of major policies does not in itself get the board of directors into day-by-day

[1] *The Practice of Management,* Harper & Row, New York, 1954, p. 63.

decision making. This is a point of crucial importance. The author found that many of the operating executives who disagreed with his proposals failed to make this distinction, thinking that the power to make policies in a given area implied that the board would make all the detailed decisions in that area.

Company policies should be reviewed from time to time to make certain that they fit the new environment in which a company continually operates. It is more dangerous for a company to operate under obsolete policies than with obsolete plant and equipment, since policies so forcefully guide and shape management thinking and decision making.

There are many types of major policies over which the board should exercise power of approval. Also, as in the case of most other types of plans, the board should expect that analyses and recommendations be submitted to it by the operating executives. Perhaps the most important kind of major policies on which board approval should be provided are the following:

1. *New Product and Research & Development Policies.* This area of activity will determine very largely the future nature of the company. Therefore the board should approve what general kind of planning it would like to see undertaken in this field. There may be a question of whether a company's policy should be to engage in basic research or only in applied research, whether it will be an innovator in product ideas or choose to be an imitator. Another question is the extent to which a company should balance defense products with commercial products, or whether it should be in one business or the other at all. Another kind of policy determination might be whether all new products should fit the company's present marketing capabilities.

2. *Basic Marketing Policy.* Marketing is closely related to product development in its controlling impact on a company's future. This has been particularly true in the past decade, as the world of competition has turned from a seller's market to a buyer's market. Policy questions in this field might be concerned with whether a company should sell direct through its own marketing force or through representatives or distributors. Another basic policy matter might have to

do with whether a company with trademark merchandise should engage in private-label business.

The crux in determining what marketing policies should be approved by the board of directors is whether the policy applies company-wide and molds the company's total marketing effort. In a divisionalized company, it may even be that a single division or group of divisions is so important that its marketing policies should be approved by the board. This is true with the automobile companies, who would unquestionably not allow any division to change its system of distribution of automobiles through franchised retailers without board discussion and approval, even though the company might have certain product lines in other divisions where the impact of marketing approaches would not justify board attention.

3. *Pricing Policy.* Where pricing policies have material impact on the company's total operations and future, their determination should normally be a board matter. In a defense business, for example, the question of whether a company should (if it has a choice) engage only in fixed-price business or in cost-plus-fixed-fee business, or operate on an incentive contract basis, might very well be exceptionally important. Also, in commerical companies, whether a company attempts to sell on fair-trade prices or on an open-competition basis without influence over resellers would normally be important. Moreover, blending of marketing and pricing policy would be required where a company has a policy of high advertising and sales-promotion expense which is usually accompanied by a policy against selling on price.

4. *Capital Procurement Policies.* Certainly the board has a primary role in determining the company's policy with respect to procurement of funds for the operation and growth of the company. Whether funds are obtained through borrowing, through lease of property, or through equity financing is a major policy matter on which board action can hardly be avoided.

5. *Cash Utilization Policies.* In most cases, the effective board should devote some attention to determining guidelines in major areas of cash utilization. Among the most important of these are policies with regard to production for order versus for inventory, the amount of speculation to encourage in buying against price rises, the

question of utilizing cash for buying major facilities versus leasing them, and those dealing with possible deferral of taxes under accelerated depreciation or other programs.

6. *Disposition Policies.* Since the disposal of profits, whether through dividend payout or reinvestment, are decision matters that boards cannot avoid under the law, it follows clearly that any policy determination in this area should be made by the board. Few boards have made the policy determination that the company will pay out no cash, reinvesting earnings completely; most boards have a fairly clear policy on cash payout, ranging from 50 percent to 70 percent of earnings. Obviously, any change in these policies should be a matter for careful board consideration.

7. *Personnel Policies.* Since people provide the principal focus of management effort, it is not surprising that more than half of company policies customarily have to do with personnel. Part of this emphasis has been forced on company managers by the militant labor movement of the past three decades, part by an enlightened attitude toward the human factor in business operations. Although boards of directors too seldom get involved in the approval of personnel policies, and although many areas of personnel policy and procedure should properly be the domain of operating executives, certain significant areas of personnel policy should be approved by the board.

In general, the board should approve those major personnel and labor relations policies that shape the essential character of personnel and labor relations in the company. If it were to get concerned with all personnel policies, this might impose too heavy a burden and also entangle the members in far too many operating matters. Nonetheless, the author has seen many instances where all personnel policies are periodically reviewed by the board of directors to make sure operating management is keeping them up-to-date with new personnel trends and to gain understanding of the nature of personnel and labor-union relations in the company.

Without attempting to be exhaustive, there are certain personnel policies on which the board should be given the right of approval. Among these are policies guiding relationships with unions, retirement policies, employment and executive insurance benefit policies and the question of the extent of company contribution, profit-sharing policies, policy on promotion from within versus open competition for available positions, patent and secrecy agreement policies, and organization policies involving such matters as nature and extent of delegation, clarity of position descriptions, use of divisional versus functional organizational pattern, and other organizational matters that shape the character of the company's operations.

In addition, often one of the major policies of a firm concerns its attitude toward how much and how to give company information to both managerial and non-managerial personnel. Since companies differ in their willingness to disclose such information and since this appears to be a company-wide problem of a basic nature, the board of directors should probably be allowed to approve the policy in this area.

8. *Executive Compensation and Development Policies.* There can hardly be any doubt that the board of directors must take responsibility for policy with respect to executive compensation and should approve policy regarding executive development. With regard to executive compensation, policy tends to treat with determining whether a company has a bonus plan and what kind, whether it issues stock options and to what levels of executives, what fringe benefits should be given to executives and to what levels, what basic approaches should be made to executive appraisals, and how this will be expected to relate to salaries and bonuses. In most companies, for example, boards limit stock options to those executives and key staff managers who can materially affect profit, and bonuses may be given to any managerial or staff personnel beyond this group with salaries exceeding a certain amount (say, $12,000) per year. The best-operated plans provide that bonus awards be approved by a committee of the board and allocated on the basis of demonstrated individual performance.

While a board can hardly be expected to take part directly in implementing executive development policy, the assurance that executives are being developed along certain lines appears to be a key responsibility of an effective board. Thus, it might determine that executive development efforts be devoted to all managerial personnel at all levels, including the top executives, be aimed at self-development, and be related to needs for improvement demonstrated by adequate management appraisal.

In better-managed companies, it has become customary for both bonus and stock-option policy and executive development policy to be geared to a policy of management appraisal. For example, a board might require that management appraisal be based upon appraisal by performance against goals plus an analysis of performance of individuals as managers.

9. *Outside Relationships.* Boards in well-managed companies have for a number of years given increasing attention to company policy with respect to outside relationships. This goes beyond customary policies regarding public and stockholder relations and may include policy regarding adherence to antitrust laws, defining conflict of interests, and policing gratuities and entertainment. With greater attention being paid to conflict of interest and influence through accepting excessive gratuities or entertainment, an increasing number of boards have properly insisted upon definite policies in this area and careful policing of their application. As representatives of the owners of the company with their interest in the long-run welfare of its operations, boards can hardly avoid scrutinizing and approving such policies, since they have to do with the position of a company in the society in which it operates.

APPROVAL OF COMPANY ORGANIZATION

Although it need not be concerned with detailed company organization planning or changes, an effective board should reserve to itself final approval of *basic* company organization pattern and major authority delegation. Whether a company will develop along the lines of a divisionalized, territorial, or product organization, whether it will develop organizational tools to make it marketing-oriented, or whether it will maintain a functional form of organization are among those organizational matters important in shaping the future of the internal company environment.

Recommendations for these patterns should come from operating management, but a board of directors should be in a position to know what pattern is being adopted, what plans are being made for the future, and when operating managers intend to change a pattern. In one company, for example, the board of directors had long held to the principle that it was better to have the company organized in a number of divisionalized profit centers with focus on products and markets. They had reached this conclusion through the firm belief, demonstrated by experience and analysis, that individual profit motivation obtained by a series of "small" integrated units within a larger company would be the surest road towards profits. A new president who was heavily engineering-oriented came into the company, saw immediately that there were some duplicate staff operations in purchasing, accounting, and engineering, and proceeded to reorganize the company into functional departments, giving up the divisional profit centers. The resultant loss in motivation to the company was serious. Had the board of directors been given an opportunity to analyze the basic changes, it is doubtful whether they would have been permitted.

Another area where a board should approve organization is the overall delegation of authority within the enterprise. This is necessary to determine the division of decision authority between the board and the chief executive and other members of top management. It likewise seems desirable as a means of seeing the pattern of decentralization in a company. It can be accomplished very easily by simply requiring periodic board review of the chart of approval authorizations described in Chapter 3.

OFFICERS AND MAJOR MANAGERS

In the discussion of basic board authority and functions it was pointed out that the board had an inescapable legal responsibility to elect company officers. It was likewise stated that there were compelling reasons why a board should approve appointment of major managers, primarily those reporting to the president who might not have officer status. By doing so, the board would also be in the position of setting or approving recommendations for salary levels of these persons.

In addition, most boards find it desirable to approve salaries of any employees above certain levels. In a small company, the hiring of any individual at a salary of more than $12,000 per year might go to the board. In a larger company the board might only ask to approve salaries abve $20,000 a year, and in a very large company above $35,000 per year.

There are two major reasons for this practice. In the first place, paying higher-level salaries in a company involves an important expenditure of funds and usually an implied commitment for keeping the person in the company as an essential part of the top management or staff team. In the second place, the board may be concerned that the company is maintaining a reasonable and consistent top-level salary structure.

TOP-MANAGEMENT COMPENSATION

One area worthy of special note is the board's role in administering company bonus or stock-option programs. Simple considerations of possible conflict of interests demand that the board should decide bonuses and options for all officer-directors, preferably through a committee of directors none of whom will benefit. In addition, in order to make sure that these special compensation programs are working for the benefit of the company as a whole, there is much to be said for this special compensation committee to review and recommend full board action on actual bonus and stock-option awards. Otherwise, there may be some grounds for an often expressed stockholder suspicion that the insider group is lining its own pockets at the expense of the corporation. Although this is difficult to prove and may be untrue even where appearances are subject to suspicion, a certain major company with a totally inside board of directors became the object of understandable stockholder and investment-community suspicion a few years ago when its inside board happened to comprise seven of the ten highest-paid executives in the country.

One of the most successful compensation programs in American industry over the years has been that of the General Motors Corporation. Not only have executives been paid handsome bonuses and gained from stock options, but the shareholders as well have received great benefits from mounting dividends and stock prices. Also, in this company, the bonus program has applied further down the line in the organization structure than in almost any other major company. This plan has been operated for many years under the general direction of a compensation committee of the board of directors, wholly made up of board members who do not participate. This board committee carefully reviews the reasonableness and justice of bonus awards to the top management group and assures itself that recommendations for bonus awards at lower levels are being considered in the light of performance factors of eligible persons. This committee has also taken an active role in guiding the corporation's executive compensation policies over the years. With this experience and approach, it can hardly be said that this area involves too much work and time for boards of directors of smaller companies.

APPROVAL OF BUDGETS

One of the most useful ways of assuring that plans are designed to meet objectives is for the board to give final approval to budgets, often more diplomatically entitled profit plans. Budgets, whether applying to cash, revenues, expenses, capital expenditures, or number of employees, are essentially planning instruments whereby plans are reduced to numerical terms. If properly prepared, they then become "windows" through which a board can see the impact and coordination of the major planning programs of operating management. Likewise, after adopted, they are standards against which actual performance may be measured for a given period in the future. To the extent that they are focused on overall corporate affairs, as would be the case of budget summaries for an enterprise, they should be matters for board approval.

However, any board of directors must take care that in approving budgets it does not freeze into inflexible compartments the underlying details and inputs that support them. Sometimes—particularly in public enterprises—budget approvals become so detailed that even slight changes from detailed budget classifications must be approved by the board, resulting in unreasonable interference with managerial discretion.

Approval of Summary Operating Budgets. While the board should not be interested in the detail of operating expense budgets, it should be given an opportunity to review and approve summary budgets showing sales forecasts for the company as a whole and for its divisions, along with operating expenses by major categories, and planned profit.

Without being able to look through this "window" of operating plans, a board tends, when it reviews financial statements, to be in the position of simply performing a post-mortem on past results. To meet its basic responsibility for planning and control to assure over-all company results, a board must have an opportunity to review these summary operating budgets.

There are some top executives who feel that this is involving a board in operating details of the business. There is a danger that some boards, like many legislative bodies in their review of government budgets, may pick at details of expenditure. On the other hand, if the focus of budget information is to show how major planning programs will operate in their effect upon expenses and profits for a future period of time, they offer one of the best ways of seeing how planning has been done and what expected results are.

Approving Variable Budgets. If a company operates under a variable or flexible budget [2] the resulting information becomes espe-

[2] This is the type of budget where expenses are divided between those that are "stand-by" or "fixed" (and related to the very fact that a company is in business), and expenses—including even overhead and general and administrative expenses—which tend to vary with volume of business. On the basis of this division, then, the budget indicates what expenses are *expected* to be at various volume levels of operation, with this volume expressed in sales per month, or direct labor hours, or some other appropriate measure. The advantage of the variable budget is that it forces an early study of what expenses *should* be at various volume levels and gives an automatic way of reviewing the entire expense structure of a

cially meaningful, since it relates expenditures and planned profit to various volume levels. Indeed, a board member should insist that his company utilize variable budgeting if it has not done so. By forcing an early study of cost-profit-volume relationships, and accompanying this technique with a philosophy of programming profit (that is, a philosophy which looks upon profit not as a residual but as an amount that can be planned), an entire company can develop a sense of commitment to desired costs and profits. Also, this technique furnishes a regular means of review of what costs *should* be at various levels of operations, and information is readily available for studying regularly the total operations of a company under varying volume and product-mix situations.

While this should be done even with fixed budgeting, there is a natural tendency for executives utilizing this type of budgeting to look only at the amount by which budgets are increased each year without reviewing the entire level and character of expenditures. A board of directors should not only insist upon a variable budget program but should, in order to have maximum visibility of expected results, review the variable budget itself. As a matter of fact, when this is done, review of operating budgets is actually little more than looking at the validity of sales or other volume forecasts.

Approval of Capital Budgets. Although available information indicates that not enough boards of directors make thorough and formal reviews of summary operating budgets or variable budgets, it is common practice for them to approve capital expenditure budgets. Since capital expenditures are regarded as using funds of the corporation and committing them in given directions for varying periods of years in the future before they can be recovered through depreciation allowances and profits, board authority in approving capital expenditures has tended to be rather extensive.

Even boards to whom no capital expenditure budget is submitted

---

company with changes in volume. For more information on variable budgets, see Koontz and O'Donnell, *Principles of Management, op. cit.,* pp. 551–553; Robert Beyer, *Profitability Accounting for Planning and Control,* The Ronald Press Company, New York, 1963, Chapters 6 and 7; or any of the standard books on budgeting.

will typically approve major expenditures, and some have even insisted on approving rather small ones. In one large company involving sales of approximately $500 million, for example, the author ob-
served that it was customary for both the budget and all individual
capital expenditures of more than $5,000 to go to the board of
directors.

However, what a board should be most interested in is the total
program of capital expenditures for a specified period of time in the
future, normally one year. This gives board members a chance to see
how the operating management intends to utilize corporate funds. It
is also an important means of requiring executives to plan capital
expenditures. The normal procedure is for the board to approve
capital expenditure programs quarterly, with budgets submitted for
at least four quarters in advance. Sometimes the full four quarters of
expenditures are approved, the board retaining the right of further
review each quarter. In other cases, a board approves expenditures
for the immediate quarter, plus expenditures with long lead times in
succeeding quarters, and approves in principle, subject to review,
expenditures in succeeding quarters.

Where the board of directors has approved a capital expenditure
budget, there is an understandable tendency to submit only very
large individual expenditure items to the board for final review and
approval. On the other hand, it is common company practice to require board approval for relatively low expenditures if they have not
been budgeted. The primary reason for this is to force upon operating executives the planning needed in this key area of company
operation.

MAJOR PLANS AND COMMITMENTS

In addition to establishing basic policy in key areas, the effective
board should review and approve major company plans. As in the
case of authority delegation, it is difficult to draw any arbitrary dis-
tinctions between the specific kinds of plans a board should approve
and those which should be left to operating management. Most
plans are properly guided and controlled by establishing major poli-

cies and by the visibility provided when summary operating and capital expenditure budgets are reviewed. There are, however, certain programs of great importance to the company, affecting its long-range profitablity, which should be reviewed and approved by the board.

There can be no doubt of the board's interest in programs of financing, merger, consolidation, or acquisition. Likewise, as indicated above, plans with respect to top-management compensation, company organization, and management development should be reviewed by the board. Additionally, plans for major plant facilities must be brought to the board if for no other reason than that they normally involve expenditures of considerable amounts and relatively inflexible long-term commitments.

Moreover, it appears desirable for the board at least to be regularly informed and perhaps be given approval authority on new-product-development programs, especially those which anticipate getting into a new product line. There are strong reasons for giving this area special board attention. Perhaps the most important one is to provide a constant reminder to operating executives embroiled in day-to-day operations that this means of future company stability and growth should not be overlooked. Planning to go into a new product line may also change the very nature of the company and impose material obligations and risks with respect to capital expenditures, larger inventories, and receivables, as well as the building up of marketing organizations and expansion of other facilities and obligations of the company.

It is also desirable that major marketing programs be submitted to the board, at least for review and comment. If a company, for example, plans to change its method of distribution from use of representatives or distributors to direct sales, this may be a serious and important step which the board ought to review. The chief executive of the company should welcome a rigorous review of so major a step. Or, if a company plans on embarking upon an unusually heavy program of advertising expenditures, such as many consumer products involve, it might well submit these to the board in view of the volume of expenditures and the risk involved.

Occasionally, also, a board should ask for review, although not necessarily approval, of specific personnel programs of all kinds. The purpose of this is to assure themselves that the management of the company is not overlooking this critical area of operations with its great impact for the future.

Better-managed companies also submit their long-range planning to the board of directors for review, comment and approval. While this may not be done more than once a year, it is an important safeguard which a board should impose on operating management to assure itself that those in charge of running the company are not overlooking the future and are taking a rational approach toward long-range company goals.

Review of capital budgets and major programs will go far toward covering desirable board approval of major commitments in the form of funds. However, as indicated above, it has been customary and probably desirable for boards of directors to approve large capital-expenditure items, even though they have been budgeted, and approve much smaller capital expenditure items which have not been budgeted.

It is often asked why a board should approve a capital expenditure budget and then, in addition, approve individual large expenditures. The reason is that the board may wish to exercise particularly close control in capital expenditures and, for large items, may desire a second look before final approval. As one board member put it to the author, the capital expenditure budget is a "hunting license," but in important cases a board should see to it that the operating managers are actually hunting the right game before they are allowed to make the kill.

OUTSIDE AUDITORS AND LEGAL COUNSEL

Best practice requires that, as a minimum, the board selects and approves hiring outside auditors. In many corporations, the auditing firm charged with examination of the books of account is even approved by the stockholders. Since the audit of accounts is designed to check upon the integrity, honesty, and accuracy of corporate assets, liabilities, and operating profits, it is both reasonable and logical that these independent auditors be at least selected by the directors, and there is much to be said for them to be responsible to and therefore selected by the stockholders. However, in the modern corporation, with stockholders taking relatively small interest in a business so long as it operates acceptably, it is probably more realistic and useful to have the auditors appointed by the directors.

Even though director or stockholder approval of auditors is fairly general, the fact is that auditors tend to regard themselves as reporting to the chief financial officer of the company, largely because he is the one with whom they deal, who has probably recommended their appointment, and who is likely to study their reports most thoroughly. The practical existence of this situation may be traced to the fact that directors themselves pay rather little, and shareholders even less, attention to the audit except to review the company's final balance sheet and income statement results.

Steps should be taken for more responsibility by directors in this area. An increasing number of companies have their outside auditors issue a special report to the board of directors on the adequacy of accounting procedures and key accounting personnel. The very issuance of this special "white paper" to the board of directors has in many cases resulted in desirable changes that might otherwise not have occurred to the responsible heads of the company. It is, therefore, a practice to be encouraged.

Corporate legal counsel should also be selected by and report to the board of directors. Since the members of the board carry immediate responsibility for the legal position of the corporation, both as individuals and in their capacity as trustees for the stockholders, they should have legal counsel who regard their primary loyalty and obligation to the board. General legal counsel normally work also for operating executives of the company, and it may be difficult to enforce a loyalty to the board of directors for the same reasons advanced in connection with outside public accountants. Nevertheless, an effective board of directors should take steps to assure this.

Moreover, it is highly desirable practice for the corporate legal counsel to attend board meetings for counsel and advice on actions of board members. This furnishes a needed safeguard against directors taking positions that could lead to personal liability or to legal difficulties for the company.

COMPANY REPRESENTATIVES

There are in practice wide differences in the board's role in selecting company representatives, such as those in sales, purchasing, or acquisitions. Since these representatives are often given authority to commit the company as agents, it is usually desirable for the board to have some hand in approving their selection and their contract terms.

Many a board has awakened belatedly to the fact that a licensee or a sales representative has an uncancellable contract to represent the company in a certain area long after his usefulness has ceased and the company finds it desirable to appoint another agent or to take over manufacture or sales itself. Also, many a corporation director has been surprised, on finally approving an acquisition, to find that a "finder's fee" or consultant's compensation is due to a third party with whom the president or some vice-president has made a specific or implied contract. That these contractual commitments which bind the company in an important way are of significance to boards is obvious.

However, in many company operations, it is not feasible for the board to approve each and every contract with representatives who have some power to commit the company. This is particularly true with sales representatives, who in a typical company may number in the hundreds. In these cases, the board of directors could discharge its responsibility by approving the basic form and substance of the contracts, and perhaps by requiring the company's legal counsel to approve actual contracts.

MATTERS WHERE SHAREHOLDERS' ACTION IS REQUIRED

There are a number of matters typically requiring shareholders' action which, by their very nature, should be approved by the board before submission to shareholders. These include original authorization of stock, mortgaging of corporate assets, and the issuance of new types of securities, although issuance of securities other than stock in most jurisdictions is given either by charter or by-laws to the board.

Another area where shareholders' action may be required is the size of the board of directors. However, in many states, and with many boards of directors, shareholder approval is granted for a variable number of directors, say six to nine, thereby giving the board the power at any given time to determine the actual number within these limits. This has a considerable advantage in terms of corporate stability when the board might be faced with the desirability of electing an additional member during the interim between stockholders' meetings and where, at the time of the stockholders' meeting, a board might not have a full slate of qualified and available directors to be nominated. If stockholders were more active in the election of directors and in the other prerequisites of their ownership, this latter advantage of variable numbers of directors would not exist. But there are many occasions where, without this variable number, a board might have to fill the full slate hastily or take the risk of some shareholder's nominating and electing an undesirable director to the board.

With the exception of the board's normal power to fill vacancies on the board between stockholder meetings, stockholders naturally have the right to elect directors. This right is exercised at the usual annual stockholders' meeting. It must be admitted, however, that, because of the lack of stockholder participation in their elections and the existence of proxy machinery, a publicly held corporation board is almost certain to be nominated and effectively selected by the existing board members or, in many cases, by the president or a small group of inside officers who actually control the proxy machinery. This is not unusual in democratic processes. We see the same phenomenon in city, state, and national elections. With disorganization of voters as individuals, the need for some special leadership to take responsibility for nomination and selection is apparent.

Stockholder action is required in the case of mergers, consolidations, and sales of company assets. These, therefore, would almost invariably call for board-of-directors approval before their submission. On the other hand, as has been pointed out, when one company acquires another either through exchange of stock or cash, stockholders' approval is not normally necessary unless additional shares of authorized stock or a special type of stock are required. But certainly any such acquisition would be a basic function of the board of directors.

Obviously, any change in a corporation charter must be made by approval of the stockholders. However, the board's power to adopt and amend by-laws varies. Most modern corporate charters give the board of directors power to amend by-laws within certain limitations set forth in the charter. Nevertheless, because power to adopt and amend by-laws is basically a power of stockholders, those who own the corporation may change any by-law by proper vote at any time they wish. It is customary, however, for by-laws themselves to provide for method of amendment; a common provision is that by-laws may be "amended or repealed, or new by-laws may be made and adopted, at any annual or special meeting of stockholders called for that purpose, by the vote or written consent of stockholders representing [a certain percentage] of the subscribed capital stock, or by the vote of a majority of the board of directors at a regular or special meeting of the board." Therefore, even though a board may have a function of submitting by-law amendments to the stockholders, and approving them before submission—in some jurisdictions and under certain corporate charters it is required to do so—this is generally a matter on which the board itself has authority.

THE BOARD AND THE SMALL COMPANY

In the smaller company there are a number of special decision areas in which the board may become involved. Such a board may feel it wise to get into more detailed management matters, such as the review of engineering effort, detailed review of product programs, decisions on competitive price changes, and other matters which would be handled by company executives in larger companies. Moreover, smaller companies almost invariably set lower limits of approval for company executives in such areas as capital expenditures and sales commitments, with the result that smaller matters are referred to the board of directors.

Since smaller companies usually do not have adequate staff for advice in such fields as accounting, budgeting, sales and marketing, financing, and production, the small company board of directors often finds itself used as an advisory agency in these areas. As a matter of fact, this is one of the major advantages of having well-selected outside board members in a small company. Individuals will often serve on a board of directors who could not or would not serve, even for pay, as a consultant to a company. The advice and assistance which operating executives and particularly the president of the smaller company can receive from an effective small company board can, therefore, be considerable.

A board can make an especially important contribution to a small company by insisting on more adequate planning. The typical small-company chief executive and his operating management, since they are not likely to have adequate staff to assist them, are prone to be involved more than usual in day-to-day problems and to overlook planning. This is nowhere more prominent than in the lack of cash planning usually encountered in the smaller company. Estimates by bank loan officers in California, given to the author over the years, indicate that only about 10 percent to 12 percent of small companies do a reasonably adequate job of cash planning. This, of course, is dangerous, since availability of necessary cash is the *sine qua non* of company existence. A board member, merely by insisting upon cash planning—and sometimes showing a company how to do it—may make a vital contribution to the success and continued existence of the firm.

In many other planning areas, also, questioning what is being done can have a very great influence. In such subjects as new-product planning, marketing planning, and new-facility planning, the board, by becoming involved and by perhaps giving actual assistance, can do much to improve the quality and extent of planning in the smaller company.

Another area where board members can make an important contribution to the smaller company is in helping to make sure that authority is properly delegated. It is typical of small companies, notably those operated by founder pioneers, that the pioneer, having originally done everything in the company, hesitates to delegate authority properly as the company grows. The resulting management bottlenecks throttle effective and efficient operation. Often a company successfully launched by some non-managerial genius in production, engineering, or marketing, may fail to continue its profitable growth. By diplomatically suggesting that authority be delegated here or there, by insisting upon an organization chart, and by asking management to prepare a chart of approval authorization, much can be done to remove these bottlenecks and make for more effective delegation.

Another major responsibility which tends to fall on the smaller company board of directors is that of management succession. Management in the smaller company is understandably likely to be much "thinner" than in larger companies. Also, the smaller-company top executives tend not to give much attention to the problem of bringing management along and preparing for possible retirement or other displacement of top-management personnel. Here again, a board member, particularly an outsider, can, by assistance and continuing suggestion, often see that this deficiency is provided for before it causes problems.

It has been the author's experience, one which has been confirmed by many others working in small-company boards, that outside members must often act as arbiters of disputes among insiders. It is commonplace that a small company may be started by two, three, or four individuals who operate very much in the way of a general partnership, although each may be given a different officer title. Being stockholders in the company, and having operated for a number of years as virtual partners, such men, even though completely honest and highly competent, may become embroiled, indeed as marriages or other partnerships do, in internal disputes. Sometimes this is merely healthy argument, but often it gives rise to a very strong set of feelings which, on occasion, can endanger the continued existence of the company.

In these cases, a level-headed outside director, who can gain the confidence of the warring parties, can act as an arbiter. Individuals who regard themselves as equals may be unwilling to back down from conflicting positions once taken in argument among themselves; but often they will back down with good grace in a face-saving agreement arbitrated by a person in whom all have confidence and who has no axe to grind in the resulting decision.

chapter 5

DIRECTORS'
LIABILITIES

A proper and increasingly felt concern of those who serve as company directors is the kind and extent of their personal liability. Particularly in the case of an outside director, compensation for serving is seldom great enough to justify considerable personal risk. Yet, in all kinds of human activities, and especially those of a positive nature which contribute to human progress, exposure to risks is inevitable.

The director who takes his duties seriously should, however, be aware of his risks. Above all, he should be aware of what the law expects of him as a director. While no attempt can be made here to discuss the problems of directors' liability in detail,[1] and no treatise on directors' liabilities can take the place of competent legal advice, their general character is outlined here. As will be seen, these liabilities are essentially a reflection of common sense applicable to a situation where a person undertakes to represent the investment of others and to face the public as a representative of those who own a corporation.

BASIC RESPONSIBILITY OF DIRECTORS

As already indicated in earlier chapters, the basic responsibility of the board of directors is to represent the shareholders generally in

---

[1] This has been done elsewhere. See, for example, Mortimer Feuer, *Personal Liabilities of Corporate Officers and Directors,* Prentice-Hall, Inc., Englewood Cliffs, N.J., 1961; Mortimer Feuer, *Handbook for*

assuring them that the corporation is well managed. But a director's obligation extends beyond the narrow self-interest of owners of a corporation. In their position of representing the owners of the corporation, directors hold themselves out to third parties as being the responsible source of power (and therefore action) in a corporation. This position may cause them to be liable not only to the state for actions undertaken by themselves and the corporation but also to such outside parties as creditors and customers with whom the corporation deals.

Although directors are not trustees in the ordinary sense of the word, since they do not hold the assets of the corporation in trust for the stockholders, the law requires them to act with reasonable business judgment, honesty, and independence of judgment. Many courts have stated the standard of a director's conduct as that of a "prudent man in handling his own property"—the standard normally applied to a trustee. However, as a matter of fact, courts apply the "business judgment" standard. This, rather than the "prudent man" rule is regarded as the prevailing law.

For example, in one leading case, the court stated that "the test in each case is whether corporate action is the result of exercise by the directors of their unbiased judgment in determining that such action will promote the corporate interests." [2] In another case, the court held that "the internal affairs, questions of policy of management, and expediency of contracts of a corporation are subject to the control of a board of directors, and in so far as those directors are honest, capable, and independent, their judgment is final." [3] Even the

---

Corporate Directors, Prentice-Hall, Inc., Englewood Cliffs, N.J., 1965; W. J. Grange and T. C. Woodbury, *Corporation Law: Operating Procedures for Officers and Directors*, The Ronald Press Company, New York, 1964.

[2] *Chelrob, Inc. v. Barrett*, 293 N.Y. 442, 460; 57 N.E.2d 825, 833 (1944).

[3] *Turner v. American Metal Co. Ltd. et al.*, 268 App.Div. 239, 259; 50 N.Y.S.2d 800, 819 (1944).

strict California Code provides only that "directors and officers shall exercise their powers in good faith and with a view to the interests of the corporation." [4]

It is true that some of the cases say that directors are trustees for the benefit of stockholders and creditors.[5] But, as a matter of fact, the courts do not go so far, or impose as strict a requirement, as they do in trust situations.

With the exception of certain matters specifically prohibited by law, the courts have applied this "reasonable man" doctrine in the absence of fraud or gross negligence. In other words, the courts have not held directors responsible in cases where only poor business judgment was displayed. They have recognized that reasonable men take risks, sometimes of a very dangerous character, and make mistakes which often appear inexcusable in retrospect. They have understood that punishment for mistakes of directors' judgment would constitute an unwarranted interference with the free-enterprise system. The courts have tended, therefore, when actions seemed reasonable under the circumstances, to decide cases of liability by giving the benefit of any doubt to accused directors.

As one authority has stated:

A director who behaves fairly and honorably, who makes full disclosure of possible conflicts of interest, and who acts, or creates the appearance of acting, diligently, is not likely to be subjected to personal liability for his conduct, even though, when his co-fiduciaries behave otherwise, he may well be caught in the web of, and be obliged to defend himself against, undifferentiated charges. This last can, of course, be distasteful and burdensome, and suggests that one who is invited to serve on a board of directors would do well to give more than passing consideration to the propensities of his prospective associates.[6]

[4] Section 620.

[5] See, for example, *Saracco Tank and Welding Co. v. Platz*, 150 P.2d 918; 65 Cal.App.2d 306 (1964).

[6] Feuer, *Handbook for Corporate Directors, op. cit.*, p. 143.

BASIC NATURE OF LIABILITIES

Major areas of directors' liabilities are discussed in succeeding pages. As will be seen, the basic nature of a director's liability follows from his position in the company and the "reasonable business judgment" doctrine which has been generally applied to his actions. However, it must be pointed out that the laws of various jurisdictions vary, in some instances rather radically. A director, therefore, should address himself to the specific laws applicable to his corporation's operations.

Liabilities to Outsiders or to the Corporation. Distinction must be drawn between liabilities of directors to outsiders and to the corporation itself. In their position as representatives of all the shareholders, directors may be held liable to outsiders, whether the state, creditors, vendors, or others, for certain of their actions. Typical of these are actions beyond corporate powers, the misuse of corporate funds for such purposes as loans to themselves or officers, declaring unearned dividends with resultant insolvency and loss to creditors, and certain corporate wrongs, such as antitrust behavior assented to or perpetrated by directors.

In reality, by far the largest number of liabilities involve obligations to the corporation (and its shareholders). Under the principle that directors are expected to operate in the best interest of the corporation, those liabilities arising under conflict of interest, and most of those resulting from the state and federal securities laws, provide for liability running to the corporation which is assumed to be the aggrieved party.

Fraud and Negligence. As has been pointed out, with the exception of actions specifically prohibited by law, the courts have tended not to hold directors liable for their business decisions in the absence of fraud or gross negligence. Fraudulent action depends upon whether the director knowingly and on the basis of improper motives took action which would cheat shareholders, the corporation, or a third party. Was he attempting to conceal facts to his benefit?

Did he understand that his action would lead to damage of another party and to his benefit? The elements of fraud depend upon rather clear facts in each case. And no director with any understanding of moral or ethical practice should have any doubt when he is committing fraud.

Gross negligence is, on the other hand, a more difficult matter. When is a director being so negligent as to be liable for his actions? As in other areas of the law, the courts have decided this question by reference to the "reasonable man" principle. In these cases, the courts have been generally quite sympathetic with honest mistakes of judgment. In other words, they have not expected directors to be specialists in any particular field like doctors or lawyers, or even necessarily to be specialists in the business itself, but only to act honestly and diligently with at least ordinary knowledge and skill.

There are some areas where courts have held directors to be negligent. Among these are complete failure to attend board meetings, to examine books or results, or to keep reasonably abreast of the course of business. Even in these cases, actual liability for negligence must arise from a showing that the damage alleged and the director's lack of attention had a direct relationship. In other words, if directors simply overlook the facts as they exist, or make no attempt to find out appropriate facts before taking a decision related to them, their action would not be in accordance with that expected of an individual using good business judgment, and therefore the director might be held negligent to the point of incurring liability.

One of the most widely quoted concepts of the law was that given in a New York State Court of Appeals case in 1880. In the case, the court stated:

When one deposits money in a savings bank or takes stock in a corporation, thus divesting himself of the immediate control of his property, he expects, and has the right to expect, that the trustees or directors, who are chosen to take his place in the management or control of his property, will exercise ordinary care and prudence in the trust committed to them —the same degree of care and prudence that men prompted by self-interest generally exercise in their own affairs. When one voluntarily takes the position of trustee or director of a corporation, good faith, exact justice, and public policy unite in requiring of him such a degree of care and prudence, and it is a gross breach of duty—*crassa negligentia*—not to bestow them.

It is impossible to give the measure of culpable negligence in all cases, as the degree of care required depends upon the subject to which it is applied. . . . There is a classification of negligence to be found in the books, not always of practical value and yet sometimes serviceable, into slight negligence, gross negligence, and to that degree of negligence intermediate the two, attributed to the absence of ordinary care; and the claim on behalf of these trustees is that they can only be held responsible in this action in consequence of gross negligence according to this classification. If gross negligence be taken according to its ordinary meaning —as something nearly approaching fraud or bad faith—I cannot yield to this claim; and if there are any authorities upholding the claim, I emphatically dissent from them. . . .[7]

And in a more recent case, the point of negligence is put in the following way:

In the last analysis, the question of whether a corporate director has become liable for losses to the corporation through neglect of duty is determined by the circumstances. If he has recklessly reposed confidence in an obviously untrustworthy employee, has refused or neglected cavalierly to perform his duty as a director, or has ignored either willfully or through inattention obvious danger signs of employee wrongdoing, the law will cast the burden of liability upon him. This is not the case at bar, however, for as soon as it became evident that there were grounds for suspicion, the Board acted promptly to end it and prevent its recurrence.[8]

ACTION BEYOND CORPORATE POWERS

One of the specific areas of directors' responsibility is action beyond corporate powers, usually referred to as *ultra vires* acts. As

---

[7] *Hun v. Cary*, 82 N.Y. 65, at pp. 71–72 (1880). It should be noted that this early case uses the "prudent man" rule—which, as pointed out above, is not actually the applicable standard of law.

[8] *Graham v. Allis-Chalmers Mfg. Co.*, 188 A.2d 125 (Del., 1963), at p. 130.

will be recalled, a corporation is established for certain purposes which are spelled out in its certificate of incorporation, as well as in the laws existing at the time of incorporation or which may be passed pursuant to a government's police power. If a corporation embarks on activities beyond its specifically delegated powers, it is, of course, acting *ultra vires*, and the directors may clearly be held responsible.

In general, since it has been the practice in recent years to draw up certificates of incorporation so broadly that the corporation can engage in virtually any activity except those specifically forbidden by law or given by law to certain qualified corporations (for example, banking), there is little likelihood that a board will act beyond its corporate powers. One exception which has received much attention in recent years is making contributions for philanthropic and educational purposes. This has sometimes been held to be beyond the powers of the corporation, although the courts have generally held that reasonable contributions which inure to the benefit of employees or to the corporation's position as a good citizen in the market it serves are valid corporate activities. In addition, particularly after corporate contributions were questioned in such well-known states as New York and Delaware, many states now permit corporations by statute to make contributions in a reasonable amount for "public purposes" which the directors regard as "reasonable and in the best interests of the corporation."

Needless to say, in the area of actions beyond corporate powers, directors cannot claim protection from the "reasonable man" doctrine if the action is clearly not permitted by the corporation charter. In other words, the directors, as a minimum, are expected to know what is permitted and not permitted under the charter.

USE OF CORPORATE FUNDS

Since directors are representatives of the corporation, it is understandable that much emphasis should be placed on their handling and disposing of corporate funds. Public interest here goes beyond protection of shareholders. The corporation, as an artificial entity, was devised to make possible perpetual life not controlled by natural life-spans and to separate the investors' personal liability from stockholder and corporate liability. By the same token, the very existence of the corporation and the resulting limited liability of stockholders imply that company funds will not be unreasonably dissipated and that a creditor may rely on the investment of shareholders as a kind of warranty for his offering credit. There are a number of places where this principle applies and directors' liability may arise, mainly in the areas of dividend payment, loans to insiders, and expenditure of funds for personal purposes, such as proxy contests. Also, there have been cases where the corporate "veil" has been pierced and where creditors have been able to get to shareholders as individuals.

Payment of Dividends. Although statutory provisions and their interpretations vary, it may generally be said that directors are personally liable for declaration of dividends which impair capital. In other words, the intent of this provision is that dividends only be paid from "surplus" and essentially from *earned* surplus. However, most statutes do not limit the dividend source to earned surplus, thereby making paid-in surplus available for at least certain dividends, and a few even allow payments from surplus created by reevaluation of company assets or other means. Nevertheless, an increasing number of states [9] are attempting to close this loophole. And under all prevailing law, dividends cannot be declared if the company is insolvent or becomes insolvent as the result of the declaration.

Obviously, if the time-honored reason behind payment of dividends from earnings and the desire to avoid impairment of capital are to be served, statutes should be changed to make clear that the

[9] According to Feuer, *Personal Liabilities of Corporate Officers and Directors, op. cit.,* p. 123, n. 6, earlier statutes did not generally prohibit the use of paid-in surplus for dividend payments or limit the discretion of directors in this area. But statutes in such states as California, Illinois, Louisiana, Maryland, Minnesota, Missouri, Oklahoma, Pennsylvania, and Wisconsin provide that cash dividends may be paid from paid-in surplus only for dividends on preferred stock and after notice as to the source of dividends.

dividends should ordinarily arise from earned surplus only. Clearly, however, in the case of "wasting asset" companies, such as oil wells and mines, it is not unreasonable to allow dividends to be paid other than from earnings. However, in this case, it should be made clear to stockholders that to the extent dividends are paid from sources other than earnings, they represent a liquidation of the assets of the company.

An interesting reverse twist to the problem of directors' liability in paying dividends other than from surplus, is the case of possible directors' liability for *not* paying dividends. Under the Internal Revenue Code, Section 531, the Federal Government may levy an accumulated earnings tax on a corporation if it is found that the company has improperly accumulated income and has not paid dividends in order to avoid taxes by shareholders. This provision was, of course, designed to force the payment of dividends in closely held corporations where the shareholders had a tax reason for receiving income only through salaries and bonuses rather than dividends. In closely held corporations, Section 531 can be a problem where the corporation is holding on to cash to avoid income taxes by shareholders, but in publicly held companies the Internal Revenue Service has found it difficult to apply this Section successfully. If the I.R.S. should successfully hold that a company has unreasonably accumulated earnings for the purpose of avoiding tax upon dividends paid to shareholders, and if, as a result, a penalty tax were levied on the company, there could be a potential directors' liability from failing to exercise care in acting so as to avoid this penalty.

Loans to Insiders. As can readily be seen, if a corporation is not—like a bank—in the business of making loans, a corporate loan to a director, an officer, or a shareholder is likely to be automatically a case of *ultra vires* action. Such loans must also raise serious question as to whether directors are operating in the interests of the shareholders whom they represent. Although this is generally the law, there are wide differences in its interpretation.

Statutes and courts have excluded incidental loans, such as ordinary expense-account advances and loans clearly made in the usual course of business. Some prohibit only loans to stockholders, while others prohibit only loans to directors and officers and make no reference to stockholders. Still others provide that, if the loan is adequately secured, bears reasonable interest, and is approved by a majority of disinterested directors, it does not involve liability.

In general, while state jurisdictions differ considerably, directors would appear to be well advised to follow common-law principles by which loans to insiders should normally not be made, the only exception being incidental and relatively unimportant loans or advances made in the usual course of business operations. Any other action would appear to be open to question.

At the same time, there are instances where it might be in the shareholders' interests for the company to make loans to certain inside officers and to key employees. One of these is the case of exercise of qualified stock options. Since the Revenue Act of 1964, option terms are limited to five years and the holding period for capital-gains treatment has been extended to thirty-six months. To make options meaningful under these severe restrictions, it may be of interest to the company to assist persons to whom options are given to aid in financing purchase of stock under them. Another case is where a company makes temporary loans to an employee who has incurred considerable expense in changing residences on a company-induced move. Although legal advice should be sought by boards of directors in these and similar instances in order to avoid liability, it would appear that, where circumstances indicate that such loans are well secured and are in the interests of the company and its operations, liability may be avoidable in many jurisdictions.

At the same time, statutory provisions vary widely on the question of making loans for stock-option exercise, even when secured. In California, for example, the statute absolutely prohibits any loans to directors, officers, or any other person upon security of the shares of the company unless two-thirds of the shareholders, with or without voting rights and excluding shares held by the borrower, approve.[10] Delaware, on the other hand, adopted a statute immediately after the Revenue Act of 1964 permitting loans on the security of op-

[10] General Corporation Law, Section 823.

tioned shares.[11] Although these loans appear to this author to be in the interests of the corporation and its shareholders, directors should clearly tread very carefully and never make this kind of loan without legal guidance.

Use of Funds for Personal Purposes. The use of corporation funds for personal purposes by directors, shareholders, or key officers and employees will normally and properly involve directors' liabilities. However, in the case of expending corporate funds in a proxy contest, it is not always easy to ascertain whether the funds have been spent for personal purposes or to protect the company against what is believed to be undesirable interference on the part of outside interests. In general, if the contest involves a question of policies pursued by the existing management group, a corporate purpose exists in spending company funds for a proxy contest.

It may well be true funds are expended in some proxy contests for personal purposes, the obvious one being the maintenance of present directors and officers in their positions. Nevertheless, it should not be difficult for any director-officer group defending itself in a proxy contest to argue that the proxy contest involves company policy, not the personal interests of the group.

LIABILITY FOR CORPORATE WRONGDOING

Although a corporation is an artificial person, it may, like natural persons, be held liable for wrongdoing. It may, for example, be held liable for breaching a contract, for malicious or oppressive acts against third persons, for damage due to its action, for breaking the antitrust or fair trade laws, for patent infringement, or for other wrongdoings which could subject any individual to liability.

By the same token, a corporation must necessarily act through its agents—its officers and employees. In general, the principle of law is that whenever an individual working for a corporation is operating under such circumstances as to imply performance of duties on be-

[11] General Corporation Law, Section 143.

half of the company, he is operating as an agent, and the corporation as well as the agent may be found personally liable for wrongdoing. The question of directors' liability is far less pervasive. Unless the law makes provisions to the contrary, directors are not held personally liable for wrongdoing of their agents unless they engaged in the wrongdoing themselves, encouraged or abetted it, or through negligence allowed it to exist. In other words, the same general principles of reasonable discretion and action apply here as elsewhere in determining directors' liabilities.

The major exception to the application of this principle is in cases where the law specifically makes directors liable even for wrongdoing of agents of the company. In this category are such instances as liabilities which may be imposed on directors by the various antitrust laws of the Federal Government or by the securities laws, which generally require full and accurate disclosure of information. It is interesting that, between 1950 and 1960 the Federal Government brought a number of successful suits against corporation executives, many of whom were directors, for antitrust violations, with fines of approximately $750,000 being assessed against 356 executives.[12]

CONFLICT OF INTEREST

One of the major areas of directors' liability arises from application of conflict-of-interest doctrine. The law with respect to company directors quite uniformly applies what is usually referred to as the principle of "undivided loyalty." Since a director is in a position of trust through his representation of the shareholders generally, courts have understandably held that the director must be loyal to the corporation in all matters involving transactions of the corporation in which he has an interest not consistent with that of the corporation. On becoming a director, he accepts an obligation to

[12] From Herbert C. Brook, "Executive Liability—Personally Speaking," *The President's Forum*, pp. 30–32, Spring–Summer, 1965, as quoted in J. M. Juran and J. K. Louden, *The Corporate Director*, The American Management Association, Inc., New York, 1966, p. 300.

subordinate his personal interests to those of the corporation where these two conflict. As Justice Benjamin Cardozo said in a leading New York case:

> Many forms of conduct permissible in a workaday world for those acting at arm's length, are forbidden to those bound by fiduciary ties. A trustee is held to something stricter than the morals of the market place. Not honesty alone, but the punctilio of an honor the most sensitive, is then the standard of behavior. As to this there has developed a tradition that is unbending and inveterate. Uncompromising rigidity has been the attitude of courts of equity when petitioned to undermine the rule of undivided loyalty by the 'disintegrating erosion' of particular exceptions. Only thus has the level of the conduct for fiduciaries been kept at a level higher than that trodden by the crowd.[13]

Yet, it is inconceivable in the modern business corporation that there would not be a number of situations productive of conflict. One of the most obvious is compensation of directors. Another is transactions between the company on whose board a particular director sits and another company with whom he has some affiliation. In the large company, particularly, it would be unusual indeed if an outside director, at least, did not have *some* relationship as a vendor or customer with another company with whom the first corporation did business or with whom it had some competitive relationship. To apply this doctrine strictly and without exception would be to exclude from board memberships a large number of very competent individuals who can make important contributions. The essential point is not really the question of whether some *possible* conflict of interest is involved, but rather whether the potential conflict operates to the detriment of the corporation on whose board the member sits. That this can go to unreasonable extremes in a government agency is indicated by the author's experience as a member of the board of commissioners of a government body. Although pressing as a commissioner for a higher rental rate on public land owned by the government agency and leased to a large private company, and despite the fact that the author owned only 0.003 percent of the widely held public stock of the private company, he and all the rest of the

---

[13] *Meinhard v. Salmon*, 249 N.Y. 458, at p. 464 (1928).

commission were disqualified to vote on the lease because of a "conflict of interest."

In general, it can be said that the main dangers and legal liabilities of such incipient conflicts can be avoided by several actions. In the first place, the director with a possible division of loyalty should make his interests crystal clear to his fellow directors. In the second place, the director should avoid taking any part in the discussion of the matter involving a potential conflict and preferably should not even be present in the board room during the discussion. In the third place, care must be taken to make certain that the divided loyalty is not utilized to the detriment of the company on which the board member sits.

In summary, if the decisions made by the board are such as would be made without the existence of possible divided loyalty and are based upon considerations other than the self-interest of the director in another situation, there would appear to be no ethical or legal liability involved. In most jurisdictions, transactions involving divided loyalty will be sanctioned if: (1) the interested director has made full disclosure; (2) the decision has been made on the basis of disinterested and independent representation (a majority of the board, none of which has an interest, or a majority of shareholders), and (3) the transaction is fair to the corporation.[14]

Vendor-Customer Relationships. The most common form of conflict of interest exists when a company in which a director has some interest either sells to or buys from a corporation on whose board he sits. In general, most courts adopt the rule that contracts so made are valid if approved by a majority of the directors acting for company interests honestly and in good faith and with full knowledge of

[14] In the California statute, transactions involving a conflict of interest are approved if (1) the fact of common directorship or financial interest is disclosed or known to the board and noted in the minutes and the board approves the transaction in good faith by a vote sufficient for the purpose without counting the vote of the interested party, or (2) the interest is known to the shareholders and they approve or ratify the transaction in good faith by a majority vote, or (3) the contract or transaction is just and reasonable to the corporation at the time it is authorized or approved.

the matter; except, naturally, for cases of fraud or clear unfairness. In these cases, if a contract is attacked as involving a conflict of interest, the burden of proof must be upon the directors to prove that the contract is indeed a fair one, and any implication of unfairness is normally sufficient ground for voiding it. Even in such cases, a contract between the director and his company may be upheld by the courts if approved by a majority of the stockholders, and many companies do submit such contracts to the stockholders.

At the same time, some courts take the position that a contract between a director and the company is, upon any attack whatsoever, voidable without any inquiry as to fairness.[15] This strict view has, however, been yielding to the more sensible and practical view of looking at the fairness of a transaction, while resting the burden of proof of fairness upon the interested director.

Without the safeguards outlined above in transactions involving a possible conflict of interest, such contracts are voidable. Moreover, a director may be individually liable for any unfair gain he may have obtained.[16]

Executive Compensation. One of the unavoidable instances of conflict of interest built into corporate operations is the matter of executive compensation. Not only are outside directors in a position of conflict in fixing their compensation, but, even more so, inside directors who act as officers of the corporation are in a position to sit in judgment on their own salary and other compensation arrangements.

One of the more delicate conflict situations is that where the board members fix their own fees for services on the board. This is especially true in view of the common-law rule that, in the absence of some provision to the contrary, directors, like other fiduciaries,

---

[15] W. J. Grange and T. C. Woodbury, *Corporation Law: Operating Procedures for Officers and Directors*, 2d ed., The Ronald Press Company, New York, 1965, pp. 298–299.

[16] For a discussion of the basic principles involving conflict of interest see Mortimer Feuer, *Personal Liabilities of Corporate Officers and Directors, op. cit.*, pp. 31–49.

render their services gratuitously. As a practical matter, either through statutory provision or by provision of the corporate charter or by-laws, directors are normally given authority to establish their own fees. In some cases, particularly where the law is not clear or appropriate by-law provisions are not made, directors may submit the matter of their fees to stockholders for approval. Fortunately, despite their obvious conflict-of-interest position, there is no evidence of any consequence that directors' fees have, in fact, ever been excessive.

An even more difficult problem exists with an officer-director in fixing his salary and other compensation arrangements. Except for unusual cases, courts have tended to give wide latitude to the judgment of independent representatives—outside board members or a majority of the stockholders. Where compensation has been approved by such disinterested parties, the presumption of reasonableness exists and the burden of proof must rest with those who attack the compensation. On the other hand, where such disinterested approval does not exist, the burden of proving fairness must lie with the interested directors.

There has been one major exception to this general principle. In a leading case of the United States Supreme Court [17] where compensation was so large as to be regarded as a corporate waste, the court did step in to reverse the action of directors, despite approval of a majority of the stockholders. However, only in extreme cases where compensation is so large as to be wholly unreasonable will the courts interfere with the judgment of independent representatives of the corporation.

Most of the questions regarding compensation have arisen as a result of stock options. Although there have been many court cases dealing with options, in the absence of fraud and with approval of a disinterested majority of the board of directors or shareholders the courts have not interfered with directors' actions.[18]

[17] *Rogers v. Hill,* 289 U.S. 582 (1933).

[18] Mortimer Feuer, *ibid.,* pp. 50–70. For a thorough discussion of this point, the reader is referred to this source.

Corporate Opportunities. One of the most difficult problems arising under the principle of undivided loyalty is that of corporate opportunity. In general, a director may not take for himself an opportunity which has been offered to the corporation. In other words, if an opportunity to make a profitable arrangement is presented to a corporation in the line of its ordinary business, a director may not take this opportunity for his own personal gain unless the corporation decides for good and proper reasons not to pursue the opportunity itself.

There is always serious question as to whether such an opportunity comes to the attention of a director in his capacity of director or as a part of his outside interests. An outside director, particularly, is expected to have interests other than those of the corporation on whose board he sits. If an opportunity comes to him to purchase some real estate, to engage in a new business, or to acquire a business interest, there is always question as to whether or not any of these was a corporate opportunity and whether the director, as a consequence, is liable to the corporation for any profits he might make.

In general, these matters are decided on the basis of pertinent facts in every given situation. Among these facts is whether or not the opportunity was one in the line of the corporation's business and one it would normally be able to exploit. Another consideration is whether the corporation would have had financial ability to develop the opportunity for its own advantage. Still another is whether the individual director was able by his directorial inside information to take advantage of an opportunity which would normally have been offered to the company.

Needless to say, in looking at the whole picture of a questioned transaction, it usually is clear whether the opportunity for gain was a "corporate" one or an "individual" one which any individual outside of the corporation might be expected to have. The question is one of fairness, intent, and circumstances. However, any director faced with this situation would do well to disclose it to his associates and to seek legal advice before subjecting himself to embarrassment and possible liability for taking advantage of what might be called a "corporate" opportunity.

Directors with Competitive Interests. Any undertaking by a director in competition with the corporation on whose board he sits is likely to have a negative effect upon the company's business and profits and thereby to represent a conflict of interest. Nevertheless, for the non-officer-director, it is interesting that the courts have generally held that it is neither illegal nor immoral for a non-officer-director even to operate a competitive enterprise for profit.[19] In these cases, the courts generally hold that a director must still act in good faith as a fiduciary of the corporation of which he is a director. This is not always easy in practice. Consequently, if the competition is at all significant, the customary and proper course is for directors not to serve on the boards of competitive companies.

The right of a director to engage in a competitive enterprise is not usually extended to an officer-director. While not often a legal matter unless expressed or implied in an employment contract, this is true largely because an officer is expected to give his full time and attention to the company with whom he holds a position. Unquestionably, any outside business activity might interfere with this obligation, but the incompatibility becomes intolerable when the outside activity is competitive.

INTERLOCKING DIRECTORATES

Closely related to the entire problem of conflict of interest is the long-publicized problem of interlocking directorates. A director may be considered to be interlocking when he sits on the board of two or more companies who have some business arrangements with each other. Thus, many cases of inter-company conflict of interest involve interlocking directorates. An individual who is an officer or director of a bank or underwriting firm with which a company does business may be regarded as having some degree of conflict of interest between his financial institution and the corporation on whose board he serves. Likewise, if a director sits on the boards of two or more companies which are in competition with each other, there is a

[19] For cases quoted on this position, see Feuer, *op. cit.*, pp. 95–97.

strong presumption that he may be in a position to dull the effects of competition. Other forms of interlocking, of course, occur when an individual is a director of companies who do business with each other as vendor and customer.

As can readily be seen, it would be a rare director indeed who, sitting on the boards of two very large companies with wide business interests, would not have some degree of interlocking. For example, almost any large company would likely have some kind of business interest, even though relatively small, with the General Motors Company, and any outside director of that corporation with any significant business interests would have some degree of interlocking interests. Again, it would be virtually impossible for an outside director of the American Telephone and Telegraph Company not to be in a company using AT&T's services.

Interlocking Directorates and Anti-monopoly Laws. As a part of the anti-monopoly legislation introduced into the United States over a half-century ago, the Clayton Act of 1914 prohibited certain interlocking directorates. In the case of industrial corporations, this prohibition applied only where one of the two companies involved had capital, surplus, and undivided profits aggregating more than $1 million, and where the companies had been competing in interstate commerce. Likewise, interlocking directorates between banks, banking associations, and trust companies were forbidden where the banks were organized under Federal law and where the total deposits, capital, surplus, and undivided profits aggregated more than $5 million. This law, which has been essentially unchanged since 1914, applied only to cases where the same individual served on the boards of two companies and where these companies were actual rather than potential competitors.

Through legislation in 1920, 1935, 1938, 1940 and 1949, interlocking directorates have been forbidden in common carriers in the field of railroads, oil pipelines, water carriers, motor carriers, and air carriers, unless the particular interlocking arrangements are specifically approved by the appropriate federal regulatory commission. This provision was designed to prevent management ties which might substantially reduce competition in transportation. Similar provisions have been made by other legislation, including banking acts, the Federal Communications Act, the Federal Power Act, and the Holding Company Act of 1938. All these have had the intent of implementing the well-known policy of the United States to maintain competition.

The provision against interlocking directorates has been of questionable effect. In the first place, most interlocks in the transportation field for which permission has been applied have been granted. In the second place, the Department of Justice has prosecuted rather few interlocking directorate cases under the Clayton Act.[20]

The Celler Committee Report. As the result of a staff report of the Anti-trust Subcommittee of the Committee of Judiciary of the House of Representatives, generally referred to as the Celler Committee,[21] new interest in outlawing interlocking directorates has arisen. On the basis of this investigation, it has been proposed that, without specific approval of the Department of Justice, no person, directly or indirectly, at the same time, may be a director, officer, or employee with management functions in any two or more corporations in interstate commerce: (1) where any one of which has capital, surplus, and undivided profits of more than $1 million, excluding subsidiary or related companies in which one company owns 50 percent or more of the stock, and (2) where there are any actual or potential interlocks with competitors, customers, suppliers or sources of capital. Note that the purpose of this recommendation is to outlaw both horizontal and vertical interlocks of a very broad kind, whether actual or potential.

Although the Staff Report found that 1,480 directors and officers of seventy-four companies had 4,428 common management connec-

[20] For a complete report on this legislation and actions taken under it, see *Interlocks in Corporate Management,* a Staff Report to the Anti-trust Subcommittee of the Committee of the Judiciary, House of Representatives, March 12, 1965, 89th Congress, 1st Session (U.S. Government Printing Office, Washington, D.C., 1965).

[21] *Ibid.*

tions with various companies,[22] the Report found no evidence "demonstrating specific abuses that have resulted from management interlocks." Nevertheless, it curiously indicated that "common sense, practical observation, and abstract reasoning all support the conclusion that such effects should follow." [23] The Report goes on to say, "It would be naive to think that the ability of two corporations to compete is not impaired by common management members; that individuals who occupy top-management positions in corporations that deal with each other will not have their judgments beclouded by considerations that affect their own financial interests; and that an individual who is too busy to appear at both board meetings does not debase the management of the corporations he serves. Conclusions supported by common sense, practical observation, and abstract reasoning, should not lightly be disregarded in the absence of convincing evidence that there is error."

If this recommended legislation should go into effect, and its enactment seems improbable, the result would be to make multiple directorates among larger companies virtually impossible. In other words, the makeup of company boards would almost certainly be greatly changed, and a large percentage of outside directors now on company boards would be forced to resign.

While this new proposal is unlikely to be enacted into law, and the findings are drawn from data subject to serious question [24] and do not show evidence of any abuses, it is clear that conflict-of-interest problems, along with possible dangers to public interests, are matters of important public concern. It does, therefore, behoove corporate directors to pay increasing attention to meaningful conflicts of interest involved in interlocking relationships and to their legal and moral position as fiduciaries representing the various private and public interests in the modern corporation.

[22] *Ibid.*, p. 228.

[23] *Ibid.*, p. 230.

[24] This report has been very thoroughly analyzed and severely criticized by A. R. Towl, "Outside Directors Under Attack," *Harvard Business Review*, Vol. 43, No. 5, pp. 135–147, September–October, 1965.

LIABILITIES UNDER SECURITIES LAWS

Even before the Federal securities laws, directors were liable for fraudulent stock promotions under state "blue sky" laws, enacted by every state except Nevada between 1911 and 1933. While differing in completeness of legislation or thoroughness of administration under various state regulatory commissions, these laws were designed primarily to avoid fraudulent security sales to the public. The Federal laws, on the other hand, have been based largely upon the requirement of "full disclosure" of information, on the assumption that the investor can take care of himself if furnished adequate information.

Blue-sky Law Liabilities. As a general rule, state blue-sky laws provide for director liability to the purchasers of securities where they have been damaged by misrepresentation, fraud, or mere selling of securities not approved by an appropriate state commission. In some cases, blue-sky laws provide for criminal as well as civil liability for officers and directors who engage in an unauthorized sale, even though they do not knowingly act in furtherance of the sale or engage in the actual selling.

Despite the emergence of the Federal security laws as the primary source of regulation of securities sales and trading, state blue-sky laws still remain in effect. In certain states such as California and Illinois, the state securities commissions are very active in regulating the issuance of new securities and in prescribing standards for their issuance. In California, for example, the Commissioner in effect sits in the position of a buyer and must affirmatively decide that the price for a stock is fair, just, and equitable. Because of this activity and the fact that securities which do not meet state standards in these stricter states simply cannot be issued or sold in them, directors' liabilities have not actually been very great, even though the laws themselves are specific and positive in their provisions.

Full Disclosure Under the Federal Securities Laws. Among the very real liabilities of directors are the full-disclosure provisions of the Securities Act of 1933 and the Securities Exchange Act of 1934. Under the former law, a corporation (except for exempt companies) wishing to offer new securities to the public must file a registration statement with the Securities and Exchange Commission. This statement, including the prospectus which must be distributed to the public, must contain considerable information concerning the finances, operations, and management of a company. Should the statement contain an untrue assertion of material fact, omit a material fact, or omit any fact in such a way as to be misleading, members of the board of directors, as well as many other persons connected with the corporation, will be held liable for losses incurred both by the first and subsequent purchasers of the security. Moreover, such losses are normally recoverable whether or not the purchaser has read the registration statement.

The law requires that the statement be signed only by a majority of the board, although every member of the board is made liable for its civil penalties. However, a director who has not signed the registration statement may escape liability if he resigns before the effective date of the statement and advises the commission that he will take no responsibility for the accuracy or completeness of facts in the statement.

According to the law, purchasers have a right of action against any or all of the following:

1. Every signer of the registration statement
2. Every director or partner in the issuing company at the time the statement was filed
3. Every person who has consented to be named in the statement as being, or as about to become, a director or partner
4. Every expert who has consented to be named in the statement as having prepared or certified data used in it and subsequently found to be faulty
5. Every underwriter of the issue
6. Every person who controls any of the above, unless after reasonable investigation he is shown to have had no knowledge of, or reasonable grounds to believe in, the facts giving rise to the liability

In addition to full-disclosure provisions of the Securities Act of 1933 applicable to newly-issued securities, similar provisions are applied by the Securities Exchange Act of 1934 to already-issued securities—originally for those traded over recognized exchanges—and by the amendments of 1964 to certain of those traded over-the-counter.[25] Under these acts, all corporations having securities listed on a regulated exchange and those over-the-counter companies covered must file reports periodically with the exchange and with the Commission, detailing extensive financial, operating, and management information similar to that required in the registration statement for new securities. The same kind of civil liabilities for false and misleading statements applies to these reports, although it is not quite so severe as in the issue of new securities. For the purchaser to recover under this law, he must prove that he relied on the false or misleading statement in purchasing the securities of the company filing the report.

Profiting from Inside Information. For the purpose of preventing unfair use of corporate information by insiders, the Securities and Exchange Act of 1934, as well as its amendments in 1964, regulates trading in a corporation stock, either over a regulated exchange or in the over-the-counter market (for companies of more than $1 million in assets or 500 or more shareholders), by directors, officers, or persons owning directly or indirectly more than 10 percent of any class of the company's stock. Such persons are prohibited from engaging in short sales of the corporation's stock. As for buying long, should a person buy stock and sell it within six months, the law presumes that such a person is operating on the basis of inside information and makes the profit so realized recoverable to the company.

In order to police this provision and to give other investors information concerning the financial stake of their officers and directors, the law provides that insiders must file information monthly with the appropriate exchange and with the Federal Securities and Exchange Commission if their ownership in the company has changed during that month.

[25] The over-the-counter companies covered are those with total assets of more than $1 million and 500 or more shareholders of record.

In addition, insiders are effectively limited in their sales of company stock if, through exercise of share options or through receipt of stock in an acquisition, they have obtained such stock under an "investment letter." In order to avoid the expense of registration, stock sold under option, or given in exchange for assets or other share interest acquired, is often not registered but is issued with the understanding with the individual that he has purchased it for investment and not for resale. Although certain circumstances are acceptable in proving that an individual might "change his mind" and sell the stock so obtained (including litigation forcing disposal of stock, such as divorce proceedings, and unusual hardship), in general the insider may not sell his stock, except for a very small amount periodically, without having it registered. How soon a person is released from his investment letter intent is open to question and the Securities and Exchange Commission has refused to say. Most competent legal opinion indicates that a period of at least two and preferably five years should elapse before a person can legally change his mind. The effect of this position, along with certain liabilities discussed in the following section, is to limit severely the liquidity of directors of many companies and other "controllers" in their holding of shares.

Liabilities under the Securities Laws. Except for certain criminal liabilities under the state-blue sky laws, generally the liabilities of directors under the state laws are primarily civil and those under the Federal laws are limited either to profits made on short-term swings or to losses incurred by purchasers. But these liabilities can be considerable. And the requirements of the securities acts, particularly those involving limitations of sales of securities and the full disclosure requirements of the Federal laws, are severe and significant.

Under Rule 10b-5, promulgated under the Securities and Exchange Act, any person, whether he be an officer, director, ten-percent shareholder, or other responsible insider is violating the law if he (1) employs any device, scheme, or artifice to defraud, (2) makes any untrue statement of a material fact, or (3) engages in any act, practice, or course of business which operates or would operate as a fraud or deceit upon a person in connection with the purchase or sale of his company's securities. This rule can hit directors severely. Not only is a violation of the law involved, but, more importantly, a finding of violation establishes virtually incontrovertible evidence for a civil suit by an injured buyer or seller. Corporation lawyers face great difficulty in advising any director or other insider how to act if he is buying or selling his company's securities. There is even danger that *not* talking may even give rise to a cause of action.

The power of the Securities and Exchange Commission and its control of insider trading is indicated by the well-publicized suit of the Commission against thirteen Texas Gulf Sulphur Company officials. Apparently, the company had preliminary indications in the late fall of 1963 that a certain Canadian ore field had promise. Despite this and the fact that information of the find leaked out, the company issued a press release on April 12, 1964, indicating that news of the find had been greatly exaggerated. However, a few days later, the vastness of the find was confirmed and announced. In the meanwhile, not only did the company president and the general counsel accept stock options between the date when company geologists saw the result of the first test hole on the site and the date when the find was announced, but a number of company officials and employees purchased shares. Some of these purchased shares between the date of the first indication of the find and the time when the find was announced, and some immediately after the start of the press conference announcing the find but before the news was on the wire.

In a Federal District Court decision in 1966 [26] all but two of the insiders were released from liability. The company president and general counsel were absolved of liability on the judge's finding that, while corporate officials have a duty to disclose "material facts" even before accepting stock options, the new ore developments were held to be too remotely related to the actual granting of stock options. Likewise, the six officials of the company who purchased stock be-

[26] Findings are reported in "Where the Texas Gulf Ruling Could Lead," *Business Week*, pp. 112–114, August 27, 1966. Also see "Texas Gulf, Most Individuals Cleared of Violating Securities Regulations," *The Wall Street Journal*, August 22, 1966, p. 4.

tween the date of the first test-hole indications and the last test hole confirming the finding of a considerable volume of ore, were absolved of liability on the grounds that the insider information they had was "too remote" to affect the market price of the stock.

Furthermore, those insiders who purchased shares after the press conference announcing the find, but before the news was on the wire, were absolved of liability on the grounds that the facts became public when they were told to reporters and the insiders' quick reaction to the news was permissible. The only two defendants who were found liable for violation of the disclosure rule were those who purchased shares in the one-week period (April 9–16, 1964) between the date of the final test hole confirming the find and the press conference announcing the find. The court concluded that these shares were purchased on the basis of inside information of a material nature.

Consequently, the court, on the one hand, agreed with the Securities and Exchange Commission in principle that an insider who gains from non-public information because of his special relationship with the company and buys securities while in the possession of undisclosed "material facts" is liable for the profitable advantage he gains. On the other hand, the court took a conservative interpretation of other considerations in the case, including the use of information which at the time had no material affect on the market, the company's action in issuing a press release minimizing the prospects of the find on the ground that this was a reasonable business position for the company to take, and the fact that insiders had no obligation to wait for their trading until the public absorbed the news, the press conference being adequate evidence of public information.

This case is being appealed, and ones similar to it may be before the courts for some time. While such cases indicate an increasingly aggressive attitude by the Securities and Exchange Commission in applying the rules against insider information, the decisions to date do not seem to expand the liability impact of the law. In fact, if the Texas Gulf Sulphur finding is upheld on appeal, the full-disclosure requirements on insiders will have been given a very conservative application.

DIRECTORS' INDEMNIFICATION

As the above summary of liabilities of directors implies, there are many possibilities for company directors to be subject to legal action, either by the corporation itself, more likely by a stockholder on behalf of the corporation, by a third party such as a creditor, or by a state or Federal Government agency. While there are no data to prove an increase of suits involving directors, many lawyers believe that the number of stockholder suits at least are definitely on the rise.[27]

Even though a company director may be held blameless, and it has been seen that courts under the "reasonable judgment" philosophy generally give directors the benefit of any reasonable doubt, litigation can be costly and time-consuming and can often involve publicity damaging to the directors involved. On the latter point, it is a commonplace that a law suit itself is news, while an acquittal or a failure by a plaintiff to follow up on a suit may get rather little publicity.

As a result of wider recognition of the problem of directors' liabilities and the costs involved in defending against suits which may legally have little substance, indemnification of directors and other corporate executives has become increasingly common. Approximately half of the states, and almost all of those in important industrial areas, permit reimbursement from the corporate treasury. Provisions vary, and any director is advised to have a careful examination made of applicable statutes in order to determine both his liabilities and the possibilities of indemnification by the company. But generally it can be said that the director will be indemnified if he is successful in defending the case, if a court has ordered indemnification, or if indemnification is authorized by the certificate of incorporation, the by-laws, a board resolution, or a stockholders' resolution. However, in most instances, the law permits indemnifica-

---

[27] "A Shield Against Stockholder Suits," *Business Week*, p. 56, July 2, 1966.

tion only so long as the director has not been adjudged guilty of fraudulent conduct or gross negligence. Nevertheless, there are some states where indemnification by a company for a director's legal bills in defending a case is not permitted.

As a result of increasing recognition of directors' liability and the costs involved in suits, protection against these costs has become available through insurance. Lloyds of London, which pioneered this type of insurance some twenty-five years ago, still handles most of the policies. However, in recent years a number of American companies have been offering directors' and officers' insurance. In general, these policies are made available only to well-known companies, provide for deductible provisions, generally of $20,000, and give insurance coverage limited usually to 95 percent of the cost and losses involved. Coverage is commonly written to apply to errors and omissions in decision making, negligence, and breach of duty, but usually excludes reimbursement for loss in criminal suits, libel and slander, adjudicated dishonesty, or cases where directors are adjudged to have gained a personal profit or advantage.

In other words, typical insurance coverage, as currently developed, applies to cost of defense and losses incurred due to factors other than fraudulent or clearly unethical behavior. As a matter of fact, except for cases of negligence or mismanagement without fraudulent intent or result, insurance coverage tends to be no broader than the typical statutory provisions for corporate indemnification of directors.

The costs of insurance vary considerably with the size and reputation of the company and the type of industry in which the company is engaged. Thus, a small but highly respected company in commercial business might receive as much as $5 million of insurance coverage for as little as $3,000 per year, while larger-company fees might involve premiums of $15,000 to $50,000 per year. Also, because the coverage is relatively new and shareholders may not understand why they should be called on to finance insurance for directors and officers who might be found guilty of acts caused by negligence and omission, the number of policies issued has not been large. However, there is every indication that the number of companies considering this kind of policy is growing.

Sale of directors' and officers' liability insurance is also likely to increase. This is primarily because a director or officer may obtain insurance for costs and losses which under certain state laws could not be reimbursed. For example, the New York Business Corporation law does not permit a corporation to reimburse a director or executive who makes a settlement in a pending or threatened suit brought on behalf of the company. If the suit is successfully defended, the indemnification is permitted, but settlements are not recognized as reimbursable. In cases like this, insurance company policies normally cover the cost of settlements. Since it is in the interests of most directors and executives to settle nuisance suits without spending the time to defend them to the end and to avoid continuing publicity, there are obvious benefits in insurance in this case.

However, there are serious questions as to the validity of this kind of insurance. One authority on the problem believes that, in New York, "insurance paid for by the corporation and used to provide a reimbursement that it could not make directly would not stand up in court." [28] The question of director and officer indemnification, either directly by the corporation or through insurance, needs much clarification both in terms of the statutes and court cases and the kind of coverage and incurred expenses of insurance companies.

Also, it is well known that many persons interested in securities regulation, including the Securities and Exchange Commission, take a jaundiced view of director and officer indemnification. Their position is that no company treasury should be called upon to foot the bills for unlawful or injurious conduct by those to whom the management of a corporation is entrusted. While this position has a persuasive ring, it is also true that the law on liability is not always clear and suits or other action may be taken against directors or officers despite their conscientious attention to duty and their exercise of reasonable business judgment. Even though few actions succeed, it is not unreasonable for a corporation to give protection from these actions to those entrusted with its management.

[28] "A Shield Against Stockholder Suits," *Business Week*, p. 57, July 2, 1966.

But all directors and officers must be aware of the attitude of certain of their regulators. The Securities and Exchange Commission is particularly anxious to prevent indemnification for liabilities arising under the Federal laws, although this has not been actually done to date. It has, however, required that prospectuses give notice of indemnification provisions and has indicated that indemnification for securities-law violations may be against public policy. In California, for example, the Securities and Exchange Commission requires the typical prospectus to state as follows:

Section 830 of the California Corporations Code authorizes the board of directors of the company to award indemnity to directors and officers under certain circumstances. In the opinion of the Securities and Exchange Commission, said Section of the California Corporations Code may contravene public policy as expressed in the Securities Act of 1933 to the extent that it permits indemnification against liability under said Act. In the event that application is made under said Code Section or otherwise by a director or officer of the company for such indemnification against liability arising out of the sale of the securities registered hereunder, the company will, unless in the opinion of its counsel the question has already been settled by controlling precedent, submit such question of public policy to a court of appropriate jurisdiction and will be governed by the final adjudication of such issue.

AVOIDING PERSONAL LIABILITY

Although the matter of directors' liability is real, and any director must take care to understand the exact nature of his liability, generally the responsible, honest, and ethical director has little to fear. This is particularly true if provision can be made for the corporation, through direct indemnification or insurance, to cover litigation expenses involved in the suits which may be entered against a director regardless of his attention to duty. As one authoritative study concluded:

Furthermore, though the legal restrictions sound strict—so that observers now and then worry that their apparent severity discourages good men from serving as directors—the truth is that directors are very rarely subjected to onerous civil liability or to any criminal penalties except in cases where their behavior was clearly proved to be dishonorable or irresponsible. As regards the "business judgement rule," for instance, courts are uniformly reluctant to substitute their own hindsight judgements for decisions made by directors in the midst of the complexities, pressures, and uncertainties of actually managing a business. Usually, only strong proof of clear dereliction of duty will overcome this reluctance. Directors who act honestly, carefully, and in good faith have little to fear.[29]

In general, a director who takes his duties seriously as a governing representative of the long-term interests of stockholders will not be subjected to liability. If he has ordinary knowledge of the laws under which he operates, takes advantage regularly of advice of competent corporate counsel on his actions, and associates himself with other individuals who act ethically and responsibly, his liability should be minimal.

In summary, one might list a number of precautions for a director. They are the following: [30]

1. Read and understand the state's general corporation law provisions for directors' liability.

2. Read and understand the corporation's charter and by-laws.

3. Gain basic understanding of the major provisions of the antitrust and fair trade laws and federal and state securities laws.

4. Obtain assurances that accounting and auditing practices meet the high standards of accuracy and integrity required for financial visibility, and insist that the certified public accountants report to the board of directors.

5. Regularly and carefully examine corporate financial statements, and seek competent legal counsel to assure the full legality of dividend payments.

[29] John R. Kinley, *Corporate Directorship Practices*, Business Policy Study No. 103, National Industrial Conference Board, New York, 1962, p. 103.

[30] The author is indebted for certain assistance to the excellent study summarizing this problem by J. M. Charlton, "Directors: The Duty to Manage," *Mississippi Valley Journal of Business and Economics*, Vol. 1, No. 2, pp. 36–51, Spring, 1966.

6. Utilizing such expert advice as may be necessary, including particularly the certification of public accountants and advice of legal counsel, assure that all statements filed with the Securities and Exchange Commission accurately reflect the company's status and the directors' share interest.

7. Take steps to make certain that corporate officers accurately perform agreements authorized by the board.

8. Acquaint yourself with your duties as a fiduciary and take care, with appropriate advice of legal counsel, to put the corporate interests ahead of personal or other interests in dealings related to the corporation's business.

9. Exercise independent judgment as a director with full realization that directors have authority to act for the corporation and are not mere management advisers, or representatives of interests other than those of all the shareholders.

10. Regularly attend at least three-fourths of the meetings of the board of directors.

11. Recognize that the long-range interests of shareholders require awareness of the demands of the social, legal, political, economic, and technological environment of the enterprise, and that social responsibility is simply an appropriate response to this environment.

chapter 6

BOARD COMPOSITION

Central to the effectiveness of any board of directors is the composition of its membership. This problem has a number of facets—size, the number of inside and outside board members, the age and retirement of members, individual qualifications, compensation, and other incentives. All these elements of board composition present difficult issues in practice. Nevertheless, keeping in mind that a board is essentially a group of individuals working together, its effectiveness and strength will depend more on its composition than any other single factor.

It is proposed in this chapter not only to discuss experience which studies have found in American boards of directors, but also to analyze some of the underlying considerations which should make for an effective board. While there is no standard applicable to all companies and to all boards of directors, there are a number of basic considerations which any company should consider in tailoring its board for its own purposes.

BOARD SIZE

Fortunately, through studies by the National Industrial Conference Board dealing with a significant sample of American companies since 1938, we have fairly representative data on board composition in the United States.

Experience and Trends. Data on the size of board memberships from 1953 to 1961 are shown in Tables 1, 2, and 3. It will be noted that, in manufacturing companies, board memberships vary from the expected minimum of three members to boards with more than

115

twenty members. It is interesting, however, that the median average of board memberships in manufacturing companies was nine in 1953 and eleven in 1958 and 1961. Examination of the data for manufacturing companies given in Table 1 will indicate also that, while the

TABLE 1   Size of Board Membership, 1953–1961, Manufacturing Companies

(Based on 244 companies in 1953 and 331 companies in 1958 and 1961)

Number of Board Members	Percent of Companies		
	1953	1958	1961
3	0.8	0.6	1.2
4	1.2	0.3	
5	9.4	4.5	2.7
6	4.1	1.5	3.0
7	13.9	10.9	8.8
8	5.3	4.8	3.9
9	M⟶ 17.6	14.2	13.0
10	6.6	7.3	9.1
11	9.4	M⟶ 11.5	M⟶ 13.0
12	8.6	11.2	14.2
13	8.3	7.3	6.3
14	6.1	5.7	6.1
15	6.6	7.9	8.8
16	1.7	4.2	3.6
17	1.7	3.9	3.3
18	0.8	0.6	1.2
19	0.8	1.5	0.6
20 and over	2.1	2.1	1.2
	100.0	100.0	100.0

M⟶ = Median

SOURCES: National Industrial Conference Board, *Corporate Directorship Practices,* Studies in Business Policy No. 90 and No. 103 (1959), p. 7, and No. 103 (1962), p. 4.

board average has risen from nine to eleven, there has been perceptible movement away from the very small or the very large boards to a size that experience has indicated is more workable.

Data in Tables 2 and 3 show that board membership in nonmanufacturing companies is much larger than in manufacturing companies. For all nonmanufacturing companies (see Table 3) the median average of boards in both 1958 and 1961 was fifteen members and

TABLE 2 Size of Board Membership, 1958–1961, Nonmanufacturing Companies

Type of Company	Average Number on Board	
	1958	1961
Public utility and transportation companies (138 companies in 1958, 150 in 1961)	12	12
Commercial banks (43 companies in 1958, 46 in 1961)	24	24
Insurance companies (48 companies in 1958, 51 in 1961)	16	18
Merchandising companies (37 companies in 1958, 42 in 1961)	11	11

SOURCE: National Industrial Conference Board, *Corporate Directorship Practices*, Studies in Business Policy No. 90 (1959), pp. 13–14, and No. 103 (1962), pp. 5–7.

the size of boards ran from a minimum of six members to a maximum of thirty-six. As these data are more carefully analyzed, it may be noted that the larger boards are in the commercial banks and insurance companies, while merchandising companies and public utility and transportation companies have boards of about the same size as those of manufacturing companies. If one separates public utility companies from transportation companies, data for which are available for 1961,[1] public utility boards are seen to average eleven

[1] National Industrial Conference Board, *Corporate Directorship Practices*, Studies in Business Policy No. 103, p. 7.

TABLE 3   Size of Board Membership, 1958–1961,
Nonmanufacturing Companies
(*Based on 155 companies*)

Number of Board Members	Percent of Companies 1958	Percent of Companies 1961
6		0.6
7	2.6	0.6
8	0.6	
9	9.0	6.4
10	2.6	3.9
11	12.3	13.6
12	5.8	7.7
13	3.9	5.2
14	5.8	3.2
15	M —→ 16.2	M —→ 18.1
16	3.9	3.9
17	3.2	2.6
18	1.9	3.9
19	6.4	2.6
20	2.6	3.9
21	4.6	3.9
22	1.3	3.9
23	2.6	0.6
24	3.2	3.9
25	9.0	9.0
27	0.6	0.6
30	0.6	0.6
36	1.3	1.3
	100.0	100.0

M —→ = Median

SOURCE: National Industrial Conference Board, *Corporate Directorship Practices*, Studies in Business Policy No. 103 (1962), p. 7.

members, like those of manufacturing companies, while transportation company boards averaged fifteen. Examination of the data for nonmanufacturing companies (see Table 3) does indicate a trend away from smaller boards but no significant trend away from boards larger than the average of fifteen.

The larger board membership among the commercial banks and insurance companies, which accounts primarily for the indication of larger boards in nonmanufacturing companies, is an interesting phenomenon. There seems to be no doubt that these larger boards are dictated by desire on the part of such companies to have wider geographic, business, and public representation on their boards. To some extent this can be explained by the greater and more immediate public interest in boards of financially oriented companies, but unquestionably some of the influence has to do with the public-relations value they place on board membership.

As might be expected, data indicate that the size of company boards varies with the size of the company. Data summarized in Table 4 for manufacturing companies show that, for companies with assets of less than $10 million the average board is seven members. In the asset grouping of $10 million to $24 million, the average moves to nine members, to eleven for the ranges of $25 million to $99 million, and to twelve members in the ranges of $100 million to $499 million in assets. Those companies with assets of more than $500 million show an average of fifteen directors.

The Ideal Size. Although it is easy to state in principle the ideal size of a board of directors, it is less easy to put this principle into actual numbers. A board should neither be too small to permit proper representation of varied experiences and points of view, nor too large and unwieldy to allow adequate free discussion of issues before the board. In general, since the board is a plural executive and therefore a committee, experience with committees is generally applicable to boards. As pointed out in discussing the plural executive in Chapter 3, the consensus of most experts is that the effective committee should have no less than five or six members in order to obtain adequate deliberation and representation of varied points of view, and no more than fifteen or sixteen members in order to avoid the problems of adequate discussion and to provide the time

TABLE 4   Size of Corporate Boards by Company Assets, 1961, 592 Manufacturing Companies

Asset Group	Total Number of Companies	Number of Members on Board																	
		3	4	5	6	7	8	9	10	11	12	13	14	15	16	17	18	19	20 and over
Under $10 Million	72	3	...	10	6	23	5	12	3	3	5	2	...	...	...	...	...	...	...
$10-24 Million	81	1	...	1	2	10	8	23	9	13	7	2	3	2	...	...	...	...	...
$25-29 Million	101	...	1	3	4	9	2	18	13	17	12	9	5	7	...	...	1	...	...
$50-99 Million	112	...	...	1	3	4	8	16	12	21	14	9	10	5	7	1	1	...	...
$100-199 Million	96	...	...	...	...	1	7	5	7	15	17	5	5	13	10	6	1	2	2
$200-499 Million	62	...	...	...	1	...	1	3	6	10	10	6	7	3	5	5	2	1	2
$500-999 Million	40	...	...	...	...	...	...	1	1	3	5	5	1	12	5	3	1	1	2
$1,000 Million and over	28	...	...	...	...	...	...	2	2	1	4	3	1	5	2	2	2	2	2
TOTAL	592	4	1	15	16	47	31	80	53	83	74	41	32	47	29	17	8	6	8

SOURCE: National Industrial Conference Board, *Corporate Directorship Practices*, Studies in Business Policy No. 103 (1962), p. 4.

necessary for every person to make his contribution. In general, the author agrees with this consensus. He feels that a board of less than five members can hardly be effective and would be inclined to limit a board to thirteen members in order to obtain the free discussion and deliberative interplay which board decisions require.

Admittedly, there are factors other than effective group action which affect size, although this should be given major consideration. There are instances, as in financial companies, where it may be highly desirable if not indeed essential to have a larger number of directors in order to get adequate representation of various interests. In addition, there have been many cases of mergers or consolidations where the board of the merged company might have to be larger than desirable, at least initially, in order to accommodate the ownership interests involved.

There are also cases where a group of inside executives has founded or built a company and placed themselves on the board. Since these executives are usually unwilling to retire from the board to make room for outside members, the only answer that has been found in such instances, in order to add outsiders, is to enlarge the size of the board. The same kind of consideration may exist where board members exceed the age of their greatest effectiveness. With a tendency to resist forced retirement of directors, sometimes the only real alternative is to increase the size of the board, at least temporarily, to make room for younger members.

Except for the compelling reasons of representation which may force a board to be larger than desirable, other reasons for excessive size should be relatively temporary. In these cases, those who lead large boards should look toward future reduction of the board to a workable size.

Board Size and Use of Committees. When practical circumstances require that a board be too large for effective operation as a single group, it can be broken down into various committees. As will be pointed out in the following chapter on board operation, the most commonly used committee to handle corporate matters for which a full board might be unwieldy or unsuitable is the executive committee. Normally endowed with broad powers, usually with certain limitations either provided by its delegation, by by-laws, or by statute, the executive committee may act for the entire board.

If committees are used and the results of their deliberations are reported to the full board, it can be seen that the actual size of a full board may, at times, not be too significant. On the other hand, since individual directors have an obligation for the management of a corporation and share personal liability for action the board takes, many board members understandably dislike to see the board's powers and action dissipated through the use of committees.

INSIDE VERSUS OUTSIDE DIRECTORS

Perhaps the most contentious issue related to composition of boards of directors is the question of how many directors should be company insiders and how many should be outsiders. Even the definition of what is an insider or an outsider varies. One authority includes as inside directors not only full-time officers of a company who also serve as directors, but also those who have formerly served as officers but are now retired as well as directors who have a "significant personal investment" in the company.[2] Among many elements of the investment community, insiders are also thought of as including large shareholders as well as directors. This is essentially consistent with the position of the Securities and Exchange Commission, which uses the term "corporate insiders" to refer to all officers, directors, and "controlling stockholders."

However, the most usual definition and the one which will be used here refers to "inside" directors as those who are full-time employees of the company and "outside" directors as those who do not have a full-time employment commitment to the company. This appears to be the way the National Industrial Conference Board has classified directors in its studies over the years. However, in adopting this definition, one must recognize that many directors are classified as "outsiders" who really have an "inside" interest. For example, a partner of a legal or management firm under contract to the company officers is, in a very real sense, an employee of the firm.

[2] Stanley C. Vance, *Boards of Directors: Structure and Performance*, University of Oregon Press, Eugene, Oregon, 1964, p. 5.

All this means that the concept of "insider" and "outsider" is not at all clear. As will be shown in the succeeding sections, perhaps what is really meant is whether the individual director is under the dominance of the inside executive group. The real question is one of independence and the ability to give an "outside" look at company problems.

Experience and Trends. In comparing studies of corporate boards from 1938 through 1961,[3] a slight trend toward an increase in outside directors can be seen. The manufacturing companies surveyed in 1938 were about evenly divided between those having a majority of outside directors and those having a majority of employee-directors. By 1953, outside directors constituted a majority in approximately 54 percent of the manufacturing companies surveyed, a figure which increased to 57 percent in 1958 and 61 percent in 1961. Moreover, in this survey, it was found that boards of only twenty-one of the 592 manufacturing companies surveyed were comprised entirely of inside members, while in only twenty-nine companies were all the board members—with the exception of a single officer, usually the president—selected from outside the company. As will be seen from Table 5, the proportion of inside and outside directors was not materially different in companies of vastly different sizes.

However, Vance, in his study,[4] disputes the validity of the National Industrial Conference Board studies quoted here. By including within the designation of "inside" director retired company executives and interested owners, Vance finds in a sample of 103 largest manufacturing companies an actual trend since 1925 toward a slightly increasing percentage of inside directors, with 1963 showing approximately 60 percent of the directors as "inside." These findings are summarized in Table 6. Vance's study indicates that companies in only three industries—aircraft, electrical equipment, and steel—had a majority of outside directors. In addition, he found in nearly forty years of operation very little movement from inside to outside or vice versa; only one inside board became an outside

[3] National Industrial Conference Board, *Corporate Directorship Practices*, Studies in Business Policy No. 103, p. 8.

[4] *Op. cit.*, pp. 18–21.

TABLE 5 Inside Directors, by Size of Company, 1961, 592 Manufacturing Companies

Asset Group	Percentage of Board Members											Total Companies
	1.0 to 9.9	10.0 to 19.9	20.0 to 29.9	30.0 to 39.9	40.0 to 49.9	50.0 to 59.9	60.0 to 69.9	70.0 to 79.9	80.0 to 89.9	90.0 to 99.9	100	
Under $10 Million	1	4	9	9	17	13	4	5	6	...	5	73
$10-24 Million	1	4	16	22	10	14	6	6	1	...	...	80
$25-49 Million	3	4	19	20	13	20	7	6	5	1	3	101
$50-99 Million	2	15	20	22	11	14	13	7	3	1	4	112
$100-199 Million	1	10	23	14	13	12	6	12	2	1	2	96
$200-499 Million	...	5	10	11	13	9	3	4	3	1	3	62
$500-999 Million	...	6	5	8	5	5	2	3	3	1	2	40
$1,000 Million and over	2	1	3	6	3	3	5	1	2	...	2	28
TOTAL	10	49	105	112	85	90	46	44	25	5	21	592

SOURCE: National Industrial Conference Board, *Corporate Directorship Practices*, Studies in Business Policy No. 103 (1962), p. 8.

124

TABLE 6 Ratio of Inside and Outside Boards, 1925–1963, 103 Largest Manufacturing Companies

| | Number of Directors | | | | | | Percent of Inside Directors | | |
| | 1925 | | 1950 | | 1963 | | | | |
Industry	Inside	Outside	Inside	Outside	Inside	Outside	1925	1950	1963
Aircraft	60	62	62	60	64	67	0.490	0.510	0.490
Automobile	42	32	57	27	53	36	0.567	0.678	0.596
Chemicals	99	47	72	36	103	43	0.678	0.667	0.706
Electrical equipment	68	88	75	73	80	84	0.438	0.506	0.487
Farm equipment	39	32	42	33	37	32	0.549	0.560	0.536
Meat-packing	47	28	53	25	58	31	0.627	0.679	0.652
Nonferrous metals	53	36	59	43	65	41	0.595	0.579	0.613
Paper	58	38	72	39	78	45	0.604	0.648	0.634
Petroleum	109	57	129	62	119	62	0.656	0.675	0.657
Rubber	34	33	42	30	42	32	0.507	0.583	0.568
Steel	86	91	95	78	90	97	0.485	0.549	0.482
Tobacco	44	13	49	15	59	14	0.772	0.765	0.808
TOTAL	739	557	807	521	848	584	0.562	0.607	0.593
Total inside plus total outside	1,296		1,328		1,432				
Average board size	12.6		12.9		13.9				

SOURCE: Stanley C. Vance, *Boards of Directors: Structure and Performance,* University of Oregon Press, Eugene, Oregon, 1964, p. 19.

board in that period, while three outside boards became inside boards.

Because the difference in the definitions used by the Conference Board and by Vance makes a surprisingly large difference in conclusion between the two studies, semantics may be more significant in this field than is generally realized. However, as will be pointed out below, perhaps the actual count of numbers of directors is a good deal less significant than other factors. Furthermore, with interest in board problems and various pressures for increased outside representation, one would not be surprised to see a current trend in that direction.

Advantages and Disadvantages of Inside Directors. Obviously, the main advantage of the inside director rests on his familiarity with the business. With his greater knowledge of a company's operation and involvement in actions taken, as well as his personal incentive to see the company succeed, it may be true that he can make more intelligent and more highly-motivated company policy decisions. Moreover, an insider is more available for company board meetings and presumably has the time to give them necessary study, thought, and deliberation. Having no other personal interest than the company itself, and almost certainly regarding his own personal economic future as tied to the company's success, the inside member —it may be argued—can and will serve on the board of directors with great effectiveness.

On the other hand, insiders—particularly insiders other than the chief executive officer—are at a serious disadvantage. In the first place, it is difficult for any insider, especially if he has responsibility for a functional or divisional operation, to wear the hat of an internal line manager for twenty-nine days of the month and change it on the thirtieth day to that of an overall company director without such line interests and prejudices.

In the second place, an officer who is subordinate to the chief executive will normally find it very difficult to be independent of his superior, even in a board meeting where the mantle of a director makes him his own boss's superior. Despite attempts by chief executive officers to encourage independence on the part of executives who report to them, it is rare indeed that they can forget this reporting relationship. It is equally rare for a chief executive officer wholeheartedly and gracefully to accept the fact that a vice-presidential subordinate is legally, and should be actually, his own superior during the board meeting.

The result of this situation is that inside employee-directors tend to support the chief executive officer, thereby becoming "rubber stamps" for him.[5] As the National Industrial Conference Board observed in its 1939 study of boards of directors, "there is some question whether such a situation is desirable, since the board members sitting as directors are merely approving the action of the board members in their executive capacities, a situation that is faintly reminiscent of Pooh Bah's strategems in *The Mikado.*" [6]

Even though the problem of independence appears to be the paramount objection to insider membership on boards of directors, a less-noted but perhaps equally important disadvantage is the fact that insiders may be too involved with their own situations to appreciate the impact of outside forces. In other words, an "outside" look, which is really a drawing on experience outside the company plus an awareness of environmental factors external to the company, may

[5] As one director said in a conference, "We've talked about the problem of the outside director and his lack of intimate knowledge; have we talked of the problem of the inside director who carries operating responsibilities? He's a full-time member of the organization, he carries operating responsibilities, and his difficulty is not so much being objective about himself but of having to go on living with other people in management and, therefore, being quite reluctant to be as searching as he should be in his questions or in his criticisms of other members of the management who are also on the board. Therefore, he shrinks into himself and will not voice his true feeling, for fear of losing his job, obviously. Frankly, I believe that in those instances a control by part-time directors is very important to the success of the enterprise, only because the inside members are beholden to the President." See C. Brown and E. D. Smith, eds., *The Director Looks at His Job*, Columbia University Press, New York, 1957, p. 43.

[6] *Prevailing Practices Regarding Corporate Directors*, National Industrial Conference Board, New York, 1939, p. 12.

be extremely significant in corporate decisions. It is a safeguard against being too preoccupied with the trees to see the forest.

Advantages and Disadvantages of Outside Directors. The advantages and disadvantages of outside directors on company boards are essentially a mirror image of those of inside directors. One of the major advantages of the outside director is his relative independence. This advantage, however, is often exaggerated; as Gordon [7] pointed out many years ago, in many companies the inside group nominates and elects the outside members of the board and in doing so controls these outsiders as effectively as if they were members of the inside management team.

Although this is doubtless true in many instances even today, the fact that insiders do nominate and have a great deal of influence in selecting outside board members does not necessarily indicate that these outsiders have given up their independence. Men of standing who take their board membership seriously will not continue to serve on a board where they cannot exercise independent judgment. The author has served on a number of boards and has always been selected by insiders. However, he feels that he is not at all unusual in that, if he finds he is expected to be a loyal rubber stamp to the insiders, he always discovers personal "health" or other reasons for resigning from the board.

Perhaps the greatest contribution of the outsider is the "outside look" which he can bring to a company. The inclusion of outsiders on a board of directors may and should provide assurance that the corporation's leadership will have the advantage of a broader and more diversified experience, more accurately attuned to society. This is particularly true if the outside group of directors includes men drawn from a variety of fields.

On the other hand, the outside director does suffer from some disadvantages. In the first place, he cannot be expected to have the insider's intimate knowledge of a company's operations. On the other hand, it is entirely possible that too much knowledge of the company can be a detriment in deciding major policy matters and can

[7] R. A. Gordon, *Business Leadership in the Large Corporation*, The Brookings Institution, Washington, D.C., 1945, pp. 121–122.

lead to "inbred" types of decisions. Also, intelligent men of broad experience have extraordinary ability to perceive problems, particularly if their minds are not cluttered with operating details, personal loyalties, and the pressure of precedent which grows from past operating decisions. In the second place, if the outsider brings a fresh point of view to the board, he can, by raising discerning questions, easily determine whether employee executives, whether directors or not, have thought through and taken into account all aspects of proposals brought before the board.

In the third place, not being embroiled in company operations and hopefully being more widely exposed to the outside world, a properly selected group of outside directors can bring to the board a kind of freshness that few groups of insiders can furnish. The shock the automobile industry received in 1966 from Congressional investigations on safety and air pollution provides an interesting example of how inside executives, even though broad-gauged, completely competent, and devoted to their tasks, can overlook outside forces. As the Chairman of the General Motors Corporation said after reflecting on these factors, "We have got a tradition in General Motors of maybe too much sticking with our business problems." [8]

Pressures for Increasing Outside Representation. That there have been pressures for increasing outside representation on boards of directors can hardly be denied. For a number of years, the American Institute of Management, in its appraisals of the quality of management of various corporations, has rated down those corporations that do not include outside members on their boards.[9] It is interesting that the Institute has pressed so hard for outside directors in companies, particularly when one realizes that its founder, Jackson Martindell, came to the conclusion after years as an astute and successful investment counselor that effective management was the best insurance that an investor could have.

Likewise, there has been increasing pressure by the investment

[8] Dan Kordtz, "The Face in the Mirror at General Motors," *Fortune*, Vol. 24, No. 3, p. 117, August, 1966.

[9] American Institute of Management, *The Corporate Director*, Special Issue 10, 1951, p. 3.

community generally for outside representation on boards. Stockholders as well as underwriters have contributed to this pressure. Apparently, the belief is widespread that this is the best protection against insider myopia and abuse of power, and the best assurance of the necessary responsiveness of a company to the outside world in which it must live.

Likewise, virtually every study of directors has indicated the desirability of outside members. But perhaps the most telling pressure for inclusion of outside members on the board of directors came with the action of the New York Stock Exchange in 1964. In its statement of listing policies and procedures, the Exchange stated:

> Full disclosure of corporate affairs for the information of the investing public is, of course, normal and usual procedure for listing companies. Many companies have found that this procedure has been greatly aided by having at least two outside directors whose functions on the board would include particular attention to such matters. Companies not having outside directors are urged to consider the desirability of doing so, particularly where the stock has been closely held.[10]

While the New York Stock Exchange statement was listed as a "policy," there is evidence that it has been accepted as a rule. For example, since it appeared, such companies as the Bethlehem Steel Corporation, Socony-Mobil Oil Company, and Standard Oil Company of New Jersey, with long histories of exclusively inside members, have named outside directors to their boards.

Are Outside Boards Superior? Although arguments, on balance, seem to favor at least a substantial portion of outside members on boards of directors, one may well ask whether outside boards are, in fact, superior. The only study based on facts which has been made in this area is that by Professor Stanley Vance of the University of Oregon.[11] In this study, Professor Vance came to the rather startling conclusion that:

[10] *New York Stock Exchange Guide,* "Rules of Board—Listing Policies and Procedures," Par. 2459G, Commerce Clearing House, Inc., New York, 1965.

[11] *Op. cit.*

1. Inside boards are superior in performance to outside boards.

2. Outside boards, with a relatively strong management representation, are superior to those lacking such management representation.

3. Next in sequence of excellence are managements with outsiders who are predominantly "local" businessmen.

4. At the very bottom of the performance "totem pole" are firms with outside boards comprised largely of absentee directors.[12]

Because this study seems to fly in the face of prevailing trends and arguments, its findings must be looked at carefully, particularly since they have been undertaken by so competent a scholar as Professor Vance. Without any desire to undermine the scholarly work which Professor Vance has done, several questions may be raised concerning his findings. In the first place, he has included in his definition of "inside" directors, as pointed out above, not only employee directors, but retired employee directors, and directors representing a "significant" stock interest. As indicated, there is some question as to whether these individuals are truly insiders in the usual sense.

In the second place, Professor Vance has classified as "inside" boards those in which "insiders" comprise more than 60 percent of the total membership. What a board actually does and how it operates does not depend upon the actual number of directors. The author has seen a number of boards with outsiders constituting only 10–15 percent of their members that operate in the tradition of and with the full advantage of outside directors. While Professor Vance recognizes this possibility, he feels that over the large sample he has studied it would tend to be ironed out. Nevertheless, it would appear that a determination of how a board actually operates, based on the ratio of "insiders" to "outsiders," however defined, is open to serious question.

In the third place, since Professor Vance's standard of performance was understandably and properly the success of the corporation in terms of earnings, productivity, growth, and other performance factors, there is some question as to whether his study has been prejudiced by his sample. There is no question that such eminently successful companies as General Motors, Standard Oil of New Jersey, Du Pont, and Ford, all of whom he would include as

[12] *Ibid.*, p. 5.

illustrations of inside control, might tend to prejudice a sample drawn, as his was, from 103 of the nation's large-scale manufacturing enterprises, all of which rank among the top 200 companies of the country.

What Professor Vance has shown, and this is a very valuable contribution, is that one cannot determine the effectiveness of a board of directors merely by counting the number of inside and outside directors, regardless of the definition of these terms. There are other significant factors to consider.

Part-time vs. Full-time Directors. Many of the major problems with respect to both inside and outside directors are removed by having board members serve fulltime. This has been done in a few large companies, such as Standard Oil Company of New Jersey, Du Pont, and Unilever. The advantage of the full-time director is that he can give adequate time and attention to his duties and does not suffer from the dangers of part-time employee-directors.

On the other hand, there are problems in having full-time board members. In the first place, they are likely to be rather expensive, and it may be difficult to obtain adequate talent for a number of these important posts. In the second place, a full-time board member, in order to keep himself occupied, might involve himself too much with operating details, thereby undermining the basic responsibilities of top-level functional or divisional managers. In addition, having full-time directors does not offset the danger of inward thinking and lack of the outside look that a director with other business interests is more likely to bring to the company. At the same time, in the case of large and diversified companies with world-wide interests, such as Unilever or Standard Oil of New Jersey, one can say that a full-time director does, in fact, represent the diversified experience of the world and a wide number of ventures. In this sense, it is entirely possible that a full-time director might have as much of the "outside" look as could reasonably be expected from an outside director.

Directors' Time Commitment. There is much to say for expecting any director to give a reasonable time commitment to the company on whose board he serves. Whether this must be his full-time job depends upon the size and complexity of the company. However, if a board of directors is to be effective, the task of directing is almost certainly a larger one than can be discharged in short monthly meetings.

If the one major function of a board of directors is to make sure that a company is well managed, more continuous contact than that provided by a monthly meeting might well be desirable. In fact, the whole attitude toward time commitment of board members probably needs rethinking. If the requirements of effective direction as outlined in this book are correct and if they are actually put into practice, many companies may find that they call for more time than the typical outside director is accustomed to give to his duties.[13]

The problem of time and need for adequate deliberation has been solved in part by the use of committees of the board. Quite often, these are comprised of employee-directors who can devote as much time as necessary to the task. Nevertheless, this is not always a good solution, particularly if the employee-directors also have operating responsibilities. Moreover, if an inside group is to operate, in effect, as the board of directors, one may question what advantage this arrangement offers over the ordinary management committee reporting to the chief executive officer.

Balancing Representation. Virtually all analyses and discussions of board composition come to the conclusion that the ideal board should represent a balance between insiders and outsiders. This is a recognition that valuable contributions can be made by both types of directors. But it also raises questions as to what the balance should be. There are those who maintain quite persuasively that a company hardly needs more than two insiders—the chief executive officer and his second-in-command—and that to add others is merely to append names, since all other possible insiders are definitely subordinate to the chief executive officer and cannot contribute truly independent thinking. Others hold the view that any employee-director can contribute importantly to the board if he is in a posi-

[13] In the Columbia University Symposium on boards of directors, it is interesting that the group rather strongly advocated full-time directors in order to give meaningful discharge of directors' responsibilities. See C. C. Brown and E. E. Smith, eds., *The Director Looks at His Job*, pp. 91–93.

tion, through his corporate assignment, to take an overall look at the company. Thus, it has been argued that the chief financial officer and perhaps other top officers in a staff capacity with overall corporate responsibilities can make ideal employee-directors.

The real problem of course, in balancing inside and outside interests is not the exact number of directors, but rather their effectiveness. This depends in part upon the abilities and independence of individuals. Even more importantly, it depends on whether the board, as constituted and operated, develops an environment that attracts individuals of high ability and encourages them to use their abilities as directors. Thus, what constitutes an "ideal" board largely depends upon the personnel and the way the board is run. This, in turn, depends heavily upon what the leaders of the company, normally the chief executive officer and his most influential associates, want the board to be. Operating executives usually get the board they deserve.

AGES AND RETIREMENT OF BOARD MEMBERS

Martindell, in his study of corporate management, has been particularly critical of the average age of directors.[14] He found in 1950 that 57 percent of the directors of 75 large corporations were over 60 years of age, and that only 12 percent were under 50. This high average age of board members was held to indicate the honorary, rather than active, character of boards and the inevitability among boards of a certain cultural lag. This criticism, of course, is not necessarily justified in any given instance, since age is not basically a numerical thing but a matter of vigor and attitude of mind.

Over the years there has not been much indication of change in the average age of directors. In more than half of the companies

[14] See Jackson Martindell, *The Scientific Appraisal of Management,* Harper & Brothers, New York, 1950, pp. 11ff., and *The Appraisal of Management,* Harper & Brothers, New York, 1962, pp. 77–78. In his 1962 book, Martindell was not nearly as critical of the problem of age as he was in 1950. One wonders whether that author, like others of us, becomes less concerned with age as he himself becomes older.

surveyed by the Conference Board in 1953, the average age of directors was between 56 and 60, and in most of the others the average age ranged from 50 to 55 years. While this is lower than that found by Martindell, it is interesting that, in the Conference Board survey of 1959, the average age of directors in manufacturing companies was 58 and the average age of directors in utility, transportation, banking, and insurance companies was 62. Likewise, in the 1961 study, the average age of directors in manufacturing companies was still 58 and in transportation, utilities, banking, and insurance companies was between 60 and 62.

However, in recent years an increasing number of companies have undertaken means of assuring a younger board. In 1961, the Conference Board found that formal retirement policies had been adopted by a quarter of the 918 companies cooperating in the study. In 1964, the Board found that some 37 percent of 218 companies surveyed had retirement policies.[15] This increasing number of companies had developed retirement plans applicable to directors, normally with an age limit for employee-directors lower than that for outside directors, these limits being 65 for members of management and 70 for directors who are not members of management. Nevertheless, the Conference Board found that a majority of the companies surveyed controlled the tenure of directors either on a case-by-case basis or not at all.

Admittedly, introduction of a compulsory retirement age for company directors is a difficult and delicate matter. These men, after all, are the top authority of the corporation, and it is natural that they should dislike introducing a compulsory retirement age for themselves and their peers. Companies that have introduced these programs successfully have used a number of techniques. One is to make the new program of retirement not apply to those already on the board. Another is to make the program of retirement apply only after ten years from adoption of the plan for those already on the board. Still another technique is the use of the title "honorary direc-

---

[15] G. C. Thompson and F. J. Walsh, Jr., "Directors' Compensation, Fringe Benefits and Retirement," *Conference Board Record,* Vol. 11, No. 2, p. 21, February, 1965.

tor," with all privileges of a director except the right to vote, for men over the desired retirement age.

Exactly how urgent the matter of forced retirement of directors is may be open to question. Certainly, when a director has become incapacitated or has lost his ability to contribute effectively to the company, he should make way for someone with more vigor and ability. However, as in all matters of retirement, vigor and ability are not necessarily related to calendar years. Nonetheless, a retirement age of 70 or 72 for outside directors and perhaps the standard officer retirement age for inside directors appears entirely reasonable. Generally, the problem of over-age directors can be met best by bringing in younger men as vacancies occur.

QUALIFICATIONS OF BOARD MEMBERS

Far more important than a board's mere size, the age of members, or the balance of inside and outside interests, is the question of the directors' qualifications. The effective member of a board of directors will possess intelligence, judgment, ability to analyze problems and come to rational conclusions, a willingness to identify himself with the company and its stockholder interests, and an ability to speak out independently during board deliberations. Also, the effective board member must be an individual of high personal integrity who understands thoroughly the ethics of his community and the company which he is obligated to serve.

Qualities Sought in Board Candidates. In a survey of 136 companies made by the National Industrial Conference Board in 1965, the participants reported seeking a wide variety of qualities and abilities when considering candidates for membership in their boards of directors.[16] As might be expected, honesty and integrity topped the list; other qualities frequently mentioned were extensive business experience, knowledge, and capability; ability to contribute to the bal-

[16] G. C. Thompson and F. J. Walsh, Jr., "Selection of Corporate Directors," *The Conference Board Record*, Vol. 2, No. 5, pp. 8–16, May, 1965.

ance of the board; demonstrated success in the candidate's principal occupation or profession; stature in the community; maturity; interest in the company; and willingness to devote time to the job of director. In addition, a number of other qualifications were mentioned, including good business judgment, objectivity, ability to work harmoniously with other board members, ability to contribute to the company's future progress, absence of conflicting interests, broad and significant business contracts, ability to advise and appraise management, and memberships in other boards of directors.

The pattern of responses on each of the major qualities and abilities identified in this survey was interesting enough to warrant summarizing here.

1. *Business Experience, Knowledge, and Capability.* Although this quality was placed high on the list by the survey participants, there was wide variation in types of knowledge and experience sought. Some companies expressed interest in a director's all-round executive ability and his capacity to consider questions broadly. Other companies preferred board members with specific types of business experience and knowledge. Some felt that prior knowledge of the problems of the company's industry were important. Others felt that a director should be familiar, not necessarily with the particular business of the company, but at least with a related field. Still other companies expressed preference for board members with experience in related businesses rather than in their own industry so as to bring to the board a breadth of experience not available in the company. Many companies felt that experience in specific operating functions such as marketing, manufacturing, or finance was desirable for board memberships, while other companies felt that this kind of experience, being available within the company, would not be particularly helpful in a director.

2. *Ability to Contribute to Board Balance.* A considerable number of companies in the Conference Board survey felt that directors should be chosen with an eye to enhancing the balance of the board. In general, these companies wished to balance the strength and weaknesses of their inside members with complementary abilities on the part of outsiders. For example, one company president stated:

When choosing a new director we first look at the qualifications and talents of the other board members and try and select a man who can contribute something additional. We believe a good board of directors should be made up of men who are specialists in their various fields, so that the sum total covers all the areas in which our business might be involved. This would include financial, engineering, manufacturing, legal, etc.[17]

3. Success in Principal Field of Endeavor. Approximately one-third of the survey respondents believe that a potential director should have a record of proven success in his principal occupation or profession, attesting to his ability to meet and deal successfully with problems.

4. Stature in the Community. A considerable number of the survey participants believed that a board member should be a person of stature in the community. Such a director, they reason, would enhance the company's reputation and would enjoy stockholders' confidence.

5. Maturity. Some of the companies surveyed indicated that the age and maturity of the potential director is important. Companies appeared to desire directors who were experienced in handling problems but who were also young enough so that they could be counted on for a reasonably long period of directorship service. Those companies who felt that age was important generally placed the desirable age bracket at 40 to 55.

6. Interest in the Company. One of the major qualifications offered by the respondents of the survey was that a potential director should have shown interest in the company and its affairs. He is presumed to have such interest if he owns stock in the company or represents certain large stockholders, is a key member of company management, or has had a close business relationship with the company in some capacity—e.g., as an underwriter.

7. Willingness to Spend Time. Approximately one of eight companies surveyed emphasized the importance of a potential director's

[17] *Ibid.,* p. 13.

having the time available to spend on the task and the willingness to spend it as a director.

What Companies Actually Do. It can fairly be assumed that the above listing of qualities and abilities sought in recruiting new directors represents a fair statement of what companies desire in present board members. Moreover, there is little to argue with in these requirements, although, particularly with respect to general business experience, there are wide differences in what companies really wish.

In the survey made by the National Industrial Conference Board in 1961, a sample of 456 manufacturing companies indicated that employee-directors predominantly held general-management positions, as opposed to management of a function, although approximately 10 percent of the directors of vice-presidential rank whose functions were specified were from such functional fields as sales and marketing, manufacturing and production, engineering and research, industrial and public relations, legal, purchasing, and similar positions. These data are presented in Table 7.

The Board found in the same study a wide variety of principal occupations of outside directors from a sample of 431 manufacturing companies. As indicated in Table 8, the largest single group of directors was bankers, followed by attorneys, corporate presidents, retired businessmen, prominent businessmen, retired or former officers, and others. What is interesting in these data is that, other than for bankers and attorneys, by far the largest group are business executives from other companies. Noteworthy is the relative absence of professional persons who, it might be expected, could make a major contribution to a company board of directors.

A recent study made by an executive recruiting firm, involving a sample of approximately 320 companies drawn from manufacturing, transportation, merchandising, life insurance, and banks, depicts somewhat similar results. These data, summarized in Table 9, show that a majority of inside board members, particularly in transportation and utilities and banking and insurance, are drawn from the general management, financial, and legal positions in management, and far fewer from the operating specialties.

TABLE 7   Positions Held by Employee-Directors, 1961, 456 Manufacturing Companies [1]

Position	Number of Directors	Number of Companies
Chairman of board	215	215
Vice-chairman and committee chairman	47	42
Presidents	435	435
Executive vice-presidents	164	143
Senior vice-presidents	38	31
Vice-presidents, specified [2]		
Divisional, regional, operations	96	61
Sales and marketing	82	73
Manufacturing and production	70	64
Engineering/research/development	33	32
Finance	31	31
Industrial and public relations	17	16
Administration and control	13	11
Legal-counsel	12	12
Purchasing	11	11
Various other [3]	17	14
Vice-presidents, unspecified	475	193
Secretaries, treasurers, controllers		
Secretaries [4]	79	79
Secretary and treasurers [5]	29	29
Secretary and controllers	4	4
Treasurers [6]	106	106
Controllers [7]	21	21
Financial, other	14	12
Managers and other operating	127	72
Parent company and subsidiary officers [8]	100	71
Assistants to chairmen, presidents, others	28	20
Consultants and specialists	22	19
Total	2,286	

SOURCE: National Industrial Conference Board, *Corporate Directorship Practices*, Studies in Business Policy No. 103, p. 16.

[1] Highest title only tabulated: *e.g.*, "Chairman and President" (one individual) tabulated only as Chairman.
[2] Excluding 80 vice-presidents holding secretarial and treasurer titles.
[3] Including: personnel (4), advertising (3), assistant to chairman (2), and real estate, coordination, traffic, general services, export, assistant to president, supply and transportation, and planning and economics (one each).
[4] Including 25 vice-presidents.   [6] Including 45 vice-presidents.
[5] Including 2 vice-presidents.   [7] Including 8 vice-presidents.
[8] Including officers designated "president" of divisions and subsidiary companies.

TABLE 8   Principal Occupations of Outside Directors, 1961, 431
Manufacturing Companies [1]

Occupation	Number of Directors	Number of Companies
Bankers (commercial, investment, private)	416	256
Attorneys	330	258
Corporate presidents	327	173
Retired businessmen [2]	225	148
Prominent businessmen, not otherwise classified	159	81
Retired or former officers	154	86
Industrialists and manufacturers	150	78
Corporate chairmen, vice-chairmen and committee chairmen	129	87
Brokers (investment, real estate, commodity)	101	86
Investment and financial counsellors, financiers	82	67
Consultants	75	64
Corporate vice-presidents	70	58
Board directors	60	35
Insurance executives	56	52
Educators	31	29
Housewives [3]	21	16
Trustees, foundation and institutional	20	19
Farmers and ranchers	18	16
Managers and other operating executives	17	16
Professions other than law and education	16	15
Government and military	9	9
Total	2,466	

SOURCE: National Industrial Conference Board, *Corporate Directorship Practices*, Studies in Business Policy No. 103, p. 16.

[1] No director is tabulated more than once: *e.g.*, a banker may be president of his bank and also an investment counsellor, but he is counted only as banker.
[2] Includes all directors identified as retired (other than retired former employees), regardless of previous occupation.
[3] Frequently, majority of substantial stockholders.

TABLE 9   Source of Board Members, 1965
         Percentage of Directors from Various Backgrounds, 320
         Companies

Background	Manufac- turing	Transporta- tion and Utilities	Wholesale and Retail	Banking and Insurance
Inside directors:				
General management	30.4%	41.1%	32.0%	50.0%
Financial	16.8	16.2	21.3	17.3
Legal	8.2	10.3	4.2	5.5
Marketing	13.7	7.4	23.4	9.1
All other	30.9	25.0	19.1	18.1
Outside directors:				
General management	25.8%	19.3%	20.5%	22.1%
Financial	26.5	22.0	25.0	18.0
Legal	17.5	16.5	16.0	19.4
Marketing	6.8	7.3	11.4	7.8
All other	23.4	34.9	27.1	32.7

SOURCE: Survey by Heidrick & Struggles, as reported in "What It Takes to Make the Board," *Business Week,* pp. 93–94, March 12, 1966.

The conclusion might be drawn (as was done in the reporting of the survey [18]) that inside directors tend to be "jack-of-all-trades" management men while outsiders tend more often to be specialists. However, as already indicated, financial and legal personnel in the typical corporation are by the nature of their duties more likely to fill a position with a corporation-wide concern than executives identified with marketing, production, or engineering and research. Thus, one can draw the conclusion that the study indicates a heavy weighting of inside directors in the general-management area. Likewise, a conclusion could be drawn that outsiders are more often specialists. When one considers only those with an interest in general management, the study would indicate this. However, since outside members with financial or legal backgrounds are likely to hold

[18] "What It Takes to Make the Board," *Business Week,* March 12, 1966, pp. 93–94.

general-management positions in other firms, as would be the case with insider officers, this conclusion might be questioned. Indeed, the only solid inference one can draw from both studies is that a majority of directors appear to have had general business experience.

The Question of Specialists. Although no one seriously challenges the desirability of considerable experience and judgment in a director, and most would agree that a substantial business background is advisable, opinions differ widely as to how heavily the board should be weighted with specialists in such fields as law, finance, marketing, production, engineering, personnel, and transportation and supply. Nevertheless, there is something to be said for balancing specialized talents on boards so that a degree of expertise may be brought to bear on a wide range of major policy decisions.

On the other hand, there are those who argue persuasively that specialized talents and advice can be purchased, and that a board member should be selected on the basis of his ability to look at the company and its problems as a whole. For example, one student of company directorates has stated that:

A man should not be chosen if he can contribute only the kind of help that can be hired unless, in a small company, he provides specialized services that the company could not afford otherwise. Lawyers, management consultants, accountants, and the like, can be hired; generally a board will not be strengthened if such men are added for their occupational qualifications alone.[19]

The sound position for a company to take would be to select persons who can contribute most effectively to board deliberations and decisions, giving heavy emphasis to individuals with broad qualifications, particularly in the field of general management. However, if an individual is otherwise qualified by the breadth of his experience and point of view, there may be an additional benefit, particularly in the case of outside directors, if varied functional viewpoints can also be represented—especially since some of them, such as marketing

[19] "The Role of the Director," *The Corporate Director*, Vol. 9, No. 13, p. 3, January, 1965. This is known to be the confirmed opinion of Jackson Martindell, President of the American Institute of Management, which publishes *The Corporate Director*.

and product development, are currently receiving such heavy emphasis. Likewise, a company with a heavy stake in production or engineering and research would certainly find it desirable to have some specialized talent reflecting this on the board.

Desirability of specialized talent does not apply with equal force to employee-directors. Particularly where a company is functionally organized (with its major activities under operations such as marketing, production, and engineering and research), it could be difficult for a functional officer in a company to be as objective and general in viewpoint as board membership requires. This is not intended in any way as a criticism of functional department heads. On the contrary, as most business executives realize, a competent functional department head should be expected to have a strong prejudice in favor of the function for which he is responsible.

There is serious question as to whether persons with certain special interests should be on the board. It is almost always unwise to have major customers or suppliers represented on the board, and the advisability of having a representative of a bank that is a vendor of credit to the company may well be questioned. This question applies with less force to investment bankers, however, since they are not so much vendors as representatives of the company in the securities market and with security holders to whom the company's shares or bonds may have been sold.

In addition, there are serious questions as to whether the company general counsel, particularly if representing an outside legal firm, should be on the board. In his position of adviser to the board on key legal matters, such a legal counselor may prefer to keep himself independent so he may limit his opinions and thinking to legal matters and thereby serve the company better. As a matter of fact, an increasing number of prominent legal firms now prohibit members of their firms from serving on the boards of companies they represent as counsel, although they may be permitted to serve as corporate secretary.

Should a Director Be a Stockholder? Another point on which opinion differs is whether a director should be a stockholder of the company. One can understand the attitude of stockholders who wish their company directors to be owner of at least a small amount of stock. In a minority of states, statutes specifically provide that directors must be stockholders. The large majority of statutes provide, however, that directors need not be stockholders unless this is required by the charter or by-laws; and relatively few company charters or by-laws require stock ownership on the part of directors. Nonetheless, in many companies without such requirements, it is traditional that a director purchase at least a few shares as a means of displaying interest in the company—and, above all, for the benefit of good stockholder relations.

It may be argued that holding a small amount of stock does not give a director a significantly greater incentive to enhance the welfare of the enterprise. It may also be argued that, if directors hold too much stock, they may be more interested in short-term stock speculation than in long-term company growth and profits. Many company executives attach little importance to the matter of whether directors own stock. However, some stock ownership is probably desirable, not only from the standpoint of good stockholder relations, but to encourage the director to have more of an owner's interest in the company's profitable growth.

THE PROFESSIONAL DIRECTOR

To increase board effectiveness by bringing in outsiders of unusual competence who will give the required time and attention to their task, proposals have often been made for broadening the practice of employing professional directors. The professional director is an individual who devotes all or most of his time to being a director, usually of several non-competing companies in which he holds no other executive position, and from each of which he receives a fairly handsome retainer. This practice has long been followed in England, where it is not unusual for an experienced business or professional man to hold six or seven directorships, each of which may bring a retainer of from $5,000 to $15,000 per year.

English experience with the professional director has not always been too satisfactory. In some cases the salary and title have been used to pension members of an owning family or bring to a board the prestige of one of the nobility, thus trading an annual stipend for the advertising value of a prominent name. In a great many cases, on the other hand, experts in general management and in various functional fields have served British corporations with great distinction.

Professional directors have not been widely utilized in the United States, although there is a currently a slight tendency to compensate more outside directors on an annual retainer basis. In a study made by the National Industrial Conference Board in 1939, approximately 85 percent of the responding executives opposed the use of professional directors.[20] Similar resistance was expressed in the survey made in 1959.[21]

Apparently much of this opposition is aroused by the connotations of the term "professional": those questioned felt that such an expert would mix unduly in the administrative affairs of the business, or would command a fee larger than he would earn, or would be an anomaly somewhere between an employee-director and an outside board member. Since the Conference Board studies have been directed mainly to company officers, they may report biased evidence. As a matter of fact, a study made by the Board in 1946 used other terminology. At that time, slightly more than half of the persons queried favored the idea of having some directors who would represent no particular group, would hold directorships in a number of non-competing corporations on an annual salary basis, and would be able to give more time than the usual outside director to board functions.[22]

The apparent opposition in the United States to professional directors is a curious anomaly. There is, as we have seen, a very strong opinion favoring full-time directors, as well as a considerable body of opinion that outside directors should spend more time on their task and become more knowledgeable with respect to company

[20] *Prevailing Practices Regarding Corporation Directors, op. cit.*, p. 9.

[21] *Corporate Directorship Practices, op. cit.*, pp. 18–19.

[22] P. W. Dickson, *Compensation and Duties of Corporate Directors,* Studies in Business Policy No. 16, 1946, pp. 17–19.

affairs. In one symposium on company boards, the consensus was that a full-time board "held a great deal of appeal" for a number of the members of the study group and that it "had the attractive quality of providing a knowledgeable group in whose judgment management might have greater confidence, on whom it might rely to a greater extent because of its familiarity with the firm's operations, even though the actual organizational arrangements might tend to blur somewhat the lines dividing directorial from management functions."[23] In addition, as will be seen presently, companies have shown an increasing tendency to place outside directors on annual retainers, and these retainers have been increasing as the years go by. Thus, there is evidence that American business is, in practice, favoring something approaching a professional director, while vehemently rejecting this device when identified as such.

BOARD COMPENSATION

It has long been recognized that directors as a group, despite their position at the top of companies and the importance of their role in assuring the long-term stability, growth, and profitability of the companies, are among the lowest-paid segments of the American managerial hierarchy.

Meeting Fees. In 1938, the National Industrial Conference Board reported that of 468 companies with outside directors on their boards, 318 companies, or 68 percent, paid them less than $25 per meeting attended, with $20 being the usual fee; and only 2.3 percent of the companies studied paid $100 or more per meeting.[24] The average amount paid per year to outside directors was $285, in contrast to an average of approximately $5,000 for 19 English companies reported in the study.

[23] C. C. Brown and E. E. Smith, *op. cit.*, pp. 92–93.

[24] National Industrial Conference Board, *Prevailing Practices Regarding Top Corporation Directors*, Studies in Administrative Control, No. 2, 1939, pp. 16–17.

In 1945, the Conference Board reported that board fees had risen somewhat, with the average fee for more than 500 companies being $50 per meeting, and with one-sixth paying meeting fees of $100 or more.[25] On an annual basis, outside directors realized an average of $850 in fees, including compensation for special board committee meetings. A 1953 survey disclosed a tendency for directors' compensation to continue its upward move. An increasing number of companies paid a fee of $100 per meeting, and some of the larger companies paid fees from $200 to $500 per meeting.[26] By 1961, board compensation had risen to an average per-meeting compensation of $200, with 29 percent of the firms reporting pay ranging from $300 to $750 per meeting.[27]

In a further survey made by the National Industrial Conference Board in 1964, directors' compensation has continued upward. Of the 211 companies surveyed that paid outside directors in 1964, the median per-meeting compensation for each director was $250, with forty companies paying only annual retainers a median of $450 per meeting resulted, and for an additional sixty-three companies paying both a per-meeting fee and an annual retainer, the median was $450.[28]

Board Retainers. As significant, perhaps, as the rise in meeting fees is a steady increase in the number and size of directors' retainers. In 1938, the Conference Board found that only nineteen of 468 companies placed outside board members on an annual salary, while in 1945 a total of eighty of 479 companies followed this practice; but by 1961, 251 of the 538 manufacturing companies reporting used

[25] Dickson, *op. cit.*, pp. 6–8.

[26] J. H. Watson, III, *The Corporate Directorship*, Studies in Business Policy No. 63, National Industrial Conference Board, New York, 1953, p. 13.

[27] *Corporate Directorship Practices, op. cit.*, p. 31.

[28] G. C. Thompson and F. J. Walsh, Jr., "Directors' Compensation, Fringe Benefits and Retirement," *Conference Board Record*, Vol. II, No. 2, pp. 13–19, February, 1965.

annual retainers for outside directors. In 1964, 109 of a total of 232 companies were paying annual retainers.

In addition, the size of retainers has materially increased. By 1961, the median retainer paid outside directors was $2,500 per year, although retainers ranging to $5,000 were not uncommon and a few companies paid retainers as high as $10,000 or $15,000. These had risen slightly by 1964, with the median retainer going above $2,500.

Justification for employing retainers as a method of compensating directors is based upon the view that, if outside directors are to keep well informed and are to be used for advice from time to time, they should be compensated more adequately. It is also believed that, in view of the high requirements for outside directors and their importance in contributing to efficient and profitable operation, fees should be made more attractive. Moreover, many believe that a retainer gives a director a greater sense of obligation to the company, and that he will more than earn it, through greater time, effort, and availability. If high-quality service is to be rendered by an outside director, even a retainer of $10,000 per year would appear to be rather modest.

At the same time, it is probably true that most directors do not serve primarily for money. Anyone looking at the history of directors' fees, in fact, would be hard put to maintain that the able and conscientious director is not principally motivated by other considerations.

Committee Fees. The Conference Board studies also indicate that approximately 40 percent of the reporting companies compensate outside directors for serving on committees of the board of directors, most frequently on a per-meeting basis, in addition to paying them their regular board fees. Perhaps this unexpectedly low percentage of companies paying fees for committee service reflects the fact that relatively few outside directors serve on important committees of the board. As service increases on such committees as the executive or finance committee, one would expect an increased incidence of payment for these services.

Pay for Employee-Directors. As for employee-directors, practice varies. It is the prevailing custom for companies not to pay employee-directors additional fees for board service. The Conference Board report for 1961 indicated that only approximately one-third of manufacturing companies and only 37 percent of non-manufacturing companies paid employee-directors for board services. The 1964 report for manufacturing companies showed a decline to less than one-quarter of the companies paying employee-directors meeting fees. Of those who do pay, approximately one-third set employee-directors' fees lower than those given outside directors. Employee-directors, of course, seldom receive retainers.

Arguments can be made either way with respect to payment of employee-directors. Perhaps the most persuasive point is that employee-directors are paid through their salary and other compensation for their full-time service to the company and should not expect board fees in addition. On the other hand, there is some foundation for the position that, if an employee-director is to feel his position as a director and to operate as such, the payment of fees is a small reward for this more effective service.

Fringe Benefits. A small but increasing portion of nonemployee directors are further compensated by participating in such employee fringe benefits as group life and travel insurance, group medical and health programs, profit-sharing and bonus plans, deferred compensation arrangements, and company matching of gifts to educational institutions. The Conference Board found that 17 percent of reporting companies in 1964, compared to less than 8 percent in 1961, provided some type of employee fringe benefits to outside directors.

Group life insurance is the most common form of benefit offered to outside board members, with provision for contribution, if any, following that provided company executives. Coverage of $25,000 or less is most common, but in some companies insurance as high as $100,000 is furnished.

It has been argued by many company executives that outside directors should not participate in these employee benefits. One reason given is that this creates a conflict of interest, since benefit programs are usually passed upon by a committee of outside members. Another is that outside directors customarily already have these benefits from their own companies.

The objections to offering outside directors employee fringe benefits are understandable but they are not too persuasive. Certain fringe benefits such as life or travel insurance tend to be fairly general in companies and can furnish a strong inducement at little company cost to outside members whose personal tax situation may make current compensation less attractive.

Adequacy of Directors' Compensation. Serving on boards does provide rewards other than money. Board memberships, particularly in well-known companies, have high status value. Also, participation in company boards may enable an outside director to gain knowledge and experience useful in his primary business or professional life. In addition, many individuals feel that they are making a contribution to the private enterprise system and to the successful growth of a company by serving on a board.

Nevertheless, financial compensation should not be overlooked—and indeed it has not been, as the growth in fees and the increased use of annual retainers indicate. If, in the interest of good management, companies wish to foster the kind of effective boards of directors for which the author argues, they must look more thoroughly toward the high qualifications and time-and-effort commitments required of outside members. By the same token, more attention should be given to increasing the compensation of those who carry responsibility for effective board operation.

OBTAINING BOARD MEMBERS

In virtually every boardroom in the country, the question is raised, "Where can we secure the kind of person who can do an effective job as a director?" There are more than 1 million active business corporations in the United States; assuming the average board comprises seven members, simple arithmetic indicates that there are over 7 million directors' positions. Even if only the very large companies are considered, the number of directors is significant. It has been estimated that there are over 400 companies with sales of more than $100 million per year. If it can be assumed that the average board for these firms is thirteen members, this would indicate a total board membership of 5,200 for these companies alone. Furthermore, if it can be assumed that half of the board members are outsiders, the requirement for these very large corporations is over 2,600. If the assumptions that half of the board members should be outsiders were applied to all business corporations, this would indicate a requirement of 3.5 million outside board members in the United States.

In the years immediately ahead, the problem of manning boards of directors is likely to become even more severe than these data indicate. In the first place, if—as this author believes—the demand for more effective boards of directors will increase, the requirements for board membership will become more exacting and many people now serving will be unwilling or unable to serve. Moreover, the increased application of retirement rules and the probable drive for younger average ages in company boardrooms, will increase the number of new directors needed.

Like any staffing problem, the recruitment of board members calls for specialized attention. Ordinarily, board members are suggested by the chairman or the president from among men they know personally or through business connections. However, in order to obtain a better and more thorough list of candidates, it has been recommended that the board establish a nominating committee consisting of the chairman or president plus two to four outside directors. This committee would be given responsibility for seeking out likely board candidates, presenting their names and qualifications to the whole board for ratification, and approaching candidates found to be acceptable.

But this leaves open the problem of where to find qualified men. Certainly, the traditional reliance on persons well known to members of the board or to senior managers of the company will not produce enough candidates. Rather, the nominating committee of the board may well decide to seek out names of potential candidates by searching through stockholder lists, combing such biographical dictionaries as the *Directory of Directors* or *Who's Who,* or soliciting suggestions from bankers, legal counsel, or other business advisers.

On the basis of this search, lists of potential candidates may be prepared, complete with biographical data; the qualifications of these persons can be compared to standards established by the company for desirable board membership. Through preliminary inquiries, the availability and further qualification of candidates may be ascertained. Then a limited list of most-desirable candidates may be presented to the full board for its confidential consideration and personal investigation, if desired. In addition, some companies find it useful to call upon the services of a top-management recruiting firm for an investigation of possible candidates.

As can be seen, this selection procedure, even at best, is a difficult and time-consuming task, and it does not guarantee that many promising candidates will not be overlooked or that selection will not be made only from well-known individuals who are often already over-committed. A more effective system of director recruitment is needed, it would seem. One approach is for companies to use the same executive recruiting firms they may employ in recruiting key executives, although few of these firms have developed a file of available and qualified board candidates and a program for director search. Another possibility is for a specialized recruiting agency, perhaps one supported by an industrial trade association, to develop a confidential pool of possible candidates who would consider themselves available for outside directorships and whose qualifications might be investigated and analyzed. That this would cost a company money there can be no doubt. However, selection of a qualified outside director is so important that any reasonable expenditure made in this kind of search is well justified.

One of the major problems of recruitment is faced by the smaller company. A large company with considerable standing in the business community normally has no difficulty in attracting top talent to its board. On the other hand, a less well-known medium-sized or smaller company may have considerable difficulty in ferreting out desirable candidates. Yet, it is inconceivable that there are not adequate qualified persons who would be willing and able to serve effectively on any company board where proper use is made of an outside director. Plainly, specialized clearing houses are needed for smaller companies in particular. Perhaps this task could be undertaken by local universities, Chambers of Commerce, various local business associations, or some recruiting firms. The need clearly exists. All that is required now is someone with the imagination to fill it.

chapter 7

BOARD OPERATION

A number of steps may be taken to assure the effectiveness of the board of directors in operation. It must ever be remembered that a board, being a plural executive, should act only as a group. Moreover, since the board is a plural executive, specific steps must be taken to see that the board meeting accomplishes its essential role at the top of the corporate management hierarchy.

In this chapter, the major areas of board operation will be discussed. In the following chapter, the particular role of the chairman of the board will be treated, while Chapter 9 will take up the relationship of the board to the operating executive group of the company.

FREQUENCY OF MEETINGS

Frequency of board meetings differs considerably. There are those who feel that company size has much to do with it. Two specialists in the field have indicated in a recent study that frequency tends to follow size.[1] They find the following "phases" of board evolution: (1) Under $5 million in sales—annual meetings with occasional special meetings; (2) $2 million to $20 million in sales and closely held ownership—annual or quarterly meetings with periodic special meetings; (3) $5 million to $50 million in sales with stock closely held—quarterly or monthly meetings; (4) $10 million to $100 million in sales with public ownership—quarterly or monthly meetings; (5) $50 million to $500 million with wide public ownership—

[1] J. M. Juran and J. K. Louden, *The Corporate Director*, American Management Association, Inc., New York, 1966, pp. 238–239.

monthly board meetings with interim committee meetings; and (6) in very large public corporations, extensive board activity with wide delegation to committees. These authors find that small companies with closely held shares tend to have primarily inside boards, and board-type matters are decided in conferences without a board meeting.

This pattern is not reflected in the National Industrial Conference Board studies. The 1962 study showed that approximately half of the 918 companies reporting from all industry groups in 1961 had at least ten to twelve regular board meetings per year.[2] Aproximately the same practice was found in the Board's 1965 study.[3] Among financial-type companies, 75 percent of the companies held regular board meetings at least ten times a year, as did 49 percent of manufacturing companies, 38 percent of merchandising companies, and 67 percent of utility and transportation companies.

The 1962 report also indicated that directors of smaller companies, being more likely to be active officers of the company, tend to have fewer formal meetings per year than larger companies, but that half the manufacturing companies with assets under $10 million had more than five meetings a year. Virtually all large manufacturing companies had regular board meetings ten to twelve times a year. The study also revealed that very few—less than 2 percent—of all reporting companies held meetings less often than four times a year.

If a board is to be effective and if its members are to exercise due care and prudence in directing the affairs of a company, it is difficult to see how, under normal circumstances, board responsibilities can be discharged without at least ten or twelve meetings per year. As a matter of fact, there are many outside directors, including the author, who will not serve on a company board that does not meet at least ten times per year.

[2] John R. Kinley, *Corporate Directorship Practices*, National Industrial Conference Board, New York, 1962, pp. 104–105.

[3] G. C. Thompson and F. J. Walsh, "Directors' Compensation, Fringe Benefits, and Retirement," *Conference Board Record*, Vol. II, No. 2, pp. 14–18, February, 1965.

To be sure, there are circumstances where monthly meetings may not be required for a board member to maintain appropriate contact with a company, its plans, and its operations. In the first place, regular meetings may be supplemented by enough special meetings to give a director adequate contact with the company. Second, companies with wholly inside boards may need only a few regular board meetings each year to satisfy legal requirements. In most of these cases, one wonders whether a board meeting is necessary at all, since what is really held is a management meeting—and most companies have far more than ten or twelve of these each year. A third factor is that a number of companies operate through executive and other committees, so that the real work of the board is done by these committees; in this event, the whole board may not find it necessary to meet more than quarterly. Nevertheless, outside directors not members of these special committees are in danger of abdicating their directorial responsibilities.

Another limitation on holding board meetings is the difficulty and expense, in some cases, of holding meetings on a monthly basis. For example, certain American companies operating joint ventures overseas may find it convenient only to hold meetings, say, quarterly, particularly where nationals of two or more countries are represented on the board. Even in these cases, there is a danger that too much time can elapse between board meetings; directors may lose appropriate contact with the company's plans, its operations, and its progress.

Approximately half of the states, including such states as Delaware, Connecticut, Michigan, Ohio, and Pennsylvania, with a considerable corporate population, permit directors to take action without a formal meeting, providing all directors agree in writing to the action. In addition, courts have sometimes permitted shareholders to allow directors to vote without a formal meeting, if this is specifically provided by shareholder approval. On the other hand, when one considers that the basic concept of a board involves *collective* action, presumably after analysis and deliberation, it is clear that effective board operation requires board action to be taken in duly constituted meetings, except in the rarest of circumstances.

DURATION OF MEETINGS

There are those who believe that board meetings should be short, usually not more than two hours. Typical is the comment of an outside director who remarked to the author, "If a board sticks to its business and proposals are properly researched and studied by individual board members before meeting, I cannot see how the matters coming before a monthly meeting cannot be discussed and disposed of in two hours. Indeed, my experience is that if meetings last much longer directors tend to get into too much detail, argue points of little consequence, and use the board room as a forum for longwinded discussion."

Although data are not available, it does seem fairly common for board meetings to last only one-half day. At the other end of the spectrum, however, are many boards of directors whose meetings last as long as a day, often preceded by several hours or possibly even a full day of informal briefing sessions on matters coming before the board. Some companies have made it a practice to have board meetings, at least quarterly, at various divisional or plant locations, where a day is spent briefing directors on particular company operations and problems and another day in the actual board meeting.

A board meeting should last long enough for the board to properly undertake its functions. How long this is will depend largely upon how well matters are researched and presented, how well directors are informed before the meeting as to matters to be discussed, how well the members do their homework, and how well the chairman runs the meeting. Therefore, an ideal length of time can hardly be specified. Nonetheless, if a board is to be effective, it is difficult to see how it can complete its task in less than a half-day and more likely a full day. And it is reasonable to expect that the time commitment for directorial duties will tend to increase in the future, despite measures taken to increase the efficiency of the meetings themselves.

IMPORTANCE OF AGENDAS AND INFORMATION

In view of the nature of a board's task and the limited time it has available to do it, the effective board meeting will depend largely upon how material is organized and presented and how adequate the information available to board members is both before and during the meeting.

The Agenda. No meeting can be well conducted without a carefully constructed agenda, preferably distributed in advance. In such an agenda, the matters to be considered by the board must be organized in logical sequence. For example, consideration of a marketing plan and sales forecast should precede consideration of operating and capital budgets. Again, review of a financial plan should precede consideration of specific lending or stock financing actions.

Advance Reporting. Particularly for the benefit of outside directors who cannot have daily contacts with the company, well-managed companies regularly send advance reports to non-employee directors incorporating much of the performance information the board should have. This is usually of a financial nature, including balance sheets and income statements supplemented by such data as comparisons of actual to budgeted performance, cash and inventory levels, and accounts receivable and aging summaries. In addition, many companies provide outside directors with at least preliminary draft minutes of the previous meeting and minutes of interim executive and other committee meetings, as well as newsworthy items concerning the company's operations, such as press releases and company publications.

So that the outside director may do his homework, effective board operation dictates that advance copies of the agenda of the forthcoming meeting be provided, as well as copies of proposals to be considered by the board, with appropriate staff reports and other necessary background information. This gives individual members time to digest and consider the usual mass of information and recommendations, so that the board meeting itself may be occupied more with questions and deliberation than with learning.

Importance of Completed Staff Work. There is probably nothing more frustrating to a board or more wasteful of its time than a proposal for action submitted without adequate staff work. Conscientious board members can hardly be expected to deliberate properly or come to conclusions on proposals which have been inadequately analyzed, without clearly spelled-out recommendations or enumeration of major advantages and disadvantages.

This means that someone in the company, preferably the chairman or chief executive officer, usually with the assistance of the corporate secretary, must take responsibility for seeing that proposals submitted represent completed staff work. If this is not done, a board member is completely within his rights to insist that the matter be tabled until such appropriate information is available. Where directors, particularly outside directors, take this hard-nosed attitude in meetings, experience has shown that it is not long until operating managers who are ordinarily responsible for presenting proposals to the board see that they have properly researched and presented proposals for board action.

As any experienced director knows, it takes only a few leading or discerning questions to tell whether a proposal has been properly researched and considered in the broader environment of total company operation, rather than as a single isolated problem. While internal management myopia can understandably cause conscientious executives to present proposals which have not been thoroughly researched and thought out, the practice of insisting upon thorough analysis and clear recommendation will not only sharpen the quality of company planning but will make the board meeting itself much more efficient and effective.

Access to Information. When it is considered that a board member is the highest authority in a company through his election as a representative of the shareholders, it is clear that he should have unlimited access to all kinds of company information. As one company executive stated, "The directors elect the management, so what right does management have to make any rules about access to plans or operating data?"

Nevertheless, executives have at times advanced objections to giving outside directors complete information. Some feel that a distinction should be made between the functions of the board and the functions of operating management. If the board is allowed to go into any kind of information, they argue, members might get into operating matters and undermine the authority of those entrusted with the management of the company. Others feel that certain plans may be of so confidential a nature, or that government security regulations in defense work might require such limitations on information disclosure, that it would be dangerous to make such information available to outside directors who have only a small commitment to the company and who have many other outside business interests. In addition, in circumstances where there might be dissension on the board or where a minority group might use company information to attempt to gain control of the company, it is sometimes thought that information should be limited.

There can hardly be any question that directors, whether management or outside directors, should have full access to information. It is possible that in some cases where dissident groups have representatives on the board this could lead to some abuse of the information. On balance, however, it would be difficult to deny that directors duly elected by stockholders to represent them have a clear right to whatever information they desire. Furthermore, virtually all company directors, whether inside or outside, can and will handle confidential information in the proper interests of the company, particularly if the need for such handling is made clear to them.

As for the danger that individual board members may get into operating data of no direct concern to them in handling their functions, this problem can be handled through proper reports to board members, through clarification of the authority of the board versus that of the operating management, and through diplomatic guidance by the chairman to make certain that the board members consider and pass only on items in their province. After all, it is the board members who define this area and they should be the first to be willing to limit their attention to these matters.

Briefing the Board. In addition to various kinds of advance reporting, it is probably wise for company management periodically to brief directors who cannot have as close familiarity with a company as might be desired. This can take the form of a special meeting prior to the board meeting or a special briefing session held at various times during the year. Experience with these briefing sessions has shown that they tremendously improve the understanding of board members and expedite their consideration of policy and program proposals in the meeting. How prevalent such briefing actually is cannot be said, but there is almost certainly too little of it. This is an area of effective board operation that top management would do well to consider.

MANAGEMENT CONTROL AND THE BOARD

One of the essential management functions is control to assure that plans succeed through (1) establishing standards (criteria of performance), whether only critical control points or an entire plan, (2) evaluation of performance against these standards or plans, and (3) correction of deviations by appropriate action or by restating a new course of action for the future. Control is usually attempted through studying past performance to see whether plans and goals are being accomplished, on the assumption that "what's past is prologue." However, the most effective form of control is to detect tendencies toward deviations *before* variances actually occur so that corrective action may be taken to assure the attainment of the results originally intended.

The board of directors, as a plural executive sitting at the top of a corporation, has an important control function. Since the scope of this control is defined by the board's area of planning or decision making, the kind of control information available to the board should largely be related to these areas.

Although most control data are historical, the perceptive director will look at them primarily for the light they cast on what is happening and what is likely to happen. For the best possible forward-looking control, information should be presented in the framework of plans with clear implications of what will probably happen if certain actions are not taken *now*. Such action may include any of the total of management functions—drawing up a new plan, reorganizing activities to make a more effective environment for performance, restaffing through better selection, appraisal, or training of personnel, or changing methods of guiding and leading those who are responsible for results. While board action is likely to be primarily in the areas of replanning or reorganizing, the "people" side of management being mostly left to those in executive positions, there are many occasions when a chief executive's eyes can be opened by intelligent questioning of the adequacy of performance and ability of key company managers.

Furthermore, a board, as with operating managers, should find useful as a part of control information, basic insights given by reports drawn from such techniques of future control as PERT (Program Evaluation and Review Technique) or critical path scheduling, as well as through generous use of forecasting. No effective board member can be content to sit only as a passive reviewer of past performance. Those who present control information as well as those board members receiving it should always try to present and interpret data with the future in view.

CONTROL INFORMATION FOR THE BOARD

Since much of the control information presented to a board of directors is financial, some executives have felt that board members become unduly preoccupied with financial matters. However, financial data, past and future, are essentially the means through which results and plans can be seen. The perceptive reviewer of financial data will not look upon them as simply accounting results, but rather as a reflection of what is occurring in marketing, new product development, production effort, or other facets of the business.

In addition, financial data are likely to be the best single means of adding together the "apples and oranges" of a variety of company operations and plans. This is not to say, however, that financial data are the only types of information to be presented to the board. As will be seen in the kinds of reports suggested for board review, there are many nonfinancial items as well.

Although requirements may vary as company operations and problems differ, certain types of control information should probably be made available to any board on a regular basis. Most of it should probably be made available monthly, and the rest quarterly, but all the data should be made available in terms of time averages to rule out variations resulting from seasonal factors, accounting adjustments, and other differences usually associated with monthly information. Perhaps the simplest and best device for giving perspective is the 12-month moving average. This simple technique involves the use of 12 consecutive months of information, divided by 12. It can easily be accomplished by simply adding the current month's information and dropping the similar month a year prior and dividing the total by 12. The difference in clarity may be shown by comparative data presented graphically in Figure 2.

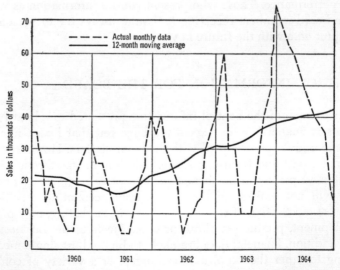

FIGURE 2   Actual Monthly Data vs. 12-month Moving Average. Sales of Company X, 1960–1964.

There are at least eight areas on which regular information should be available to the board. It will suffice to discuss each briefly.

Operating Results and Plans. Basic information on operating results and plans is best given by an income statement with its usual components: sales; cost of sales, broken down between direct labor, material, and overhead; sales expenses; engineering and research expenses; general administrative expenses; and profits before and after taxes. In addition, expense items are usefully shown as a percentage of sales, and profits both as a percentage of sales and as a return on assets employed. In order to give a director a standard by which to judge sales, expense, and profit performance, it is necessary to show forecast and budgeted amounts, preferably by the application of a variable budget.

These data should be presented in a thoroughly summarized form, with explanations of any deviations and action being taken to correct them. In this area, it is especially important that a 12-month moving average be used to supplement monthly data, because of variations in monthly information which really have nothing to do with the basic performance of the company or its major divisions.

These data should be for the company as a whole, and—except where profit-center divisions may be so numerous in very large companies that divisional data should be gathered together in groups— for company divisions. If these data are presented to the board with proper standards in terms of goals and budgets and adequate explanations of deviations and actions contemplated, this financial review should take very little time to analyze. In fact, if reports are made available to board members prior to a meeting, it is possible that regular financial reviews can be handled by dealing only with questions raised by board members.

Cash Planning and Results. No one acquainted with business can overlook the importance of adequate cash planning. Because a business can fail through lack of cash, regardless of the existence of profits or losses, cash planning is the minimum of planning any business should do. Since this fundamental resource is of such importance, a board should carefully review cash planning.

Of particular interest to a board member is the trend in inventories and receivables, plus the impact and timing of capital expenditures. The board also should be concerned with cash developed from operations and plans to raise additional cash as needed. These are areas where considerable advance planning follow-up should be done.

A board member can do much to force adequate cash planning. By insisting on cash forecasts and programs to meet cash needs, he can put pressure on management to plan for cash requirements. Moreover, presentation of cash planning information plus discerning questions by experienced and astute board members may ward off cash problems. The author has seen many instances where a few simple questions aimed at size of inventory or inventory increases or at the age of accounts receivable have brought to light deficiencies in cash management.

Capital Expenditure Plans and Results. In addition to approving the capital expenditure budget, a board should require, at least quarterly, reports on actual expenditures against plans. Most boards have found it advisable to have periodic reports on actual results achieved through capital expenditures. Usually capital expenditures are approved on the basis of economic savings foreseen, but seldom does any one question whether the savings were actually realized. On major expenditure items, the best management practice calls for actual results to be reported for a period of two or three years after the expenditure. Not only is this effective control; it can improve the quality of analyses by operating managers recommending capital expenditures.

New Product Plans and Results. Since the future of a company perhaps depends more on its new product plans and what is done about them than on any other single factor, the agenda of a board should include regular review of these plans and results. Involving futures as it does, this area can easily be forgotten in the press of current operating problems. The very act of requiring periodic reports on what is really happening on new product plans can probably do more than any other single action to assure that something actually is done. Moreover, reports of this kind are excellent means of seeing what kind of product development programs the company is pursuing and whether the company is following the product policy approved by the board.

Marketing Plans and Results. As new products furnish the material for a company's future, so marketing programs and results furnish the primary means of assuring successful exploitation of product and market opportunities. There is much that a director should wish to know concerning marketing. In the first place, assuming that marketing plans have been presented for approval, he would like to know the progress of these plans. He would certainly have questions as to the trend of the company's share of market, the possibilities of a new product's sales, or the performance of new products already introduced. Likewise, a director should have information occasionally on distribution patterns. What are the company's outlets, how is it marketing, who are its customers, and what is the company doing to meet or surpass competition?

As in the case of new products, much of the information on marketing plans and results would have to be given in special presentations, rather than in routine fashion. To be sure, some of this information, such as performance against forecasts and future expected performance, can be given in a tabular form, some can be made available in very brief tailored reports, but much may have to be given to the directors in an oral briefing either before or during the directors' meeting.

Key Personnel Policies and Practices. Although directors generally pay little attention to operation of personnel policies, it is obvious that what is happening in this area may be of very great importance. Therefore, directors should receive in summary form, probably quarterly, such pertinent personnel data as turnover, promotions from within and outside, recruiting costs, training programs, grievance volume, status of labor union relations, and other information on the "people" side of operations.

Review of Divisional Performance. In a divisionalized company, the board should occasionally be given a fairly thorough report of performance of individual divisions. In financial reports, it will be able to see divisional financial performance regularly. But in addition, once a quarter or once a year, a divisional general manager should be asked to make a presentation to the board on his division's performance, prospects, and problems. While these are admittedly operating matters, this can be an effective way of seeing how the chief executive is undertaking his task and a means of giving board exposure to key division general managers. The realization that the top authority in the company is concerned with his operations and problems, along with the necessity of preparing his presentation, can also strongly motivate the divisional general manager.

Reports Against Specific Goals of Top Executives. It should be assumed that the well-managed company today will have developed a system of verifiable quantitative and qualitative goals for responsible executives throughout the company, including the chief executive officer, the division general managers, and the key executive personnel reporting to the chief executive officer. From time to time, probably quarterly, progress against these major goals should be reported to the board of directors.

This is important for a number of reasons. In the first place, the system of verifiable goals has shown itself to be one of the best management techniques of assuring good planning and performance. In the second place, well-established goals can show more clearly and easily how key executives are doing in their jobs and give them a chance to bring to the attention of the board any obstacles to their performance which may be within the board's power to remove. In the third place, as in so many other cases, the very act of reporting progress to the board has a strong motivating force, making this system meaningful and constantly alive. The difficulty with these programs, as with most all good management techniques, is that they may die from executive malnutrition. One of the best ways of avoiding this is to have reports concerning these programs go periodically to the board.

Other Control Reports. In addition to the above reports, which would be regarded as standard for any board of directors, there are many other items on which control reports may be made. From time to time progress against long-range plans and forecasts should be reported. In addition, reports should be given to the board on organi-

zational changes, progress in license agreements where the company
is either a licensor or a licensee, economic trends affecting the company, profit contributions of individual product lines, procedure
planning and control, utilization of electronic data processing equipment, the public relations or public image of the company, the
operation of salary and wage programs, and other matters of interest to directors.

The President's Summary. One of the most useful and appreciated
reports a director can receive—particularly with respect to profit
performance, although it is quite helpful in other areas—is an analytical summary of the company's operations prepared by the chief
executive officer. If concise and objective, it can do much to point
up the significant changes, problems, and opportunities facing the
company and can give directors a capsule picture of operations and
progress by the one person who should be most concerned and most
knowledgeable on the subject. In many boards of directors this report has become a key instrument of information and control. It
should be universal.

STAFF ASSISTANCE FOR THE BOARD

A frequent suggestion for improving board effectiveness is to provide it with staff assistance directly available for its use and reporting to it, since the staff assistance made available by the chief executive and the top officers of the company is often inadequate. A
board of directors is largely at the mercy of the chief executive officer and the insiders of the company in getting analyses and recommendations. Sometimes with obvious intent and sometimes not,
inside executives are likely to submit to the board only the proposals
they wish to see considered and to make available only such information they wish the board to have.

In order to avoid this problem, there is merit in providing the
board with its own analytical assistance independent of the executives in the company. While this should be done with great diplo-
macy and tact to avoid interfering with the proper prerogatives of

managers, it could render valuable assistance by independently informing the board on problems of interest to it without the danger of any information being consciously or unconsciously filtered by the chief executive.

There are also cases where the staff work should not be done by the chief executive officer or any insider. In a sense, the work done by the public auditors in the certified financial audit is such a task. But there are also many tasks—e.g., establishment of a management compensation program, selection of a new president, selection of directors, or problems of serious dissension at the top of a company or within the board—which should be done by an independent staff reporting only to the board. In many instances, it would suffice for the board to hire special consultants or investigators for the purpose. As a matter of fact, in some of these cases a permanent staff assistant to the board might not be competent to handle an analysis and make recommendations. But such a special staff assistant would be in a position to supervise and work with the specialists called in to make the study and recommendations requested.

The staff assistance suggested here would extend beyond the administrative assistance a board normally needs for housekeeping functions such as scheduling meetings, circulating agenda and reports, and furnishing facilities and services between and during meetings. These chores may be handled as a part-time job by the corporation secretary, by an assistant to the president, by the chief executive officer, or by the chairman of the board, if he has administrative personnel to help him. This kind of assistance normally presents no problem for the board, since few matters of judgment are involved. Also, operating executives are likely to have adequate inducement by their positions to see that such needs are properly cared for, particularly if the directors make them known.

USE OF COMMITTEES

As business becomes more complex, companies grow larger, board membership increases, or a board becomes more effective in undertaking its proper duties, it often becomes impractical to have the full board consider and act on all matters. There are also transactions requiring board action which may come up between regular meetings and, particularly where outside directors are involved, it may be impracticable to call special board meetings. In addition, certain matters, such as recommendations on executive compensation or nomination of new directors, can be more effectively handled by a smaller group than the whole board.

Consequently, most boards, especially in larger corporations, set up one or more committees to undertake specific board duties. Some, like the executive, finance, audit, or compensation committees, are regular committees of the board. Others may be *ad hoc* committees charged with dealing with special problems.

What Is a Board Committee? Many top-level committees that are called board committees are actually management committees. In order to avoid confusion in this area, the term will be limited here to committees comprised wholly of directors and established (1) by statutory requirements of the state of incorporation, (2) by provision of the corporate charter or by-laws, (3) by and with stockholder action, or (4) by resolution of the board of directors.[4]

Occasionally committees are comprised of both board members and company executives who are not members of the board. This is likely to be the case with an internal management committee reporting to the president and advising him on corporate policy matters. It is often the case in executive-development committees, pension, retirement, personnel policy, or other groups on which board membership is desired but in which the non-board operating managers are essential contributors to policies or recommendations. These committees are usually composed of inside directors, although an outside board member with special interest or expertise in the area being discussed may sometimes sit in.

No distinction is made among board committees made up completely of insider board members, those comprised entirely of outsiders, and those with mixed membership. In the General Motors

---

[4] This is essentially in accordance with the definition used by the National Industrial Conference Board in its studies. See *Corporate Directorship Practices, op. cit.*, p. 113.

Corporation, for example, it is customary for the finance committee of the board to have approximately half outside directors and half inside directors. On the other hand, the executive committee is made up completely of inside members of the board, while the audit committee contains all outside board members.

Basic Types of Committees. There are three basic types of board committees. One, usually exemplified by the executive committee, is granted power to act on behalf of the board. It has the same power as the board itself in stated matters delegated to it. In some cases, its actions taken may be ratified by the full board, but this is not regarded as a practical limitation on the board's authority. While technically a board could refuse to ratify actions of this committee, ratification tends to be a formality when action has already been taken on behalf of the company. If this is not intended, the committee should not be given power to take action but only to recommend action to the whole board.

A second type of committee, such as the usual policy, appropriations, or budget committee, may be given responsibility for studying and reviewing certain operations or subjects of interest to the board and for making recommendations to the full board. They usually need more time to come to conclusions than board meetings afford. For example, review of capital appropriations may require considerable study and analysis. Budget reviews or review of divisional performance may take more time than the entire board can feasibly give. These committees, in other words, deal with matters on which the board wishes directly to be involved but cannot, as a whole, practically do so.

A third common type of top-level committee has a combination of decision-making authority and advisory responsibility. Even in an executive or finance committee, usually given extensive power to act on behalf of the board, there may be a number of matters on which the full board wishes to reserve action and therefore asks that recommendations be made to it. In addition, such committees as the audit committee may be given authority to select the auditors but only to recommend any action that the review of audit results may call for.

Extent of Committee Use. That committees of the board are used extensively is shown by the report made by the National Industrial Conference Board in 1962. Reference to Table 10 will show that, of 307 manufacturing companies and 146 non-manufacturing companies studied by the Conference Board, approximately three-fourths had executive committees, approximately one-third had salary and bonus committees, almost one-third of the manufacturing companies and one-fifth of the non-manufacturing companies had stock option committees, approximately one-sixth had audit committees, and less than one-seventh of the manufacturing companies and one-fourth of the non-manufacturing companies had finance committees. The same report indicates that 11 percent of manufacturing companies and 12 percent of non-manufacturing companies reported they had no standing committees of the board whatever.

As might be expected, board committees are more common among larger than among smaller companies. This tendency is much more pronounced in committees other than executive committees, which were reported by half the manufacturing companies with assets of less than $10 million, as well as a majority of larger corporations.

Legal Provisions for Board Committees. State laws are by no means uniform in spelling out the power of a board to delegate authority to committees, but statutes generally make some reference to the right to do so. Many states permit a board to appoint committees only if the corporate charter or by-laws so provide; others allow their appointment unless the charter or by-laws specifically deny it; and some state laws are silent on the point, relying on common law developed by the courts, which ordinarily approves of board delegation of most of its authority.

In general, while many states' statutes are silent on the point, the laws of most states, either by specific reference or by the common law arising from court cases, tend to limit matters which the board may delegate to committees. This is noteworthy in the case of executive committees. In this instance, the customary exceptions apply to declaration of dividends, changes in by-laws, issuance of corporate stock, appointment of directors to fill board vacancies, fixing of com-

TABLE 10 Use of Committees of the Board, 1961, 307 Manufacturing Companies and 146 Nonmanufacturing Companies

Asset Range	Executive	Salary & Bonus	Stock Option	Audit	Finance	Other
Manufacturing companies (307)						
Under $10 Million	9	4	6	...	...	3
$10–24 Million	21	3	4	...	5	4
$25–49 Million	37	11	14	4	2	5
$50–99 Million	57	25	23	13	11	14
$100–199 Million	41	21	18	9	6	10
$200–499 Million	27	21	13	13	7	11
$500–999 Million	18	11	8·	4	6	9
$1,000 Million and over	16	9	8	2	4	8
TOTAL	226	105	94	45	41	64
Public utilities and transportation companies (92)						
Under $100 Million	14	2	1	...	3	4
$100–199 Million	9	2	5	...	...	2
$200–499 Million	17	6	4	1	6	1
$500–999 Million	9	4	1	1	1	4
$1,000 Million and over	15	4	1	2	2	3
TOTAL	64	18	12	4	12	14
Financial companies (40)						
Under $100 Million	7	2	...	1	1	3
$100–499 Million	8	1	1	3	3	4
$500–1,999 Million	8	2	1	4	1	5
$2,000 Million and over	10	3	...	7	1	10
TOTAL	33	8	2	15	6	22
Merchandising companies (14)						
Total all ranges	11	4	3	5	4	3

SOURCE: J. R. Kinley, *Corporate Directorship Practices*, Studies in Business Policy No. 103, National Industrial Conference Board, New York, 1962, pp. 114–115.

pensation for committee members or directors, election or removal of officers, or extraordinary or unusual matters of major importance to the corporation.

Board Practice with Respect to Committees. In practice, boards tend to place specific limitations on authority of committees, whether the statute requires it or not. For example, the National Industrial Conference Board found that only 8 percent of the reporting manufacturing companies in its survey, 20 percent of the public utility and transportation companies, and 27 percent of the merchandising and financial companies place no specific limitations on executive committee authority. Most limitations were placed by provision of by-laws, although a substantial number were imposed by statute and by action of the board of directors.

Responsibility of Committees. The prevailing legal opinion appears to be that individual members of board committees have the same basic liabilities and responsibilities as board members. But it is often asked whether board members not on a given committee are responsible for action of committee members. In this case, the legal liability apparently follows principles applicable to board delegation of authority to officers. If board members have acted with prudence and due care in the selection of committee members, have properly delegated authority to the committee in accordance with requirements of the charter, by-laws, or statutes, and have exercised reasonable care and diligence in supervising operations of a committee, there seems to be no liability to non-committee directors for the actions of committee members.

It is important that a board makes certain it has not delegated authority to the committee which overriding regulations of the law or of the corporation do not permit. Courts would almost certainly hold any individual board member liable if he permitted, even by acquiescence, members of standing committees of the board to make decisions the board was not permitted to delegate. Therefore, non-committee board members should make certain that delegations to such standing committees as executive or finance committees be clearly in accordance with the requirements of a corporation's certificate of incorporation, its by-laws, or the applicable statutes.

THE EXECUTIVE COMMITTEE

As indicated by the discussion above, in most jurisdictions and in most companies executive committees operate in a wide sphere, but with certain limitations. In some companies, the executive committee is looked upon as the actual board of directors and makes virtually all of the decisions which the whole board would undertake. Far more often, the executive committee is regarded as a convenient device for handling board-level questions and transactions in the interval between regular board meetings. Also, in a large number of companies, this committee has been given special duties such as review of operating results and plans by the various division managers, including budgets and budget performance, as well as review of capital expenditures, proposals for changes in policy, and major programs which must come before the entire board.

Composition of Executive Committees. According to the National Industrial Conference Board report of 1962, executive committees most commonly comprise four to nine members. Especially in financial companies, however, their membership may vary from as few as three to as many as twenty-one (in the case of one bank).

The chairman of the executive committee is normally designated by the board of directors, although in approximately 17 percent of manufacturing companies and 36 percent of other companies he is selected by the committee itself. In a number of cases the committee chairman is designated in the company by-laws and is usually either the chairman of the board or the president.

Committee Operation. The Conference Board's report discloses a wide variety of practice with respect to the frequency of executive committee operation. Among manufacturing companies, it may meet as often as once a day or as rarely as once a year, with twelve meetings annually being most common. Similar practice is found among transportation and utility companies and among financial companies. However, in financial companies, where the executive committee normally meets whenever action is required, available data indicate that it meets more often than in manufacturing, transportation, or utility companies.

Dangers of Executive Committee Replacing the Board. There is always the danger that a company's executive committee will, in fact, replace the board of directors. Unless clear limitations are placed upon its activities, and unless these are properly supervised by the full board, the natural desire to get things done and to avoid the delays inherent in less frequent meetings of the full board has tended to lead executive committees to take over the real responsibilities and duties of the board of directors.

Much of this is unavoidable in view of the volume of work and the pressure to get decisions. On the other hand, the alert director who wishes to maintain an effective board of directors should be on guard against the tendency. An executive committee in the right functions, regularly reporting its actions to the board, and submitting appropriate analyses and recommendations to the full board, can be a valuable asset. But an executive committee operating as an inside power clique can convert the full board into a set of rubber stamps. Because of these dangers, any board should make delegations to the executive committee crystal clear and refuse to acquiesce in the committee's overstepping these bounds. Likewise, some of the need for executive committees might be eliminated by directing attention to reducing board size, changing membership, increasing the efficiency of information and proposal presentation, and other actions to assure the full board's effectiveness as an instrument of corporate trusteeship and policy.

FINANCE COMMITTEE

In virtually every case the board finance committee is established either by provision of by-laws or board resolution. While not used as frequently as the executive committee, it may be an exceedingly important body. Finance committees vary from those with limited evaluative powers in financial matters to others which have virtually final decision-making authority in their area. In most cases, however, the finance committee is subordinate in authority to the executive committee of the board.

Perhaps the strongest type of finance committee is one utilized by certain companies such as General Motors, which has authority to approve actions of the executive committee and the officers of the company that have substantial financial impact on the company. Thus, most major programs, after approval by the executive committee as being desirable from a corporate operations point of view, are submitted to the finance committee since they will almost invariably involve commitment of company funds. Except for items reserved for board approval, the finance committee has final decision-making authority and is the ultimate authority for recommending any action beyond its purview which must be submitted to the board.

At the other end of the spectrum are finance committees with purely advisory functions. Such committees may be charged with the duty of reviewing the company's financial condition and its need for funds, suggesting investment of funds and issuance of securities, recommending payment of dividends, and making final recommendations to the board on such matters as executive salaries.

Probably the most common type of finance committee has analytical and advisory functions of financial review and advice and is given final authority in approving such items as budgets, capital appropriations, and corporate investment policy.

AUDIT COMMITTEE

Except in financial companies, audit committees (often called examining committees among financial institutions) are infrequently used. However, a significant number of companies feel that supervision of financial audit is a board function which should be given special attention by a committee in order to assure that the audit is properly undertaken and reviewed. In these, the audit committee is charged with recommending or selecting outside public accountants to conduct the audit of the company's books, receiving and reviewing the auditor's report, and making appropriate recommendations to the board on the basis of this review. In a few cases, an audit committee may get into the actual operation of the audit through suggesting its scope. In addition, it is charged in some companies with working with the chief financial officer or the controller or other officers to make certain that the company's internal accounting and audit procedures are adequate to protect the integrity and accuracy of accounting records.

With their special obligation to the corporation, which is often best discharged through the window of financial records and reports, and with their special liabilities under U.S. securities regulations, boards of directors might well utilize a small board committee to give audits special attention. In far too many boards of directors, attention to the audit is limited to receiving and looking over the final audited figures and noting or approving the audit fee involved.

Although all competent auditing firms view themselves as reporting to the corporation through its board of directors, the tendency of board members to pay rather little attention to this aspect of the business has often led the auditors to report to, receive their assignments from, and recognize that their employment is dependent upon the chief financial officer. While rather few difficulties have actually come to light because of this practice, the effective board of directors should take steps to assure a closer relationship with and control over the external auditors. Also, the board should probably have closer ties than usual with the nature and quality of the internal auditing program.

SALARY AND BONUS COMMITTEE

A widely used committee of the board is the salary and bonus, or compensation, committee. This is understandable, both because recommendations on top executives' salaries and bonuses should be given considerable study and because it is indelicate and improper for inside officer-directors to sit in judgment on their own salaries and incentive compensation.

Most companies with effective board and management operation, therefore, establish a committee of outside directors to make salary recommendations to the board. In the case of bonuses, the committee may include insiders who are not eligible for bonuses. However, even in this case, in order to avoid embarrassment and possible internal politics or claims of favoritism, it is good practice for all insiders on the board to remove themselves from consideration of director-officer salaries or bonuses.

Available information indicates that companies are increasingly establishing salary and bonus committees made up exclusively of outside directors who may make final decisions in this important area. These directors should understandably be very heavily influenced by the recommendations of the chief executive officer with respect to those men reporting to him and by other top executives with respect to their subordinates. At the same time, to avoid possible internal politics and stockholder criticism of officers' voting themselves substantial salaries and bonuses, these matters should probably be handled by a committee of outside members.

STOCK OPTION COMMITTEE

Given impetus by the Revenue Act of 1950, "restricted" stock options, as defined by that Act, assured favorable capital-gains treatment for options to executives and other key employees. As a consequence, stock option plans developed very fast as an inducement and compensation for executives in a position to materially affect profits. While many of the advantages of stock options have been dulled by the changes made in the Revenue Code in 1964 (providing for shorter option periods and longer waiting periods to qualify for capital-gains treatment), they are still an important area of supplemental executive compensation.

For the same reasons that an increasing number of companies have placed top executive salaries and bonuses under a special committee of the board of directors, stock option committees have been established in a substantial number of companies. The usual task of these committees is to act as the final authority in the administration of an option plan previously approved by the board. This would involve such decisions as final determination of the persons who will receive options, the number of shares of stock optioned, and other terms and conditions of individual options.

Where inside directors are eligible for options, as they are in the very large majority of cases, establishing such a committee comprised of outside board members or members not eligible for options appears to be good board operation. As with salaries and bonuses, it is awkward for recipients of such emoluments to sit in judgment on their own cases. It is, therefore, somewhat strange that both the bonus and salary committee and the stock option committee devices are not more universally used in smaller companies as well as larger companies.

OTHER BOARD COMMITTEES

A variety of other committees of the board may be found. Boards occasionally use contributions committees to establish or recommend basic contributions policy and to consider, recommend, or decide upon major contributions—e.g., those over $1,000. Contributions always pose difficulties for companies that sincerely desire to make their fair share of contributions but cannot contribute to all worthy causes. A policy outlining the area in which contributions will be made is indispensable in such cases. In addition, because of the embarrassment which individual corporate officers may face in having to turn down a deserving charity, often backed by influential people, the anonymity of committee operations makes this kind of committee desirable.

As suggested in connection with the selection of directors above, there also seems to be considerable merit in establishing within a board a nominating committee to recommend candidates for the board. In view of what can be done by such a committee, it is somewhat surprising to find it used so seldom.

One committee fairly often used is the so-called policy committee. Although this is sometimes a group that acts more in the area of administrative committees, the task of the true policy committee is to review company policies from time to time to make sure that they are up-to-date, accurately reflect external conditions, are effective in guiding action of executive management, and relevant to and supportive of the company's long-range goals.

Among other committees found in company boards are management development committees charged with the task of assuring an adequate supply of competent executive personnel, product development committees with responsibility for reviewing product program efforts, capital appropriations committees, and budget committees. Occasionally one finds investment committees, charged with overseeing the investment of company surplus funds, and bank relations committees, empowered to handle various banking relationships and to designate appropriate officers and employees with power to sign company checks. Moreover, in many financial companies one finds a trust committee of the board with the assigned task of reviewing the policies and programs of trust department operations. Furthermore, as mentioned above, any board may set up a special committee for a given purpose. This is not unusual in cases of large capital expansions, such as new offices or plant, or in the case of developing special proposals with regard to company executive compensation policies and plans, or recommendations on many other sporadic problems where the board wishes to have control but cannot afford the necessary time.

chapter 8

THE CHAIRMAN OF THE BOARD

Key to any committee or board operation is the chairman. The effectiveness of any such group will never be greater than the skill of the chairman. The assumption made in this book is that the board can and will be an effective board, acting responsibly and intelligently as a group. And in any group operation the chairman has a key role to moderate and lead decisions and actions. This does not mean that his legal power is or should be greater than that of any other director. It does mean that his is the responsibility to see that the board functions effectively.

COMPANY PRACTICE REGARDING THE BOARD CHAIRMAN

As in other areas of management, U.S. company practice regarding the board chairman varies considerably. In some cases, the chairman of the board is merely that; presiding over the board meeting and undertaking those duties, as any committee chairman would, of assuring that agendas are properly made and distributed and that necessary reports are available to board members both before and during meetings. In other cases, the board chairman may operate as a company executive, in addition to being chairman of the board, with responsibilities varying all the way from those of a chief executive officer to specified duties such as long-range planning or stockholder relations. As might be expected from these differences, some board chairmen are part-time, spending little more time in board duties than an outside director. Others may be full-time employees of the corporation. In still other cases a company may not have a designated chairman of the board at all, and the president will normally serve as board chairman during the meetings.

What Companies Do. The most recent authoritative study of company practice with respect to board chairmen was published by the National Industrial Conference Board in 1962.[1] This study of 206 manufacturing companies disclosed that 133, or 65 percent, of these companies had an officer with the title of chairman of the board. Of the remaining seventy-three companies not having an elected board chairman, virtually all reported that the president presided at board meetings, although one company stated that a chairman was elected at each meeting from among the directors. In 117 of the 133 companies having a designated chairman of the board, the chairman and the president were two different people. In the other sixteen companies, one person held both positions. However, this understates the number of cases where the president is actually operating as chairman of the board. When it is recalled that in all but one of the seventy-three companies not having an elected chairman of the board, the president acted as chairman during the meetings, this means that in nearly one-third of the companies surveyed the president was chairman.

It is interesting, also, that company by-laws differ on requiring an elected chairman. Of the 206 companies surveyed, the by-laws of forty were silent on having a board chairman, eighty-six companies made the election of a chairman optional, and eighty companies required a board chairman to be elected. When taken in connection with data concerning the number of companies having an elected chairman, these data indicate that approximately 40 percent of the companies whose by-laws do not require it do, as a matter of fact, elect a chairman.

Various reasons are given for not having a chairman of the board. They include such explanations as those that a small company does not need a chairman, or that the president can fill these duties effec-

[1] J. R. Kinley and G. C. Thompson, "The Board Chairman—Position and Duties," *Management Record*, Vol. 19, No. 12, pp. 7–13, December, 1962.

tively, or that election of a chairman might interfere with the management hierarchy and the authority of the chief executive officer. Reflection will indicate that none of these reasons is persuasive. The author's experience suggests the main reason for not electing a chairman is often the chief executive officer's wish to chair the board himself, thereby maintaining better control over it.

The Board Chairman as Chief Executive Officer. As was pointed out, the chairman is chief executive in forty-five of the 117 companies reported in the National Industrial Conference Board study which had offices of chairman and president, and in sixteen additional companies where both offices were held by a single person, the duties of chief executive were attached to the office of chairman. If one were to take these cases as instances where the president was really chief executive officer and the cases of companies without an elected chairman where the president actually acted as chairman, one concludes from this survey of 206 companies that the chairman was chief executive of the company in only forty-five of a total of 206 companies, or less than 22 percent of the companies involved. However, another study found that more than one-quarter of all manufacturing firms on the New York Stock Exchange had chairmen who were chief executives.[2]

In a later study involving 586 manufacturing companies, the chairman was found to be chief executive in 55 percent of the companies with sales over $500 million, ranging downward to 21 percent of the cases of companies with sales of less than $50 million.[3] Moreover, this same study indicated that there was little difference among types of industries in the practice of chairmen operating as chief executives, although textile companies did show a much smaller proportion of chairmen–chief executives than other types of companies.

[2] H. Stieglitz and A. Janger, "When the Chairman Is Chief Executive," *Management Record,* National Industrial Conference Board, August, 1963, p. 7.

[3] *Ibid.,* p. 9.

REASONS FOR HAVING A BOARD CHAIRMAN

There are a number of reasons why a company should have a board chairman. Some of these were recognized in the National Industrial Conference Board Survey of 1962; [4] others have become apparent to the author in his study, observation, and experience in boards of directors.

To Chair the Board. Obviously, any effective committee, commission, panel, or board needs someone to chair the discussions. As will be seen presently, the task of chairing is not an easy one. Also, it requires skills and understanding that not many people possess.

To Lead the Board. While a board chairman legally does not have and may not in practice exercise greater authority than any other board member, his role as a leader of the board is significant. Performance of individuals operating together in a group, especially when these individuals are intended to be equal in stature, can be chaotic without a skillful leader to weld group interests and actions into a cohesive unit. To be sure, an effective chairman tends to do this. But as will be seen later in this chapter, a competent board chairman also has other roles to play.

To Comply with Organization Requirements. One good reason given for electing a chairman is to assure a clear separation between the trusteeship aspects of a corporation, as represented by the board of directors, and operating management authority. The role of directors and that of operating management, even top executives of the company, are two distinctly different ones. If the election of a board chairman helps to maintain this distinction, as it apparently does, this is a reason which can hardly be overlooked.

To Provide Management Continuity. In the Conference Board survey of the board chairman's position and duties, many respondents felt that election of a chairman provided a device for manage-

---

[4] "The Board Chairman—Position and Duties," *op. cit.*, pp. 8–9.

ment continuity when and if a change in chief executive occurs. This position is valid. Any board member who has gone through a change of top executive personnel, particularly an unplanned change resulting from death or discharge of the chief operating executive, has felt thankful for the presence of a chairman to fill the gap temporarily and to guide the board toward proper solution of the problem encountered.

A number of corporate executives further believe that a chairman can be a valuable adjunct during the break-in period of a new president. This is undoubtedly a sound observation, although there are probably many cases, particularly when a president has retired and moved to the position of chairman or when a founder has decided to give up his operating responsibilities by taking the chairmanship, where the chairman is motivated by feelings of distrust of his successor and a desire to hold on to some of the glory and power of his former position.

To Divide the Top Executive Workload. There is no question that one of the sound reasons for having a chairman is for him to share with the president the workload of the top executive. As business becomes more complex and particularly as companies grow larger, the duties usually expected of a chief executive may be so broad in scope and so time-consuming that it makes sense to divide them. This has been done in many companies, particularly larger ones where the chairman is a full-time executive.

The division of responsibility between the chairman and the president under circumstances of this kind is extremely important. In the author's observation and experience, it is rare that two people can amicably share the pressure and responsibility of the chief executive's duties without a fairly clear delineation of functions. There have been too many instances where honorable, well-intentioned, and able individuals get into each other's way, with resultant friction and dispersion of leadership at the top of the company.

Where the chairman and the president share the top officer's duties, therefore, certain decisions should be made. In the first place, it is imperative to determine which of the two is the chief executive officer. In the second place, duties should be carefully divided. It is customary in many companies, for example, for the chairman, particularly if he is chief executive officer, to have jurisdiction over finance, legal matters, public relations, and stockholder relations. Sometimes the chairman is also given responsibility for long-range planning. In these cases, the president is really chief operating officer with the usual operating functions of marketing, production, and engineering, as well as management of operating divisions reporting to him. In other cases, especially where the president is chief executive officer, the duties of the chairman of the board may be limited to shareholder and public relations, perhaps with responsibility for long-range policies and plans. If this kind of demarcation is made and understood by the men involved, there need be no problem of friction in dividing what is essentially a chief executive's functions.

To Provide an Honorary Position. The board chairman's position is often used to provide an honorary position for a retiring president or for a founder of the company who wishes to give up many of his operating responsibilities. It has also been used, as have titles such as vice chairman of the board or chairman of the executive committee, to give positions to chief executives in the event of a merger. Often one of the understandable blocks to a merger or consolidation is the respective position of the presidents of the combining companies. Because the new company has room for only one president, and because this position usually carries more status than others at the top level, many an arbiter of a merger or a consolidation (including the author) has found the titles of chairman of the board, vice chairman, or chairman of the executive committee useful status symbols for displaced presidents. Nevertheless, many of these individuals have considerable contributions to make to a company more than justifying the title and salary involved. In such cases, their assignment to these positions may be far more than a matter of bestowing honorific title.

To Maintain Contacts. The board chairmanship has also been used as a convenient means for giving a retired president a suitable title in order to take advantage of the contacts he has built up as chief executive. Like it or not, the mere title of "director," "president-retired," or "consultant" does not carry nearly the status or prestige of the chairmanship in maintaining such a man's contacts with shareholders, customers, vendors, and others. Furthermore, in many instances it has been found that a retired president or other top officer can be extremely useful as a part-time or a full-time executive in such important areas as public or stockholder relations. These are sometimes areas which chief executives, preoccupied with company problems, plans, and operations, may overlook.

To Provide a Stabilizing Force. Particularly in smaller companies, or fast-growing companies with an aggressive group of directors, ordinarily many of them employee-directors on the board, a respected and tactful chairman can operate as a significant stabilizing force on the board and in the company. Aggressive executives in a fast-moving company understandably tend to be impatient and often rather brash with their colleagues. This can sometimes lead to undesirable frictions and contention. The alert board chairman with the wisdom and patience of experience can often exercise a healthy moderating influence. This can be a significant contribution. No company can expect to proceed vigorously with passive executives or directors whose only major objective is "to get along." At the same time, no company can stand the excessive in-fighting and friction that men with ideas and drive altogether too often engender.

THE CHAIRMAN'S ROLE AS CHAIRMAN

The chairman of the board of directors has much the same duties, as chairman, as the individual who chairs any committee. The most important of these duties are outlined below.

Preparation of the Agenda. In discussing board operation in the previous chapter, we stressed the importance of a logical and well-prepared agenda, preferably distributed to board members in advance. This is a major responsibility of the chairman, even though he may have the chief executive, the company secretary, or an administrative assistant in the headquarters office, actually perform the task.

Seeing That Proposals Are Completely Researched for Presentation. Also, in discussing effective board operation in the previous chapter, the importance of having proposals completely researched and clear recommendations presented was stressed. As in the case of the agenda, it should be a major responsibility of the chairman to see that this is done.

Getting Information and Proposals to Board Members in Advance. If directors are to come to meetings prepared, having done their homework, and if the meeting is effectively to use the time of the members as a group, agenda, proposals, and reports should be made available to the members in advance. Masses of carefully prepared recommendations available for cursory study at the member's place at the table seldom meet the need for effectiveness. Yet it is amazing how many directors receive their first glimpse of material to be discussed when they find it neatly stacked on the board table in front of them. The results are as might be expected. Either the time of the group is consumed in laborious study of reports or delay while various members think aloud, or else the reports are merely accepted by the members and the recommendations railroaded by the chairman, or the meeting is postponed until a later date when the members will have had an opportunity to study the proposals.

It should be the board chairman's responsibility to assure himself that appropriate materials are sent to the board members in advance. As can be easily understood, the board chairman cannot normally do this himself. But he can and should see that it is done, with the help either of the chief executive or of other persons.

Keeping the Meeting on the Track. One of the duties of the effective chairman is constantly to take steps to keep a meeting on the track. In any group of individuals, especially as they voice their opinions and raise questions on matters, there is ever the danger that the meeting will wander from the subject. While it is sometimes difficult tactfully to bring a meeting back to the subject or to interfere with a board member's discussion or train of thought, most board members will appreciate efforts by the chairman, whether tactful or blunt, to keep discussion geared to the subject at hand. This means also that a chairman must use certain skills in keeping the meeting moving by eliminating irrelevant discussion, and particularly by discouraging the tendency of inside board members to lapse into consideration of operating matters.

Also, by asking questions and inviting comments from the right members, the skilled board chairman can tend to keep the meeting moving toward a conclusion on the matter before the board.

Setting the Tone of the Meeting. It is largely up to the board chairman to set the tone of a meeting. He may require by example and action that certain portions of the meeting be very formal or that the discussion be quite informal. Through introducing levity at the right time and seriousness when called for, he can reduce pressures at one moment and place the board under desired pressure at another.

Integrating Committee Deliberation. It usually falls to the chairman to integrate committee deliberation. Integration of ideas, as contrasted to compromise, is the building of a point of view, often quite new, from the basic positions of the group. If the chairman is a weak leader, or if he is not fully familiar with the subject matter or the way individual members think, integration of ideas is not likely to result. But if he knows the problems and analyzes the basic positions of board members, the chairman can often do much to assist in the proper integration of ideas which arise from deliberation.

Handling the Perennial Dissenter. In many committees and boards, there are perennially individuals, not always the same individual, who dissent from various kinds of proposals. Because of the desire of most groups to reach unanimous or nearly unanimous conclusions and because dissenters may tend to be vocal in their dissent and their reasons for it, such persons can consume inordinate amounts of board time. While the board chairman must take time to assure that various views on matters before the board are freely expressed and the reasons for them presented, if the perennial dissenter becomes too difficult and takes too much time, it is up to the chairman to place some controls over him. One way, of course, is to abruptly give the floor to others. Another way is to table a matter for a future meeting when time may have sapped the vigor of the dissent. One of the most effective ways is to anticipate the dissenter's objections and, by playing devil's advocate and answering the objections in advance, or calling upon individuals who will, cut the ground from under the individual.

Handling Touchy or Contentious Issues. On very touchy or contentious issues, the board chairman should try to keep individuals from taking a position too early. All of us tend to defend our position, once taken, almost to the death. Delaying the taking of positions can therefore help. Also, if the matter does not require a formal vote, the board chairman may be able to suggest a reasonable compromise as the "sense of the meeting."

Perhaps, additionally, every board chairman can learn from the old Chinese proverb, "Prepare a path for your adversary's retreat." After people have taken a position and feel personally and emotionally committed to it, even if they recognize that they might be wrong or that the other board members' position is reasonable and should be accepted, they often find it hard to back down. Bowing to defeat can be made more palatable if the chairman can find a way to give the person a face-saving "out." He might, for example, endorse the complete reasonableness of the person's position in light of certain facts but suggest that he doubtless lacked information the other members had—information, the chairman is sure should have been made available to him, an oversight for which the chairman apologizes. Or, the chairman might praise the individual for his great courage and insights, ask his cooperation, as a person whose contributions to the board have been so very great and appreciated, and urge him not to feel unhappy with what appears to be a different position of the group.

Knowing Subject Matter and People. The effective chairman must, of course, be familiar with the subject matter of the meeting and with the personalities of board members. Nothing makes a meeting drag more or gives individual directors a greater feeling of futility than an uninformed chairman. One of the most inept chairmen the author has ever observed customarily opened a board meeting with the words, "Now, let's see, what have we got on the agenda?"

The chairman must, of course, know the personalities, prejudices, limitations, and strengths of his fellow directors. For knowing people is the first step in knowing how to deal with them and how to get them to make their best contribution to a group meeting. This may mean many things. It may mean encouraging the shy and suppressing the too-eloquent. It may mean asking the most informed to lead off in a discussion, or calling upon the director whom the chairman knows has some particularly constructive and useful ideas on a subject. But it is well, too, that the chairman be something of a bird-watcher—if the author may risk the charge of facetiousness. From his observation of various boards, committees, and commissions, he has developed a list of "board birds" which he has referred to, collectively, as "Americanus Commitatus" in order to give his list proper academic respectibility. Perhaps experienced board members will recognize some of the following birds: [5]

1. *The Loud-mouthed Black Crow*—who uses the board as a forum to crow over his accomplishments.

2. *The Yellowbellied Responsibility-avoider*—who finds in the board the perfect place to exercise authority fearlessly without the danger of being held personally responsible for his actions.

3. *The Pollyannish Song Sparrow*—who sings his happy song of good fellowship and unanimous agreement to spread togetherness and avoid free discussion.

4. *The White-breasted Nuthatcher*—who hatches nutty ideas, not related to the subject, which take hours of time to dispose of.

5. *The Red-tailed Bandwagon-Jumper*—who stays on the fence until he sees how a decision is going and then hops merrily on the bandwagon.

6. *The Black-breasted Screech Owl*—who shrieks dire warnings of disaster for any course of action the board considers.

7. *The Gimlet-eyed Nitpicker*—who insists upon having every

[5] The author is indebted to Professor M. L. Mace of Harvard University for the idea of business "birds," first presented by him in "Developing the Executive of Tomorrow" in *Improving Managerial Performance*, General Management Series, No. 186, American Management Association, New York, 1957, pp. 19–24.

statement and statistic presented to the board carefully reviewed and rechecked.

8. *The After-luncheon Napper*—who finds the board a comfortable place to dream while others deliberate and reach conclusions.

9. *The Long-winded Coot*—who takes 15 minutes of board time to ask a question to which he gets the perfect answer by providing it himself.

10. *The Logger-headed Sandbagger*—who takes exception to and sandbags every constructive idea brought before the board.

11. *The Duck-billed Doubletalker*—who confuses everyone and straddles every issue by talking out of both sides of his mouth.

Needless to say, if any boards in the United States or elsewhere have such birds among their members, not only the chairman but the other members as well should be able to spot them. Bird-watching in board meetings is an interesting sport. And, perhaps, one of the best ways of detecting these birds is to use not only binoculars but also a mirror.

THE CHAIRMAN'S ROLE AS LEADER

An effective chairman will almost invariably emerge as a leader of the board of directors. While rather little may scientifically be known about leadership, we do know that individuals tend to follow another person in whom they see a means of accomplishing their own personal desires. In the board of directors, it can be fairly safely assumed that most directors wish to be effective, though independent, members of the team. The chairman who establishes an environment in which they can fill this desire cannot help but become a leader.

In addition, the chairman is likely to be cast in other leadership roles. By virtue of being chairman, in all probability he will be the primary liaison between the company executives and the other members of the board, particularly the outside members. Also, in his role as chairman, he is likely to be, and should be, an important link between the company and its stockholders. Indeed, many board chairmen, as pointed out above, have operational responsibilities in this area. With the link to stockholders, it is only natural, also, that the chairman be an important communications channel with underwriters, brokers, and security analysts.

There is also little doubt that the effective chairman will present an image of a company to such outside parties as trade associations and the general public. Likewise, even though the chief executive (if he is president rather than chairman) may be better known in the company, the chairman also, along with the board as a whole, can furnish an example or image to the executives and officers of the company. Board members seldom realize with what awe and respect they are held by managerial and non-managerial employees in the company. They also seldom realize the impact of their personal characteristics and their actions in the board on the whole company.

The author knows of one company where the board chairman, while fairly effective in his public relations and his diplomatic activities, had a tendency to be rather profligate in his expenses. Even though his expense account was routinely approved by the board for large amounts and with virtually no detail, and even though this was done in the secret confines of the boardroom, it was not long until a spirit of unlimited expenses pervaded the entire company. Likewise, in another large enterprise, the chairman and the directors were shocked to find out that their vacillations at the board level had created an atmosphere of vacillation and uncertainty throughout the organization of some 30,000 employees.

In other words, the board must recognize that it is in a leadership role. And the chairman, as leader of the board, is in a primary leadership role. This is not surprising. When one looks at the importance of overall company objectives and goals, company-wide policies, and major programs that must be approved at the board level, it is clear that the board is or should be molding the shape of the company. In so doing, it is molding the environment, the opportunities, and the possibilities of security of every person in the company.

THE CHAIRMAN AS EXECUTIVE

The chairman of the board in many companies fills the role of a full-time executive. In some cases, he is chief executive officer, in some he shares the duties of the chief executive, in other cases he undertakes some specialized company assignments, and in still other cases he retains the final chief executive officer power while essentially carrying limited company assignments.

As Chief Executive. In general, when the chairman has the authority of chief executive officer, he does not exercise it so broadly as the president. While operating as the top executive of the company, the chairman is likely to have operating functions report to the president, limiting his own responsibilities to final decisions at the executive level, major representation of the company with the board of directors, and such specialized tasks as public and stockholder relations, finance, and long-range planning.

These observations are borne out in a special study made of cases where the chairman is chief executive.[6] This study found that the president, when chief executive, is likely to be concerned with many more aspects of the business than is the chairman as chief executive. This, then, tends to mean that the chairman as chief executive usually has a far narrower span of management than the president who is chief executive. Also, as this study indicated, the chairman-chief executive "tends to concentrate more on those functions: (1) that relate to the corporation as a legal and financial entity, (2) that affect its future growth prospects, and (3) that affect the various publics with which the corporation comes into contact." [7]

When Not Chief Executive. The duties of the chairman as a company executive, when not in the position of chief executive officer, tend to be rather varied. They do often include special assignments

[6] H. Stieglitz and A. Janger, "When the President Is Chief Executive," *op. cit.*

[7] *Ibid.*, p. 9.

in long-range planning and in policy review and formulation, as well as public and stockholder relations. As a matter of fact, these are important duties which an operating executive, preoccupied with operations, is likely to find too little time to undertake. In addition to these duties, the chairman may be utilized as a general adviser to upper-level management, as a partner with the president in a review of divisional plans, programs, and results, and as an important reviewer of company budgets, capital expenditures, and cash planning programs. In some cases, also, the chairman is given operating responsibility for other areas which the chief executive might wish to delegate and feels should be handled by a top-level executive. This may include direction of overseas subsidiaries and affiliates, supervision of licensing and patent programs, and administration of executive incentive and compensation programs.

Importance of Clarifying the Roles of Chairman and President. Because both the chairman and the president are top general officers of the company, if the chairman is employed on a full-time basis it becomes extremely important to clarify their roles, even if the incumbents maintain that no such clarification is needed. Clarification, however, does not mean specifying duties in detail. It merely means separating them so that each of the incumbents clearly understands his responsibilities.

For example, in one company where the founder gave up his operating responsibilities to the president but wished to retain some overall responsibility, his basic function as chairman and chief executive officer was spelled out as follows:

Responsible to the board of directors for acting as chairman of all board and stockholders' meetings; for establishing overall corporate objectives and goals with respect to profits, product line, advertising and pricing, capital expenditures, financing, company size, organization structure, and company acquisitions and growth; for assuring that company plans and policies as developed and administered by the president are designed to effectuate these objectives and goals; for establishing basic company organization plans and policies and seeing to the proper manning of top management organization; for nominating company officers to the board, after consultation with the president; for developing plans for management compensation; for developing plans for company financing; for developing proposals for acquisitions and mergers looking toward profitable company growth; for acting as the principal stockholder relations officer of the company; for undertaking such other duties as he may deem wise and necessary in the interest of the company or as the board of directors may from time to time designate.

In the same company, the president was given the following basic responsibilities:

Responsible to the chairman of the board for planning, organizing, staffing, directing, and controlling the business of the company as a whole within the scope of the objectives and basic policies established and authority delegated by the chairman of the board and the directors; for making sure that company objectives and goals are reflected in effective divisional and departmental plans and budgets; for securing results in accordance with such plans and budgets; for establishing detailed company organization plans in accordance with basic organization plans and policies developed by the chairman; for recommending basic personnel policies and assuring the proper operation of approved policies; for directing, coordinating, and controlling company operations in marketing, sales, manufacturing, finance, international and industrial operations, and personnel; for developing plans and policies designed to maintain the financial health of the company; for undertaking necessary controls for the effective and efficient use of the company's financial resources; for developing programs and undertaking activities designed to effectuate the profitable growth of the company; and for undertaking such other duties as the chairman of the board may deem necessary in the interests of the company.

Although these are only statements of basic functions and were supplemented by a statement of authority relationships and extent of decision-making authority in committing the company, as well as by an outline of major duties, they made it possible to clarify the division of roles between these two top executives. And this was important. The new chairman of the board had long been president and chief executive of the company, accustomed to making decisions at every level and unwilling or unable effectively to delegate authority. When certain directors raised the problem of company growth and the need for a full-time operating president to take over much of the load of chief executive, the problem could only be resolved by clearly spelling out the various responsibilities of these two top officers and by making sure that they not only agreed to them but operated in accordance with these charges. More complete examples may be found in the Appendix.

SEPARATING THE CHAIRMAN'S ROLE

Although there is far from general agreement on the question, the author believes that a company president should not also act as chairman of the board. The objections already cited to a predominantly inside board seem applicable to the practice of combining the position of president and chairman. The president, particularly if he is chief executive, is in a very strong position to influence the board, since he possesses far superior information concerning the company and is likely to be the person who submits proposals for action to the board. If, to this strong position, is added another of acting as chairman, the danger of a rubber-stamp board is greatly increased. Furthermore, it tends to be difficult for the president to maintain the posture of reporting to the board if, as chairman, he is also its leader. Moreover, there is merit in taking every step possible to assure that the trusteeship position of the board is kept separate from operating management.

It may be asked whether the same considerations apply if a chairman is chief executive officer. In part they do, but to a much lesser extent, depending upon the nature of the management functions which the chairman undertakes as chief executive officer. If the chairman, for example, is concerned with overall corporate matters, such as financial control, legal policy, and long-range planning, he is sufficiently detached from the general operations of the company, and his interests are sufficiently allied with those of the board, to enable him in most instances to maintain the primary outlook required of a board member. At the same time, there is always a danger that a fully occupied chairman operating as chief executive officer may not be able to maintain the degree of objectivity and the kind of "outside look" required for effective board operation.

chapter 9

THE BOARD AND
THE CHIEF EXECUTIVE

The board of directors has done only part of its job when it has acted responsibly, wisely, and effectively in establishing goals, determining policies, and making program decisions regarded to be in the best long-run interests of the shareholders. As has been constantly emphasized, the board's primary and essential role is to see that the company is well managed. Many of the functions and responsibilities of the board, many of the techniques of managing and operating, and many of the considerations for assuring an effective board recognize the necessity of doing just this.

This means that the corporate board must have an effective relationship to the company through the chief executive. He is the essential link through which the board must operate, even though the tentacles of board power, policy determination, and control extend well beyond him. Unless this link is clear and strong, and unless a board furnishes an environment for effective performance by the chief executive in accomplishing the goals, policies, and programs approved by it, it is not an effective board.

Most chief executives want guidance and wise decision making without interference. Most ask for a clear understanding of what a board expects of them and help in meeting these expectations. Most are willing to be appraised on the results a company accomplishes, but they would like this appraisal to be fair and objective. Most are willing to concede that their tenure is contingent on their accomplishments, as reflected in company results.

To assure an effective board-chief executive relationship, three main things are required. First, a board must understand the chief executive's role and his essential functions. Second, it must establish appropriate goals for the company, goals for whose attainment the chief executive must be held responsible and against which he should be appraised. And third, the chief executive has a right, as has any subordinate in management, to obtain assistance from the board in successfully accomplishing his job.

THE CHIEF EXECUTIVE'S ROLE

The chief executive's role is essentially to take responsibility for the successful operation of a company. His is the desk where, in former President Truman's apt phrase, "the buck stops." He has a number of basic responsibilities. He is the main source of staff advice for the board on matters where it must make decisions. He is also responsible to the board for making certain that planning is done in such a way as to assure the attainment of corporate objectives. This, in turn, involves him in:

1. Making certain that, throughout the company, an environment is created where individuals can perform most effectively in meeting these goals

2. Seeing that a logical network of planning exists and planning is, in fact, done

3. Making sure that the company organization structure reflects a clear understanding of every person's part in planning and accomplishing plans

4. Taking steps to assure that the most qualified people are selected for positions and are given job inducements that will appropriately motivate them to the best possible performance

5. Developing and motivating people by nuturing at all levels of management a tradition of patient guidance, teaching, and leadership

6. Designing control techniques which will show readily and accurately where deviations from plans are occurring and seeing that steps are taken in time to correct them

In other words, the chief executive's role is to lead the company. But leading is more than inspiring, being a good example, or being in the forefront of the ranks. Effective leadership arises from effective managership. Therefore, the chief executive's role is essentially to practice and encourage managerial excellence.

ESSENTIAL FUNCTIONS OF THE CHIEF EXECUTIVE

Although too often none exists, there should be a position description for the chief executive. This involves not only a statement of major functions and duties, but also a clear description of authority and authority limits and a clear statement of goals. In any position description, however, it will be recognized that the chief executive has certain essential functions.

The functions of the chief executive naturally reflect his role as leader of the company and possessor of ultimate responsibility for its success in meeting its primary objectives—normally, profitable growth over the long run. But the long run is made up of a series of short terms, and no chief executive can expect to succeed in meeting company goals by worrying only about the long-range future or being satisfied to "look at the big picture." The future unfolds month by month and year by year. The "big picture" is made up of many small pictures.

As one astute observer of the business scene has said about the extent of information and concern of top executives,

Information may involve anything from the most minute and finite to the universal. Processing information today calls not only for distinguishing the forest from the trees, but distinguishing leaves and chlorophyl—while still not losing sight of the forest.[1]

The essential functions of the chief executive may also be summarized in the words of one company head who said, "The main responsibility of the chief executive is to make money for his company. . . . Somebody has to set objectives. Somebody has to run the organization and see to the selection of people. Somebody has to measure, gauge, and appraise performance. Somebody has to provide the climate in which the people work. Somebody has to make the final decisions."[2]

[1] Marion Harper, Jr., "A New Profession to Aid Management," *Journal of Marketing*, Vol. 25, No. 3, pp. 1–6, January, 1961.

[2] As stated by W. J. Holman, Chairman of the Board, Chicopee Manu-

In other words, the chief executive must be an effective manager of the company as a whole. This means developing goals and plans, both short-term and long-range, but not doing all of this himself; rather, seeing to it through adequate staff assistance and enlisting the full human resources of his company that planning is done. It also means both effective structuring of management roles through good organization and assuring the understanding of these roles by the people who occupy them. It likewise requires the constant assurance of management quality through proper selection, appraisal, and training of those who handle managerial tasks throughout the company. It contemplates strong leadership and example. And it proposes control techniques and information that report, hopefully in time, progress against plans and are tailored to individual job responsibilities, plans, and people.

But the essential function of the chief executive involves more than managing. He certainly has the task of seeking guidance, assistance, and decision from the board of directors. He is in a staff position to the board in the areas of its decisions. He will also do well to use the board as staff advisers for many of his own major decisions.

Furthermore, the chief executive has operating responsibilities. He is likely to be the actual head of public and stockholder relations, the company's number-one salesman, its most effective money raiser, and its personnel policy leader. He can never expect merely to establish goals, select people, and furnish an environment for performance so that others do all the work of the company. He cannot sit back and expect all the results to be accomplished by others; there is much he must do himself.

More specifically, the essential functions of the chief executive are likely to be spelled out, as one company has done in its position description for its president, which states:

Within the limits of the Certificate of Incorporation, By-Laws, and policies established or authorized by the Board of Directors and its committees, he is responsible for, and has commensurate authority to accomplish, the duties set forth below. He may delegate portions of his responsibili-

facturing Company, in "The President Looks at His Job," *Management Record*, National Industrial Conference Board, Vol. 24, No. 5, p. 11, May, 1962.

ties, consistent with sound operations and with authorized policies and procedures, together with proportionate authority for their fulfillment, but he may not delegate or relinquish any portion of his accountability for results.

1. Sees that the Board of Directors is kept fully informed on the conditions of the Corporation's several businesses and on all important factors influencing them; and sees that the Board is properly represented to employees, stockholders, investors, and the general public.

2. Sees to the execution of all decisions of the Board of Directors and its duly constituted committees, except when execution is otherwise specifically assigned by the By-Laws or by action of the Board or its committees.

3. Sees to the development of specific policies, procedures, and programs to implement the general policies established by the Board of Directors and its committees; sees that these policies, procedures, and programs are effectively administered and controlled; and authorizes all corporation-wide policies.

4. Determines the over-all objectives of the Corporation; sees to the development of operating and service division objectives which support the Corporation's objectives.

5. Develops and recommends to the Board of Directors long-range plans, consistent with the over-all objectives of the Corporation, which take full advantage of the long-range potentialities of the business; and sees to the development of divisional operating and long-range plans which are consistent with established objectives.

6. Sees that sound plans of organization, including the determination of the manageable units of the business, are developed and maintained for the Corporation and for each major component; sees that major additions, eliminations, or alterations in the organization plans of operating divisions are properly controlled; and authorizes organization plans of service divisions.

7. Authorizes entry into or departure from specific businesses, or the transfer of businesses or functions from one group or division to another.

8. Provides for optimum utilization of managers throughout the Corporation. To this end sees that the organization is staffed with competent people; that they are delegated authority and are compensated commensurately with their responsibilities; that appropriate limitations of their authority are defined and understood with respect to policy, commitments, expenditures, and action affecting personnel; and that managers are continually being developed so that qualified successors are available for major positions when needed.

9. Subject to action by the Board of Directors, authorizes the appointment, promotion, retirement, or release of officers of the Corporation.

10. Sees to the development throughout the Corporation of standards of performance in such key result areas as marketing, utilization and development of people, operating efficiency, innovation, physical and financial resources, public responsibility, and profitability. Sees to authorization of standards of performance for divisions, and to measurement of division performance; and makes sure that corrective action is initiated where necessary or desirable.

11. Sees that appropriate salary and wage structures are developed and maintained throughout the Corporation, and that the use of these structures is properly controlled.

12. Authorizes and executes such contracts and commitments as may be required by the By-Laws, the Board of Directors, or established policies.

13. Sees that effective relationships with labor organizations are maintained, and that commitments in contracts with unions are consistent with basic Corporation policies and objectives.

14. Sees to the development, authorization, and maintenance of an appropriate budgetary procedure; sees that the authorized procedure is properly administered, that its use is extended throughout the Corporation, and that the consolidated annual budget is prepared and submitted for review to the Budget Committee of the Board of Directors.

15. Sees that all funds, physical assets, and other property of the Corporation are appropriately safeguarded and administered.[3]

APPRAISING THE CHIEF EXECUTIVE
THROUGH GOAL ACCOMPLISHMENT

Reference has been made in this book to the importance, both as an operational matter and as a means of executive appraisal, of establishing verifiable quantitative and qualitative goals from time to time. The purpose of this approach to management is twofold. In the first place, no group or individual can move toward attainment of a goal which is general or vague for the simple reason that no one

[3] Drawn from the position of the President of the American Radiator and Standard Sanitary Corporation, as published in C. L. Bennet, *Defining the Manager's Job*, American Management Association, Inc., New York, 1958, pp. 143–146.

can know when he has attained the goal or whether a given program really contributes to it. In the second place, to avoid the obvious dangers of subjectivity in appraising performance, establishment of verifiable goals gives a standard against which performance can be measured with a high degree of objectivity. Also, it is worth noting that this approach to appraisal makes audit of performance an operational matter, tied in directly with the operations of a company rather than the personality or foibles of an individual.

Verifiable goals can be established for the chief executive. Moreover, this is the only way the board can really hold him responsible for performance. In addition, this approach gives meaning to the chief executive's role. As one company president told the author after a committee of his board had worked out verifiable goals for the next year, "This is the first time I have ever understood what the board expected of me as President."

An Example of Goals for a Company President. Perhaps the best way to show what is meant by verifiable goals is to cite a practical example by summarizing a set of specific objectives actually established by a board for the chief executive of a medium-sized company:

1. *Sales and Profit Goals—1966:*

Operating Division	1966 Sales	Increase over 1965
Test equipment	$ 9,500,000	12.0%
Engineering test facilities	2,400,000	15.0%
Medical equipment	6,700,000	22.0%
Control instruments	12,300,000	20.0%
Electronic components	5,100,000	24.0%
	$36,000,000	18.3%

Pre-tax Profit as Percent of Sales	Profit Before Taxes	Pre-tax Profit as Return on Investment
12.0%	$1,140,000	24.0%
10.0%	240,000	42.0%
16.2%	1,085,400	34.0%
13.6%	1,672,800	30.0%
14.8%	754,800	40.0%
13.6%	$4,893,000	30.6%

II. *An improved system of profit planning* with the following characteristics:

1. A system of variable budgets for the company as a whole, for each division, and each department designed to reach the sales and profit goals of the company and divisions.

2. A program of sales forecasts made one year in advance and revised quarterly.

3. A program of regular (not less than semi-annually) review of variable budget bases.

4. An actual monthly, twelve-month moving average, and year-to-date summary report of performance against budgets.

III. *An improved new product development program* for each major product area of the company, designed to assure an increase in company sales of 20 percent per year, with the following major features:

1. Review and selection of new products and product improvements which will be consistent with the company's financial resources, maintenance of profit levels, its engineering and production capabilities, and its marketing abilities.

2. Submission of major new product or product improvement programs, involving an expenditure of more than $20,000 in engineering, production facilities, and market test and promotion to the board of directors for approval.

3. Programming of product development projects which will assure completion within budgeted time and costs.

4. Control information flow which will give adequate information on the progress of product development projects.

5. Formal, rigorous, and regular review of new product and product improvement selection and progress.

6. Monthly summary reports of all new product and product improvements selected, of program, and progress to the board of directors.

IV. *A revised chart of executive approval authorizations,* to be submitted to the board of directors within three months and regularly (not less often than semi-annually) reviewed with a view to revision thereafter.

V. *An organization plan* for three-five years in advance based on, among other things:

1. A recognition of the importance of profit responsibility by individual managers.

2. The availability and capacities of present managerial personnel.

3. The possibilities of training of present management personnel.

4. The possibilities of recruitment of new managerial personnel.

5. The necessity of considering proper centralization of authority at top corporate levels and the need for appropriate decentralized authority to division and functional managers.

6. Consideration of the costs and advantages of divisional product, or other decentralizational and functional departmentation.

VI. *A proposed program of compensation of key managerial personnel,* including salary adjustments, the initiation of bonuses and stock options, and adequate fringe benefits.

VII. *A program of new plant facilities* for the medical equipment and control instruments divisions, including the gradual move to such facilities, which will:

1. Not materially reduce profit in the current operating years when moves must take place.

2. Improve earnings of the company in the near future (*i.e.*, within two years).

3. Provide for minimum losses on present lease obligations.

4. Provide for minimum possible losses of trained personnel.

VIII. *An acquisition program* based on the following principles:

1. The acquisition must fit the company's capabilities in marketing, engineering, manufacturing, or bring such capabilities into the company.

2. It must be within the company's financial capabilities.

3. It must improve the company's earning position:

a. It must provide, at least after integration, for a return on net assets and net worth above that now being made.

b. It must increase the earnings per share of company stock after the acquisition.

4. Normally, the acquisition must include an element of effective management, or the company must see the ability to acquire effective management for it.

Desirability of Goals for the Chief Executive. While an increasing number of companies see the benefit of establishing verifiable goals for key executives and a very few carry this goal structure down in the organization to the lowest level of management, few have apparently seen the value of establishing goals for the chief executive beyond the commonly established sales and profit goals. Yet most top company officers would rather have clear goals by which to be judged than rely on the caprice of subjective judgments. Moreover, setting such goals helps the board to determine its proper area of concern and mitigates the danger of directors getting into purely operational matters to the point of interfering with the effective management of the chief executive.

In setting up major goals for the chief executive, the board should not attempt to cover every facet of his accomplishment during a given period of time. Instead, it should select a relatively small number of major areas where special, verifiable accomplishment is expected in a given period. Most individuals who have studied a system of management by objectives believe, with some justification, that if there are too many goals established, they lose their effectiveness as major points toward which an individual can aim his activities.

It is only natural, also, that the goals for the chief executive, like those of other managers, should vary from time to time. In the example given above, a number of the goals established involved special new or improved programs which, in the directors' judgment, were especially needed by the company. After such programs have been suitably established, the directors' concern is only to see to it —assuming that the programs are suitable to the company's business —that they should not die from executive malnutrition. Many excellent new product-development programs, for example, have started out well, accomplished results, and then been allowed to wither in the aftermath of their success. While directors must be concerned with this and keep accurate reports to make sure that these programs essential to company success are maintained, it may not be necessary to include a given program every year in the primary goals of the chief executive.

EXPOSURE OF KEY EXECUTIVES

Except for the possibility of having some reporting relationships directly to the board by the chief financial officer or corporate secretary, or of the board's having certain administrative or staff assistants directly responsible to it, the major line of reporting, and usually the only one, between the board and the company is through the chief executive. However, the effective board cannot help but be concerned about the quality and the performance of other key executives at the top level, especially division general managers and the heads of major corporate staff departments in a divisional company, or the major functional department chiefs in a functionalized company. This was pointed out above in the discussion of authority delegations by the board, where it was recommended that the board be given authority to approve appointment, removal, and compensation for such key executives. Without in any way interfering with the essential responsibility of the chief executive, the board can continue its acquaintanceship with key subordinates of the chief executive through review and approval of plans and policies and through review of appraisal information on their performance when salary changes, bonuses, stock options, or other compensations of these persons are considered by the board.

A chief executive should encourage a reasonable degree of exposure of his top executive personnel to the board of directors, in view of the board's natural interest and concern with them. One of the best ways he can do this is to have them present to the board or its executive committee an accounting of their performance against budgets and other plans. Another is to have them make submissions of major planning proposals subject to board decision, rather than having these proposals always come through the chief executive. It would be well, also, for a board to receive through the chief executive, for information purposes only, a statement of the goals of key top executive personnel. In its review of divisional and top functional executive performance and plans, the board will naturally be concerned with these goals.

A chief executive should welcome this exposure of his key subordinates. In the first place, they are primarily his selections and he should be proud to display their abilities and personal growth. In the second place, he should welcome the assistance they can give in presenting proposals with which they are especially familiar and answering questions of board members. In addition, one cannot overlook the importance of morale. Such executives feel closer to the top of the company, the board of directors, because they are in fact closer.

APPRAISING THE EFFECTIVENESS OF MANAGEMENT

While appraisal of performance aganist goals is a tremendous step forward in manager appraisal, and properly deserves the enthusiasm with which it is being accepted, it is still subject to deficiencies. In the first place, a manager may reach or fail to reach his goals through circumstances largely beyond his control. In addition, there are always questions as to whether the goal structure goes down into the organization far enough and whether there is a logical and practical network of supportive goals through each echelon of management. Again, it is often extremely difficult to establish goals that cover the proper area of company operations and are reasonably attainable, with proper "push" or "stretch." Furthermore, there is always the danger that any set of goals, designed as they must be to measure performance within a reasonable time span, will tend to overemphasize short-term accomplishment at the expense of longer-term results.

In order to offset these deficiencies and to assure long-range effectiveness and success of the company, there is probably no substitute for appraising the quality of management as such. While brilliant ideas and performance in engineering, marketing, financial arrangements and manipulation, and other operating matters can make a company financially successful, there is no doubt in this author's mind that, over the long term, the single greatest assurance of success in a company is the quality of management.

Therefore, it would be useful for a company to have a program under which each manager, even the chief executive, would be assessed on his ability to manage effectively. While this may be approached in various ways, this author believes (and is experimenting in a company operating with a program supporting this belief) that the best way of appraising management is to translate the basic principles of management into questions that can be used as guides and answered with a fairly high degree of objectivity.

By taking the essential functions of management—planning, organizing, staffing, directing, and controlling—it is possible to construct a basic and fundamental checklist on what the effective manager does. For example, in the area of planning, one might ask such questions as: Does he set goals for his area of responsibility that are related in a positive way to the accomplishment of company objectives? Are his goals verifiable? Does he make sure that his goals are understood by those that report to him? Does he check his plans periodically to see that they are still consistent with revised expectations? Does he understand and guide his decision making in accordance with company policies which affect his area of operation?

In the area of organizing, such questions may be asked as these: Does he delegate authority to his subordinates in accordance with results expected of them? Does he refrain from going below the subordinate to whom he has given a task and delegated authority? Does he balance delegation of authority downward with maintenance of adequate control and reserved authority in his own position? In the area of control it may be asked: Do his control techniques report deviations promptly? Does he develop controls that point up exceptions at strategic points? Does he use control techniques, where possible, to anticipate deviations from plans? Does he keep abreast of newer techniques of planning and control and does he attempt to apply them to his operations?

However a manager is appraised with respect to his management abilities and practices, the point is that it should be undertaken. This has appropriately been called the most direct kind of control simply because qualified managers plan best for the future, undertake actions designed to assure that future goals happen, and make fewer mistakes.

While there may be questions as to how far board members should become involved in the matter of appraisal, they should be assured that an effective appraisal system does develop. This can be done directly by asking for a review of the company's appraisal program or the submission of a program to the board. Or it can be done indirectly through board review of extra compensation such as bonuses and stock options. It can be done, likewise, by asking the chief executive what attention he is giving this important subject. The president of one of America's largest industrial companies told this author he estimated that he and the chairman of the board spent 40 percent of their time appraising the performance and the quality of management of key managerial personnel throughout the enterprise. One wonders how many top executives can make such a claim.

ASSISTING THE CHIEF EXECUTIVE

The effective board must necessarily regard assistance to the chief executive of the company in his leading and operating of the business as one of its key tasks. It does this best, of course, by doing a good job as a board of directors. This means discharging its responsibilities conscientiously and wisely and making decisions in its proper area of authority promptly and clearly. It also means establishing an environment for performance by the chief executive in such fundamental ways as clarifying his objectives, removing obstacles to his performance, and helping to create effective executive inducements. In other words, by seeing that the company is well managed and taking steps to assist in assuring good management, a board will be making its most significant contribution in assisting the chief executive.

As is well known, the executive pinnacle of a company is a lonely post. Although the chief executive has available—depending, of course, upon the size and resources of a company—considerable assistance in his key operating and staff subordinates and in the organization as a whole, he cannot always count on these subordinates to speak the truth freely or to be fully objective in situations where their own positions may be affected directly or remotely by a policy matter. There are still other cases where the wise chief executive will welcome the questions and suggestions of experienced outside board members who may be able to direct his attention to strategic factors he might otherwise overlook. In all these cases, it is natural and proper that the board, either as a group or as individual members (and this approach would appear to be especially wise if the board is heavily loaded with insiders who are subordinate to the chief executive), should be available for consultation. And the intelligent chief executive will use this resource.

Perhaps one of the most effective ways in which a board assists the chief executive is through careful review and appraisal of major goals, policies and plans. By asking basic questions, the board member can do much to assure the chief executive that the program he recommends has considered all the critical variables and is developed as logically as possible. The board may ask such questions as: Will this program work? How? Is it practicable to aim for these objectives in the time-span indicated? What are competitors doing in the business we are now in or contemplate going into? What makes the management of this company feel that it can succeed in a given new program, when Company A, Company B, and Company C have made only modest profits or have suffered losses? What are the long-term financial commitments involved in the program?

Also, individual board members and the board as a whole can assist the chief executive in certain operational matters, notably stockholder and public relations. Or a board member may be very useful in negotiating with underwriters for a new security issue. The author has also seen board members with specialized talents used very effectively as consultants to operating management in such critical fields as marketing, production, and research and engineering. With his status as a member of the board of directors, and if he is properly qualified, a board member may be very useful to the chief executive in ferreting out information, finding problems, suggesting solutions, or even "selling" new approaches and ideas that even the chief executive might find difficult to sell.

A board, then, can be an exceptionally important asset for the chief executive. Although too seldom used in this role, board members, particularly outside members, can do much to help the chief executive. And the intelligent chief executive not only recognizes that he needs this help, but uses it. Playing too close to one's vest or assuming that one's judgment is infallible are hallmarks of top-executive failure.

INTELLIGENT CHIEF EXECUTIVES
WANT AN EFFECTIVE BOARD

That the intelligent chief executive appreciates a board to whom he can truly report and to whom he can present his program proposals, is true more often than is realized. In general, it is only the chief executive obsessed with monolithic power, doubtful of the soundness of his proposals or the accuracy of his judgment, and fearful about his own security and competence who opposes this reporting relationship. But the board itself must be informed, intelligent, and objective and must limit its decision making and inquiries to matters that are definitely within its purview.

As one executive said of the relationship of the top officer and the board, "He . . . needs to report to somebody. He needs to report to a body where he has to support his programs, his policies, his decisions, and the body if sympathetic will back him up until they replace him. It must be a good hardheaded group where he feels that he is on the spot to prove his case. I think without that there is something lacking. I think that any chief executive who is running a company should have the full authority, but should have that privilege of going before a board and of defending his practice." And another pointed out that a board should "have the complete respect of the chief executive, where he will be willing to go before them and say, 'I will submit my plans for your objections. I am damn sure I am right, but I want to prove it to you first.'" Still another executive stated the same idea when he said, "In addition, I believe very strongly that he (the chief executive) needs one more step if you are going to have the proper safeguards, and that is the job of proving his point to an independent group that are damn good judges, who have not been participants in the plans, but who stand aside and judge. They interfere in no way with the management, but they are judges. I think that if that element is lacking you are always in danger. And I never want to be a chief executive with that element lacking." Or as another executive pointed out, "You can walk into a group that are your judges and say, 'Now, gentlemen, this is my program.' Let them attack it, and you defend it, and when you finally come out of there, they say it's all right that you go. Then you go with confidence. But you've got to have that element." [4]

[4] All the statements quoted in this paragraph are from C. C. Brown and E. E. Smith, *The Director Looks at His Job*, Columbia University Press, New York, 1957, pp. 48–50.

chapter *10*

MAKING BOARDS
EFFECTIVE

Stockholders and the public at large hold the board of directors responsible for seeing that the corporate form is used to serve both the investors' interests and the social needs for which it was created. To think of the board of directors as an anachronism of antiquated corporation law or as an obsolete form of organization overlooks this inescapable fact.

Especially as we awaken to the realization that management is the catalytic force which must establish an environment for efficient channeling of human and material resources in any society, the basic responsibility of a board becomes an urgent matter which those interested in management can no longer treat lightly. If they do, it is not beyond the realm of possibility that society, through political action or innovation, will find a way, as it has in other areas, of dealing with an institutional device not meeting recognized needs.

As one astute observer has noted in connection with the problem of ineffective boards of directors:

If our corporations are not well run in the total sense—that is, through the effective harmonization of all interests involved—the public will not continue to believe that they are functioning in the general public interest; and, if that day comes, the politicians will be only too ready to suggest a different way of handling things. This longer-term problem is amplified by the fact that the current trend toward larger and larger enterprises will probably continue in the future—and may even be expected to accelerate because of the economics of technological development and perhaps because of military necessity. Certainly history teaches us that the public sooner or later comes to distrust large enterprises, whether they be church, government, trusts (as in Theodore Roosevelt's time), financial interests, or (as is most recently evident) labor unions. This distrust derives largely from the public's fear that too much power will come into the hands of a few individuals if an adequate system of checks and balances is not maintained. With regard to our artificial being, the soulless corporation, it is becoming increasingly obvious that the individual voting stockholder is a dying breed, and that management and the board can be self-perpetuating institutions. Thus, a widespread public distrust of large business enterprises could develop more rapidly even than a distrust of such monopolistic and powerful groups as labor unions, which are more public-relations conscious than business and hence have been able to assume a better posture in the eyes of the public. In the long run, therefore, American management must evolve a better system of checks and balances to satisfy the public that its interests are being protected.[1]

CRITICISMS OF BOARDS OF DIRECTORS

Despite the unequivocal fact that boards hold a key position in the business and social scene, efficacy of board operations has long been questioned. That raising such questions is not new is evident from the following quotation from Adam Smith, who wrote in 1776:

The trade of a joint stock company is always managed by a court of directors. This court, indeed, is frequently subject, in many respects, to the control of a general court of proprietors. But the greater part of those proprietors seldom pretend to understand anything of the business of the company; and when the spirit of faction happens not to prevail among them, give themselves no trouble about it, but receive contentedly such half or yearly dividend as the directors think proper to make to them . . . The directors of such companies, however, being the managers of other people's money than of their own, it cannot be well expected that they would watch over it with the same anxious vigilance with which the partners in private copartnery watch over their own . . . Negligence

[1] E. E. Smith, "Management's Least-used Asset: The Board of Directors," from *The Dynamics of Management*, Management Report No. 14, American Management Association, New York, 1958, p. 54.

and profusion, therefore, must always prevail, more or less, in the management of the affairs of such a company.[2]

This kind of criticism has prevailed to the present day, although it apparently reached a high-water mark in the 1930's. Typical of the kind of criticism made then is that by Justice William O. Douglas when, as a law professor in 1934, he blasted at "directors who do not direct."[3] Criticising directors for not assuming the responsibility of directing and company management for dominating an agency to check on its performance, Douglas urged that the board be divorced from management, pay closer attention to the operation of the business through proper supervision, and place greater emphasis on outside directors. He also recommended that a protective association be established to unite shareholders so that their interests would be more fully represented on boards. Likewise, in his study in 1945, Baker found that directors have been criticized as being "complacent," "rubber stamps," "back-scratchers," "log-rollers," "irresponsible," "self-dealers," "incompetent managers who do not know what their duties are and treat these perfunctorily," and "members of an exclusive club who conform to a social pattern."[4]

Even in more recent years, effectiveness of company boards has been seriously questioned. As Smith said in 1958, "In practice, however, the board of directors has in most companies become something of a legal fiction. Its role as a vital organ of the business has deteriorated, and in many companies the board has actually been deposed by operating management. This trend has gone so far, in fact, that one Professor of Business Administration recently pronounced the board to be 'dead as a dodo,' and in his own private

[2] *The Wealth of Nations*, Modern Library, Inc., New York, 1937, pp. 699–700.

[3] "Directors Who Do Not Direct," *Harvard Law Review*, Vol. 47, pp. 1305–1334, June, 1934.

[4] J. C. Baker, *Directors and Their Functions*, Harvard University Graduate School of Business Administration, Boston, 1945, pp. 20–21.

funeral rites observed that operating management was quite capable of reviewing its own actions." [5]

That these criticisms are almost certainly accurate for a large number of company boards there can be little doubt. But there is also little doubt that an increasing number of companies have improved the effectiveness of their boards. Unfortunately, boards with high standards in terms of fully discharging their responsibilities are not as numerous as they should be. But there is evidence leading this author to believe that boards in the category of pure legal fictions are declining. What must not be overlooked is that boards may vary from fictional, to useless, to ineffectual but conscientious, and finally to effective in the best sense of the word.

PRESSURES FOR MORE EFFECTIVE BOARDS

Particularly in the United States, a number of pressures are tending to increase the concern of many companies—especially those with public stockholders—for developing effective boards. Surveys of board operations made over the years disclose that more outsiders are serving on boards, qualifications of board members are being given more consideration than ever, more is being expected of boards, more and longer meetings are being held, and directors are being compensated better.

What are these pressures? At least four can be clearly identified.

The Changing Shareholder Role. Although in most publicly-owned companies insiders may still be able to elect the board of their choice through their control of proxy machinery, there is also evidence that shareholders are taking an increasing interest in boards. The rise of the large institutional investor has brought to many companies holders of large blocks of stock who, while owning nothing approaching a majority interest, have considerable power not only because of their large shareholdings but even more because of the publicity given their operations and their stock transactions. There has also been an increased incidence of stockholder rebellions

[5] E. E. Smith, *op. cit.*, p. 49.

led by dissident inside or outside groups. Enough of these have succeeded, so that few top managers any longer take the attitude toward their shareholders exemplified by one chief executive who told a dissatisfied stockholder: "If you don't like the way I'm running this company, there is a market in which you can sell your stock." And stockholder suits aimed at directors and officers have multiplied, aided and abetted by attorneys who see a chance for publicity and handsome fees through successful prosecution of claims.

In addition, general interest in the stock market in recent years, accompanied by a rapid growth in securities and companies, has increased investor interest in how companies operate and how they are managed. All these things have led top management to pay more attention to shareholder relations, to securities analysts, and to investment bankers, as well as to others in a position to influence company acceptance in the market. The result has been intensified programs of investor relations and greater sensitivity of top managers to the interests and position of stockholders.

Growing Awareness of Board Responsibilities. The increased legal responsibilities placed on board members by the securities regulations of 1933 and 1934 have played an important part in forcing them to take their role seriously, as have the criticism and suspicion aimed at business by a number of administrations in Washington during the last thirty-five years. Also, an increasing number of top managers are developing a philosophy of director trusteeship. One such credo of directorship is the following statement of F. W. Abrahms, Chairman of the Board of Standard Oil Company (New Jersey) in 1950:

We have a stewardship in a company like Jersey Standard and a personal pride. We would like to leave the company in a sounder and more assured position than when we took it over. We are not looking to the company just to support us; we want to make it healthy for future generations and for the employees that will come along. We like to feel it is a good place for people to work. We have equal responsibilities to other groups: stockholders, customers, and the public generally, including government. What is the proper balance for the claims of these different sections? Keeping the proper balance in these things is one of the most important things that boards of directors have to consider.[6]

The Management Revolution. With the revolutionary growth of interest in management, and the rise of the belief that managing is a teachable function based on an underlying science, concern with the problems of managing has understandably developed in all types of enterprises and at all levels. In view of the board's responsibility, it is hardly surprising that this new emphasis on management should extend to considering the effectiveness of boards.

Recognition of the Business as a Social Institution. There has been widespread recognition by company managers in the past three decades that a business enterprise must be attuned to the society in which it operates. The ability of an organization to endure, as now well recognized, depends largely upon the way it keeps in step with changing social objectives, technical developments, and economic and political change. Since the board of directors has as one of its major functions the maintenance of stability and growth, an alert board will be aware of the necessities of attunement to society and will judge the quality of company managers in part by the skill with which this is accomplished. It is interesting that Jackson Martindell, founder of the American Institute of Management, made this consideration a principal criterion of the quality of boards of directors.[7]

WHY WEAK BOARDS?

In the light of the role of the board of directors in the management of a corporation, imposed both by law and by practical desirability of adequate stockholder representation, it may well be asked why so many boards appear to be deficient. Why are boards so often weak? Why do so many boards fail to meet their responsibilities? Indeed, why should not have boards been the first point of the man-

[6] C. H. Maurer, "Boards of Directors," *Fortune*, Vol. 41, No. 5, p. 130, May, 1950.

[7] See appraisals of individual corporations in *The Corporate Director*.

agement structure to be "developed" in the rapidly expanding management movement of the post-World War II era? There are a number of answers.

Misunderstanding the Management Position of the Board. Perhaps the primary cause for board weakness has been failure to understand the board's responsibility for corporation management. The exact position the board occupies in management has seldom been defined beyond such generalities as "managing the corporation" or "seeing that it is well managed." Directors have sometimes forgotten that they are in fact the company's top executive group. Executive officers have likewise tended to regard the board as a nuisance which must be put up with, nothing but an honorary group tolerated for public and stockholder relations, or a mere committee of management advisors.

As one observer has pointed out: "It is ironic . . . that we in the United States have so neglected this most vital area. Every other management function, it seems, has been subjected to searching scrutiny and detailed analysis, and new concepts and methods have been developed in great number. Each management function today has its high priests who are dedicated to improving the practice of their particular speciality and to increasing our general understanding of its importance and of its relation to other management activities. Yet the responsibilities of the board and the relationship and distinction between board and management have been sorely neglected. Management literature on the subject is pitifully brief and strikingly devoid of any real depth or new ideas. It is not surprising, therefore, that there is so little recognition of the need for a truly effective board and so little effort to obtain one." [8]

Also, there has unquestionably been a failure to recognize the contributions that a board can make to a company. Through its pressure on the chief executive and, through him, the other company executives, the effective board can force establishment of clear and better goals and more logical policies and plans to assure their attainment. Through deliberation, it can greatly contribute to ade-

[8] E. E. Smith, "Management's Least-used Asset: The Board of Directors," *op. cit.*, p. 52.

quate consideration of major problems and the subtle strategic variables involved. It can, moreover, be a source of great strength and assistance to the top executive group of a company. Much of the weakness of boards stems from sheer unawareness, on the part of top company executives, of the potential of a capable board.

Insiders' Desire for Independence. As has been pointed out before, a publicly-owned corporation tends to be controlled by one or a few insiders despite the fact that they may own little or no stock in the company. This is due, of course, to a combination of stockholder apathy and lack of organization, and the power inherent in control of proxy machinery. That this is a considerable power is indicated by one case where the author was involved. A group of shareholders owning approximately 40 percent of the company's stock undertook to gain control of the board. The management had been so inept that the company earnings were less than the amount for which its owned plant and office facilities could be rented to outsiders. Yet a management group with less than 1 percent of the company's stock was able to continue control of the board through its domination of proxy machinery and ability to spend company resources to solicit proxies from the public shareholders.

The result of such power in the hands of insiders is often that the controlling group simply does not want an effective board, which might threaten their control or at least limit their freedom to run the company as their own private fief.

The same kind of desire for independence more understandably exists in companies owned completely or predominantly by an individual officer or group of inside executives. Often, seeing no sense in an effective board which might challenge their powers, they put up with the board only as a legal requirement or a showpiece. As the elder Henry Ford was reported to have remarked at one of his board meetings, which he seldom attended: "Come on, Harry, let's get the hell out of here. We'll probably change anything they do anyway." [9]

[9] Harry Bennett, *We Never Called Him Henry*, Fawcett Publications, Inc., New York, 1951, p. 167.

Boards as Creatures of the Chief Executive. Because of insider control and apathy of board members as well as stockholders, perhaps most of the boards are creatures of the chief executive, or at least of a controlling group of insiders. The chief executive normally recruits and selects directors and tends consciously or unconsciously to pick those men he "can work with." Often this means a man who will do his bidding, who will not interfere in the way he runs the company—who will, in short, be a "rubber stamp."

This is understandable. A chief executive who has risen to the top of a company naturally feels that he knows best and that his responsibility to the company itself requires that he possess the ultimate power of control. Moreover, he cannot be blamed for wanting to maintain his position of power and prestige. In such a position, no matter how much lip service he may give to the role of boards, he may not truly *want* an effective board.

While this is a fact in many, many cases, it should not be taken as a universal tendency, even where the chief executive does actually select the board. As has been pointed out in a number of instances in this book, there are chief executives who honestly see value to themselves and the company in an intelligent and powerful board. Also, the very fact that directors are nominated by the chief executive does not mean that they are always rubber stamps. Men of stature, intelligence, and experience—those usually sought for board membership even where "windowdressing" motives exist—are seldom content with the purely advisory, or, worse yet, useless board position. They are not nonentities. They do not need the status or responsibility or compensation of board memberships that badly.

But the dangers inherent in boards being creatures of the chief executive suggest that directors, and especially outside directors, should take a more active role in nominating new board members. This also points to the desirability of a chairman of the board independent of the chief executive, who can make his primary business the strengthening of the board itself through recruitment of individuals of ability who can meet their responsibilities with independence. Even though the chief executive should have the right to be consulted on nominations, and individuals totally unacceptable to him should probably not be appointed, allowing him to control the selection of directors is questionable at the very least.

Alleged Shortage of Competent Directors. One encounters throughout the literature and in statements of many executives the belief that there is such a shortage of competent directors that no practical alternatives exist but to appoint insiders or to recruit from persons with close ties to the company, such as legal counsel, business consultants, or bankers with whom the company does business. The author doubts that this shortage is nearly as real as usually perceived. It is hard to believe that there are not competent individuals among business, professional, and other ranks, whether active or retired, who can and will give a reasonable time to board service. If those in control of our companies can get away from the idea that few people have wisdom or interest, or that directors must be "big names" to adorn the company's masthead, there doubtless is a large untapped reservoir of talent available to company boards. This is particularly true if the person selected for a directorship can be given the opportunity to make a contribution he regards as significant.

But the problem does point up several things. In the first place, more attention must be given to determining what qualifications a director should have. More effort must be spent in recruiting directors. And programs for increasing the competence of directors need to be undertaken.

Exaggeration of the Time Commitment. A commonly advanced objection to having outside—and, for that matter, part-time—board members is that they cannot and will not spend time to be capable directors. It is said that directors must be prepared to spend from 10 percent to 25 percent of their time to be effective. When one considers that few executives or professional men work less than a 60-hour week, this would mean from six to fifteen hours per week. How many non-retired business or professional men can spend this much time?

While a considerable time commitment may be desirable, the amount of time necessary for being an effective director seems to be greatly exaggerated. The author has seen many men of wisdom and experience who have been effective as outside directors with a time commitment as little as four hours per month on regular board meetings and an additional two hours in homework, plus occasional special meetings or briefing sessions. Yet these men have contributed significantly to the successful operation of the company.

Much of the time commitment necessary depends upon how the board is operated. If directors do a reasonable amount of homework, if proposals are properly researched and presented, if the board chairman keeps meetings on course, and if committees of the board are appropriately used to study complex issues and present their findings to the whole membership, a board can accomplish a great deal in a half-day or full-day meeting.

Furthermore, there may even be merit in having certain directors not too thoroughly knowledgeable in some company matters. One of the advantages of a part-time outside director is that he brings to bear an "outside look," buttressed with knowledge of external forces and trends, usually superior to that of individuals fully committed to the inside operations of a company. He does not know all the reasons why a course of action cannot succeed or why another program is unquestionably "right." It is exactly this freshness and detachment which give him a high value in board deliberations. Through a few probing questions, the perceptive director can soon satisfy himself whether the proposer of a policy or a program knows what he is talking about and has considered and made provisions for critical, or strategic, variables.

Failure to Operate Efficiently and Effectively. A major cause for board weakness is simply the failure of many boards to operate efficiently and effectively *as a board.* If it has no clear understanding of what it wishes to deal with, either as a reviewer or as a decision maker, and does not stick to this task, a board will understandably waste time and not do the things it should. If half-baked proposals are presented, board members will waste time groping for facts or answers. If members regard themselves as a club where no one questions the proposals of the chief executive or other officers or directors, or where a director feels he cannot speak his mind freely, its effectiveness as a deliberating group will wither. If the chairman's lackadaisical handling of a meeting lets board members wander into meaningless or inapplicable discussion, it may never get to the matters it should consider.

Likewise, if the board is not informed as fully as possible before the meetings of the agenda and the matters to come before it, time waste is an inevitable result. If the board does not know what control information it wishes, or permits reports to be presented in an unintelligible fashion, it will almost certainly fail, either engulfed in a sea of ignorance or swamped in a deluge of meaningless data.

All this is to say that a board must know what it is doing. In addition, it and those responsible for its operations—primarily the chairman and the chief executive—must know and practice the various techniques and approaches necessary for an efficient group meeting.

BALANCING THE BOARD

Underlying various board weaknesses is the failure to balance the board. This means getting an integrated assortment of talents and points of view applicable to the company's operation and position in its industry, its economy, and society. While the concept of balance is usually limited to the undeniably important considerations of inside and outside members, there are many other factors to examine.

Balance Between Inside and Outside Members. The problem of balance between inside and outside members has been discussed in a previous chapter on board operation. The reasons for having both represented on a board are persuasive, although it is far from certain that this issue can be solved by dealing in numbers. The essential point is that the board must be looked upon in substance rather than form.

It is possible that a board composed entirely of full-time insiders without operating responsibilities can provide the breadth of knowledge and experience and the independence of action so essential in an effective board. However, there is always the danger of insularity, which might be avoided or mitigated by the use of competent and independent outsiders. Likewise, it is possible that a minority of outside part-time members can make a board essentially act like an outside-dominated board. This depends upon how the board operates and whether the outsiders are able and allowed to be effective.

By the same token, it is possible that a board with a minority of insiders will have all the characteristics of an inside board. If the outsiders are merely rubber stamps for the chief executive, this can and probably will occur. If the insider group is so strong and dominating that it seldom listens to outsiders, admits them to the "club," or allows major issues to come before the board, even a minority of insiders can so control the board as to make it for all intents and purposes an inside board.

Many are the cases where a chief executive, sensitive to shareholder and public criticisms of a board loaded with insiders, has transformed his board into a predominantly outside one without in fact changing its substance. Unless the outsiders are treated as essential elements of the board, are encouraged to contribute, are listened to, are adequately informed, are stimulated to come to independent conclusions, and are allowed to help decide basic company issues, the substance of the board is not changed. All the chief executive has done in these instances has been to change the form but not the essential quality of the board.

Balance, then, is a matter primarily of how the board operates, how it is led, and whether the officers and directors *want* an independent and effective board. It is true that there is likely to be a better chance of a board's meeting its responsibilities if it is numerically dominated by outsiders. It is likewise true that a board is likely to be better if insiders with narrow divisional or functional operating responsibilities, in contrast to the broader functions of such officers as the executive vice president, financial or legal vice president, or corporate staff officers, are excluded from the board.

Balance in Part-time and Full-time Directors. One of the criticisms advanced against almost all directors is that they give their task too little time. In practically all companies both inside and outside directors are part-time. A few of the largest companies, such as Du Pont, Standard Oil (New Jersey), and Unilever, have some or almost all directors who carry no operating responsibilities and devote their full time and energies to board service. In addition to ample time, such directors can obviously acquire intimate knowledge in depth of their company and its problems, and of the industry. Moreover, if the one dominant function of a director is to select company management and appraise it, doing so accurately and completely probably requires more contact with the company than can be had through monthly board meetings.

Especially for large and complex companies, the concept of full-time director has much to commend it. Understandably, in one study group comprised of major corporation directors, the idea of having at least some full-time directors was very favorably received.[10] It was felt that the use of full-time directors had the attraction of providing a knowledgeable group familiar with company operations while still maintaining desirable separation of the directors' task from the operating manager's job.

But there is still the problem of the possible insularity of a full-time board, and it may also be questioned whether a company can afford the cost of so heavy a full-time top management. Also, the point may be made that directors with no other assignment but to direct might find too much time on their hands and be tempted thereby to dabble in the affairs of operating management.

Possibly a better balance might be that practiced by E. I. du Pont de Nemours & Company, which has traditionally had a board composed one-third to one-half of full-time members, a small number of top operating executives such as the president (who might be regarded as a part-time insider), and the rest part-time outside directors, although a majority of these are usually retired Du Pont executives.

Balancing a board with a combination of full-time members and part-time outsiders does appear to be desirable, the number of full-time members clearly depending on the complexity and nature of the business. As pointed out by one panel of executives who studied the problem, a balance between part-time and full-time, inside and outside directors has definite advantages.[11] Such a board should

[10] C. C. Brown and E. E. Smith, *The Director Looks at His Job*, Columbia University Press, New York, 1957, pp. 57–93.

[11] *Ibid.*, pp. 99–101.

avoid using members of management who are not likely to be independent of the chief executive. It also gives certain members time to do a thorough job in analyzing proposals coming before the entire board and in reviewing operations, as well as serving on certain committees such as the executive committee. It permits the part-time outside directors to review the actions or recommendations of the full-time inside group and thereby preserves the advantages associated with outside board membership.

When one considers the cost of operating even a medium-size company, the extra cost of some full-time directors does not appear to be excessive. Perhaps this is an element of balance which deserves more study and attention than it has been given.

Balance in Experience and Expertise. Though it may be argued that expertise can be purchased through hiring consultants and does not need to be a requirement of board membership, there is much to be said for having a variety of special knowledge and experience on the board. Even though persons of broad intelligence, who are able to view corporation problems and operations in a comprehensive way, are naturally preferred to narrow specialists, this author believes that an effectively balanced board should include members of varied experience and expertise.

Almost any company would benefit by board members representing experience and knowledge in such areas as marketing, finance, and production or procurement. Companies heavily oriented towards engineering and research would do well to have a person on their boards with extensive experience and knowledge in this field. Other companies with overseas operations could gain by having a board member with special competence in international management and marketing. Most companies, judging by the composition of boards, have felt it desirable to have members with legal expertise and experience. However, this preference can be easily overdone since the law represents a number of fields of specialities and a board member attempting to function as a general or a specialized counsel may put the board in the dangerous position of a business executive who attempts to act as his own lawyer. There are also, especially in companies with considerable public prominence or which deal with large segments of the general public, advantages in having someone like a public official or a university president, dean, or professor on the board.

General management experience and expertise should be placed at the top of the list in the truly balanced board, however. Men who understand what management is and who have had experience in weighing the performance and plans of individuals with functional or divisional interests are likely to be the kind who can serve on a board most effectively. If they have been trained by experience and study to see the corporation as an integrated whole and understand how individual pieces fit together in this whole, they are likely to have the knowledge to weigh the kind of problems which the typical board faces. Such men are accustomed to utilizing the advice of specialists, fitting it into proper perspective in the total picture of operations.

But all the knowledge available on a board comes to naught if the board does not use it. Such knowledge is equally futile if individual board members will not work hard enough to understand plans and operations. Furthermore, one of the great dangers of experience is that of succumbing to the fallacy that experience repeats itself and that what worked or did not work in a time past will automatically work or fail to work in an almost certainly different future. Finally, breadth of knowledge and expertise have little meaning unless a director has the courage to express his opinions and conclusions freely.

Balance in Age and Time on the Board. The truly balanced board comprises a variety of ages and tenures. Although chronological age is often a poor measure, since individuals vary tremendously in their vigor, flexibility, and outlook, it can be said that the balanced board should include members whose ages range from approximately 40 to probably not more than 75. Younger men are not likely to have the breadth of experience or leavened judgment which time gives. Older men may not have the vigor or mental flexibility to deal with board duties and meet new problems.

One of the factors of balance often overlooked is the time individuals have spent in a given board position. Knowing the environment of past company policy decisions can be invaluable, as can understanding of past problems and progress. But, as has been indicated, too much experience can lead to closed minds, lack of aggressiveness, and limited originality. Therefore, a board of directors should bring in "new blood" from time to time. Doing so not only avoids some of the dangers of inflexibility but also can help in providing a degree of continuity among the membership.

Geographical Balance. Companies with widespread operations often believe it advisable to have on a board a balance of members from various geographical areas. The idea is that individuals from various sections of the nation or various countries will have an appreciation and understanding of the customs and attitudes of the people—employees and customers—with which the companies deal.

This tendency for geographical balance has been particularly noteworthy in such companies as transportation and insurance companies. Serving as they do a geographically wide public and being particularly sensitive to public opinion, not only from customer and employee viewpoints but perhaps more particularly from political and regulatory viewpoints, the typical boards of these companies tend to be manned by prominent citizens from various segments of the country. For example, a prominent Western railroad includes on its board industrialists and bankers from Chicago and New York, a publisher from Los Angeles, a prominent citizen from San Francisco, an oil man and a rancher from the Midwest.

Where the company's operations are sensitive to various geographic interests, such balance is probably desirable. Even though communications and transportation have shrunk the world, no one can deny the significance of regional differences.

Balance and Special Interests. In seeking balance in a board of directors, care must be taken to avoid building a board from a conglomerate of special interests. No board member should regard himself as a representative of a special interest. Instead, he must see his task as that of representing the stockholders as a whole.

Nevertheless, no board member can forget that his company lives in a community of investors, employees, customers, and the general public. To meet the best long-run interests of stockholders themselves, a company must be responsive to the society in which it operates. This is true business responsibility and consistent with the selfish interest of stockholders in long-run profitable growth. It is up to the board to see that this kind of attunement to the community is reflected in its search for profits. But to make certain, perhaps the balanced board will take special care to assure that there is a balance between their paramount responsibility for representing the stockholders and the requirements of the external environment.

INCREASING THE SUPPLY OF DIRECTORS

Although the author believes that enough qualified persons are potentially available to fill the need for effective directors, much can be done to make this supply evident and accessible.

Operate Boards Efficiently. At the top of the action list is the obvious desirability of efficiently utilizing the talent now available. This means, in turn, operating the board efficiently and effectively. Many are the directors who have left board meetings with a feeling that they have wasted their time. Many are the individuals who have hesitated to accept board assignments because of their fears, often well founded, that these duties would involve a waste of time, a resource which any knowledgeable and ambitious person holds dear. Likewise, there are many persons who have felt compelled to resign from boards whose operations were carried on inefficiently.

Recognize that a Wider Supply Exists. Basic also to increasing the supply of directors is to recognize that a wide supply of directorial talent does, in fact, exist. There are many persons of exceptional competence, wide experience, interest, and ability to give effective board service, who are not among the "big names" so regularly sought. These include not only operating executives and retired officers with five to ten years of intelligent board service still left to them, but also a number of second-level executives, public and military officers, professional men, owners of small and medium-sized businesses, foundation or association executives, and university professors, many of whom have considerable knowledge and experience in business or public life.

The potential supply of directors is far greater than most corporate officials believe, but steps must be taken to uncover it.

Use Organized Recruitment. A company faced with a need for outside executive talent generally knows exactly what to do. It may use any one of a number of the excellent executive recruitment agencies available. It may canvass its key employees for suggestions. Its executives may suggest the names of individuals with whom they have had some association either in business, in some trade association, or in a seminar or meeting of a management group. They often utilize the services of newspaper or selected journals for advertising the opening.

In essence, a director's position is no different from any other top-executive position. If the above techniques work in executive recruitment, one may ask why they should not be used for recruitment of directors. The answer is that they obviously can and that, if more companies followed an aggressive program of recruitment, more persons with good potential for directors service would let their availability be known and more recruitment firms would begin to specialize in this area. Moreover, even the superficially unthinkable approach of newspaper advertisement has been known to work. One consultant tells of actual experience in placing a "blind" advertisement for a corporate director in *The Wall Street Journal*.[12] Out of fifty-five replies received, thirteen appeared to be "good possibilities"; ten of these had had previous experience as directors, and seven were prominent enough to be listed in *Who's Who in America.*

Encourage Key Executives to Serve Other Boards. One important way of increasing the supply of directors is for companies themselves to encourage their key executives to make themselves available for one or two outside directorships. While chief executives often do serve on outside boards, apparently feeling that this adds significantly to their prestige and experience and also is an obligation which they owe the business community, a relatively smaller

[12] J. M. Juran and J. K. Louden, *The Corporate Director*, American Management Association, New York, 1966, p. 205.

number of subordinate executives appears to be available for board service.

This tendency is probably due to a number of factors. In the first place, a company almost always tends to set its sights on obtaining the top man of a company to serve on its board, often overlooking the fact that this chief executive is so committed to various company and outside activities that he cannot give much time to the company if he will serve at all. In the second place, many companies have shown a reluctance to have a key executive serve on other boards, thinking that this may dilute the time and effort they spend on their primary job. Furthermore, unquestionably many key executives, even where their company permits outside board memberships, may hesitate to accept a board post for fear of causing concern or displeasure to their employers.

In a study of 374 manufacturing, retailing, transportation, and utility firms by the National Industrial Conference Board,[13] it was found that nine out of ten companies permitted their executives to serve on the boards of directors of other business companies. The usual motives cited were the desire to develop executives through exposure to the problems of other companies, the opportunity to become better known in the business community, and the public-relations value of having officials serving on the board of successful local and nationally-known companies. These companies tend to withhold permission in particular cases where the board membership involves a possible conflict of interests, where the time commitment might be excessive, or where the board membership would not expose the executive to experience of value in his own job.

Although a very high percentage of companies *permit* executives to serve on the boards of other companies, as indicated by the survey, only 17 percent of the companies both permitted and encouraged it, while 45 percent permitted it but neither encouraged nor discouraged it and 24 percent permitted but definitely did not encourage outside board memberships. When one looks at these

[13] L. Laporte and G. C. Thompson, "Outside Directorships for Key Executives? More Than Nine Companies in Ten Say 'Yes,'" *The Conference Board Record*, Vol. II, No. 10, October, 1965.

data, the observation that more than nine-tenths of the companies surveyed stated they permit the practice is misleading. Perhaps it would be more accurate to conclude that only the one company in six that both permits and encourages outside board service truly "permits" it.

The apparent lack of interest by companies in encouraging their key top executives to accept a minimal amount of outside board membership, while understandable in the light of the self-interest of the company involved, is nonetheless discouraging and open to question. If proper conflict of interest, time, and type-of-company limitations are placed on executives, and if these are checked by requiring approval from the chief executive or the chairman of the board, much might be gained by both allowing and encouraging chief executives to serve on other company boards. The advantage of knowledge and experience to the executive involved is obvious. But equally important, even though not as obvious, is the contribution a company can make towards preservation of private enterprise through helping increase the effectiveness of boards of directors.

Recognize Questions of New Board Recruits. A company also might increase its supply of directors by recognizing another fact. A few companies are so prominent and well recognized as being effectively managed that almost anyone would be honored to accept a directorship and would make time in his schedule for giving the necessary service. However, in most cases an attractive candidate approached for a directorship is more than likely to have a number of questions. The intelligent company will not only recognize these questions but be prepared to deal with them, preferably before they are even raised.

The questions likely to be in an individual's mind before accepting a directorship might include the following: What kind of a company is it and what is its record and reputation for ethical dealing, intelligent operations, growth, aggressiveness, profitability, and good management? Who are the top executives and the other board members? What are their reputations, backgrounds and experience, personalities, interests in the company, and goals for the company's future? Are the executives and the other board members the type of persons with whom I can work and would enjoy working? How do they operate the board? Does it make significant decisions? Is the line between the province of the board and operating management clear? Does it have an effective chairman? Does it operate only as an audience or an advisor to the chief executive, or does it operate in a way to meet board responsibilities? Does it distribute an agenda in advance? Does it keep the board informed? Are proposals presented clearly?

Can I contribute something worthwhile as a board member? Do the activities of the company in any way conflict with my present commitments and duties? Can I, and am I, willing to spend the time to be an effective board member by attending meetings regularly, doing my homework, becoming fairly familiar with the company and its problems, and being reasonably available for special meetings? Why should I join? What do I expect to get out of the board membership and does it make sense to me that I should serve? Can I act independently and responsibly? Will favors be expected of me beyond conscientious and independent service?

As can be seen from this sample of questions, the intelligent and experienced individual is almost sure to wish to know a great deal about the company and his directorial and executive associates before going on a board. And he should raise these questions and insist on suitable answers. A board member's responsibility is such that he can hardly afford to accept membership without doing so.

INCREASING THE QUALITY OF DIRECTORS

One way of effectively increasing the supply of directors is to improve their quality. Enough has been said in this book to indicate that qualifications for directorships are considerable in terms of intelligence, experience, ability to conceptualize problems and come to well-designed answers, independence and courage, and high ethical standards. Enough has also been said to emphasize the point that, to have an effective board, directors should be carefully selected. But more than this is needed to assure a high quality of directors.

Need for Specialized Director Training. As has been mentioned before, the tremendous interest in management which has swept the world has led to considerable emphasis on advanced management training in order to assure that operating managers understand the nature of their task, appreciate the rapidly developing scientific knowledge underlying managing, and know how to apply the latest management techniques. It is all the more curious that there has been so little emphasis on special training for directors. A few seminars have been given by such organizations as the American Management Association, but even these have been aimed primarily at company executives—not at directors *per se,* and almost certainly not at outside directors. Moreover, few executive development programs give any time to the role of boards of directors, their proper composition, their operation, and other matters designed to teach more effective board performance.

For more than five years the author has been giving special seminars in Australia to company directors, with emphasis on outside directors, who play a significant role in many companies there. It is interesting that the idea that directors have a primary and significant role in the entire management of the company strikes many as novel. Also, emphasis on effective board operation and such things as what a board can do to improve company management and assist the chief executive seem to come as new concepts to most board members. When one considers that the individuals who come to these seminars are probably among those who least need the instruction, it is hard to avoid the conclusion that directors need management training of a general kind in order to keep up with the developments in management, and of a special kind in order to operate more efficiently and effectively as a board.

To be sure, Australia is not America, but the author's dealings with top management groups all over the world have convinced him that the United States has no corner on management quality or on management problems of significance and complexity. Accordingly, it is the author's opinion that specialized director training is long overdue.

Review of Board Performance. All effective top managers are accustomed to reviewing performance of their companies, their divisions and departments, and their subordinates. There is much to be said for carrying the technique of review to occasional review of board performance.

In a recent book, this point was emphasized.[14] It has been suggested that appraisal of board performance be systematically and regularly undertaken, that it be made someone's job to do this, and that time be reserved on the board agenda for at least an annual review of performance. It was suggested that this review might be conducted by a director, the chief executive officer, the board "agent" (secretary of the company or other administrative assistant charged with looking after the administrative matters concerning the board), by various committees of the board, by individual directors, by a special committee created for the purpose, or by inviting a "professional director" to observe the meetings and give his views on their operations.

This is a suggestion worth consideration by any board of directors. Even an inadequate review is better than none and any review is likely to disclose previously unrecognized areas of weakness. But for the best kind of review, some individual knowledgeable in board operation and independent of the board and executives is needed. The idea of having a "professional director" undertake this task is especially worthy, providing such a person spends enough time observing the board to see its normal operation. Also, there are unquestionably business and management consultants with experience in management and ability to analyze operations who could handle this task.

AFFORDING AN EFFECTIVE BOARD

Apart from compensation to officer-directors, who are presumably being already paid for their full-time service to a company, the amount of a company's resources spent for a board of directors is negligible. Rarely does a company spend as much on the fees, re-

[14] J. M. Juran and J. K. Louden, *op. cit.*, pp. 315–318.

tainers, and board expenses of all its outside members put together as it does for a single key executive. Perhaps this has some relevance to the status with which boards are held in many American business corporations.

But it is said that board members do not serve for financial compensation. Instead, they serve because they have a prominent share interest in the company, they like the glory of board membership, they enjoy association with other business executives, they can obtain wider business experience of benefit to them in their own positions, they enjoy the challenge of problem-solving at the top level, they feel an obligation to society and the enterprise system, or they believe that they or their own business may gain through company association or privileged information.

To be sure, these are strong inducements and they may be enough. But a company cannot overlook both the real and status symbol inducements involved in adequate compensation, whether by fee, retainer, or fringe benefits. That this has not been totally overlooked is apparent from the rise, slow as it may be and starting from the low base of the traditional $10 gold piece, of directors' compensation in recent years.

However, directors' compensation should be materially higher, and more companies should not only pay retainers but larger ones *if* they expect effective service from their board members. To achieve an effective board of directors will require more of a commitment from outside directors. It may even require an increase of full-time directors who give their entire time to the job of directing. In any case, even if the board compensation is substantially increased from the present level and even if many more companies find full-time directors desirable, the cost would not be high. Assuming a truly effective board meeting its responsibilities intelligently, conscientiously, and successfully, these costs would represent money well spent. The question might be raised in the reverse. Who *cannot* afford to have an effective board?

The point is sometimes made that many directors from various business firms are already so highly paid that increased compensation would have no meaning. But not all persons who would make able directors are in this class. The professional man, for example, has usually only one thing to sell—his time—and time taken for board meetings or other work required might have a high opportunity cost for him. Or a retired executive or a public official might find compensation a strong inducement.

Nor should a company overlook fringes. The author has known several companies that provide directors with company-paid life insurance equivalent to that given to top operating executives. This compensation, which can be made tax-free, operates as a strong inducement with benefits to companies far more than its cost.

One prominent management consultant who has studied boards put it well when he said: "As for that other old lament that it isn't possible to compensate a successful executive adequately for board service, I wonder if it really bears close examination. Why not use the same ingenuity that we apply to other recruiting and compensation problems? Is there any rule that says all board members must receive the same stipend? Each man we approach has a different fiscal and tax situation, so why not tailor our proposition to suit his particular requirements? In any event, financial compensation is only one of the many motivating forces that make board membership interesting and stimulating. If we really *want* to, we can certainly combine our carrots in such a way as to attract an effective team. And, instead of admitting defeat before we start, we might bear in mind that success in obtaining one good member often starts a snow-balling action and makes it easier to bring in others." [15]

THE SMALL COMPANY BOARD

Small companies have a way of thinking that their problems are unique and that what is required for effective management applies to larger companies but not to them. The grain of truth in this is a small one. Management principles apply to small as well as larger

[15] E. E. Smith, "Management's Least-used Asset: The Board of Directors," in *The Dynamics of Management*, American Management Association, New York, 1958, p. 58.

companies. Good management techniques, properly tailored to the small company just as they must be tailored for different large companies, are useful and applicable to the smaller company.

What has been said in this book about developing and maintaining the effective board applies in its fundamentals to small companies as well as large ones. It is true that some of the *applications* are different. The small company usually has all of the problems of the large company, except perhaps those caused by size and executive distance through longer organizational lines of communication. But the smaller company seldom has the executives, staff, and other resources which the large company has to deal with its problems.

This is exactly where the board differs. As pointed out in discussing board functions in decision and control areas, a small company board is likely to get deeper into management problems. It is also likely to be concerned more with advising the chief executive and the company officers in a wide variety of matters, advice and problems for which the larger company would have executive and staff personnel to handle. The small company board is likely also to be forced to take a more prominent role in company planning, executive selection, policy interpretation as well as formulation, and personnel problems.[16]

But perhaps the major problem in the smaller company is the fact that it is usually dominated by the founder-owner or a direct descendant. These men are often accustomed to running the business to suit themselves. It is understandable that a founder who has started out in a garage and clawed his way to success in the rough terrain of competition should feel that way. However, until the owner realizes that he and his company can benefit from an effective board and that he must keep board members as independent participants on the team, he cannot and will not have such a board. It is up to him. The basic requirements for board effectiveness apply as much to him and to his company as to the large publicly owned company.

[16] Still the best analysis of the small-company board of directors is the book by M. L. Mace, *The Board of Directors in Small Corporations*, Harvard Graduate School of Business Administration, Boston, 1948.

TOWARD AN EFFECTIVE BOARD

The essential requirements for an effective board are clear. That putting them into practice is difficult one cannot deny. But many companies, large and small, have done it. The main essential is that those who control the company must *want* to have such a board. Even though it may take time, particularly if a board has fallen into slovenly, irresponsible, or ineffectual ways, it can be done. And in a surprising number of instances, the changeover has come more rapidly than had been thought possible. Ordinarily, there is talent on even an ineffectual board. If challenged by doing what a board should, this talent will often rise rather quickly to the opportunities for contribution thus provided. In addition, when it is understood what a board should do and how it should do it, it becomes clear what kind of directors are needed as board vacancies occur.

Most of the requirements for an effective board add up to the need for establishing an environment for performance. These include clarification of fundamental responsibilities and duties and knowing what a board is expected to accomplish. This, in turn, demands that the role of the board in terms of decision areas be spelled out logically and understandably. No one can properly fill a role unless it is clearly defined and understood. While writing out the authorities, responsibilities, and functions of a board does not assure clarification, it is certainly the surest technique known for doing so. Supplemented by teaching, interpretation, and practice, and aided by review for adequacy and by modification as needs change, clarification of the role of directors can be attained.

The effective board must also comprehend its place in the whole management structure of the corporation. This implies not only knowing the company, but knowing what management is and what managers do. In short, the effective director should be as well versed in management fundamentals as the operating executive.

To be an effective member of a board, an individual must also be aware of the problems, weaknesses, and strengths of the plural executive. And the chairman must be selected for one primary reason

—that he will make a good chairman. For on him, as in any committee, much of the efficiency of group operation depends.

Also, steps must be taken to permit directors to act like directors. This requires not only intelligence, experience, and problem-solving ability, but the independence of position which allows these attributes to be effectively employed. It also demands that a group be used where it has its main strengths—deliberation, stimulation through interchange, bringing to bear different points of view, and probing into the dark corners of problems. These strengths can be utilized efficiently only if agenda are logical, proposals well-researched and presented, and information provided which truly informs—all points which have been repeatedly emphasized in this book.

Furthermore, the board must operate efficiently. Time is a scarce commodity. Board responsibilities are complex, varied, and important. Every director must be willing to spend the time necessary to be informed, analyze company problems falling within the province of the board, aid the chief executive in successfully operating the company, and assume some leadership for the company's performance and plans. But in spending the necessary time, steps should be taken to see that time is not spent unnecessarily.

Finally, no board member can forget that his is the responsibility to do those things at the very top of the corporation which create and maintain an environment for performance of the entire management and personnel of the company. Where a company goes, how it gets there, and whether it is doing the best possible job to utilize its human and material resources in the best long-run interest of the stockholders can be traced to this fundamental responsibility of every board member. That it is a difficult task may be readily admitted. That it is a worthwhile challenge there can be no doubt. But in serving a company well, the effective director is serving well not only those he represents—the shareholders—but society as well.

BIBLIOGRAPHY

Baker, J. C., *Directors and Their Functions*, Harvard University Graduate School of Business Administration, Boston, 1945.

Bienvenu, Bernard J., "Boards of Directors Revisited," *Business Horizons*, Vol. 5, pp. 41–50, Fall, 1962.

Brooker, R. E., "Working Together at the Top," in *Ends and Means of Modern Management*, AMA Management Report No. 30, American Management Association, New York, 1959.

Brown, C. C., and E. E. Smith, *The Director Looks at His Job*, Columbia University Press, New York, 1957.

Chamberlain, J., "Why It's Harder and Harder to Get a Good Board," *Fortune*, Vol. 66, pp. 108–113, November, 1962.

Charlton, J. M., "Directors: The Duty to Manage," *Mississippi Valley Journal of Business and Economics*, Vol. 1, No. 2, pp. 36–51, Spring, 1966.

"Company Presidents Size-up the Board: Presidents' Panel Report I," *Dun's Review and Modern Industry*, pp. 40–42, November, 1958.

"Company Presidents Size-up the Board: Presidents' Panel Report II," *Dun's Review and Modern Industry*, pp. 38–39, December, 1958.

Copeland, M. T., and A. R. Towl, *The Board of Directors and Business Management*, Harvard University Graduate School of Business Administration, Boston, 1947.

Dickson, P. W., *Compensation and Duties of Corporate Directors*, Studies in Business Policy No. 16, National Industrial Conference Board, Inc., New York, 1946.

Directors and Officers Encyclopedic Manual, Prentice-Hall, Inc., Englewood Cliffs, N.J., 1955.

"Directors' Compensation and Retirements with Table by Industry," *Conference Board Business Record*, Vol. 17, pp. 15–18 and 34–41, April, 1960.

Dolgins, Judith, "Big Change in the Boardroom," *Dun's Review and Modern Industry*, Vol. 80, pp. 51 ff, October, 1962.

Douglas, W. O., "Directors Who Do Not Direct," *Harvard Law Review*, Vol. 47, pp. 1305–1334, June, 1934.

Feuer, Mortimer, *Handbook for Corporate Directors*, Prentice-Hall, Inc., Englewood Cliffs, N.J., 1965.

Feuer, Mortimer, *Personal Liabilities of Corporate Officers and Directors*, Prentice-Hall, Inc., Englewood Cliffs, N.J., 1961.

Gordon, R. A., *Business Leadership in the Large Corporation*, Brookings Institution, Washington, D.C., 1945.

Grange, W. J., and T. C. Woodbury, *Corporation Law: Operating Procedures for Officers and Directors*, 2d ed., The Ronald Press Company, New York, 1964.

Interlocks in Corporate Management, Staff Report to the Anti-trust Subcommittee of the Committee on the Judiciary, House of Representatives, U.S. Government Printing Office, Washington, 1965.

Juran, J. M., and J. K. Louden, *The Corporate Director*, American Management Association, Inc., New York, 1966.

Kinley, J. R., *Corporate Directorship Practices*, Studies in Business Policy No. 103, National Industrial Conference Board, Inc., New York, 1962.

Kinley, J. R., and G. C. Thompson, "Board Chairman: Position and Duties," *Management Record*, Vol. 24, pp. 7–13, December, 1962.

Kinley, J. R., and G. C. Thompson, "Tenure and Retirement of Directors," *Conference Board Business Record*, Vol. 18, pp. 30–35, May, 1961.

Laporte, L., and G. C. Thompson, "Outside Directorships for Key Executives? More Than Nine Companies in Ten Say 'Yes,'" *Conference Board Record*, Vol. 2, pp. 7–13, October, 1965.

Mace, M. L., *The Board of Directors in Small Companies*, Division of Research, Graduate School of Business Administration, Harvard University, Boston, 1948.

Martindell, Jackson, *The Appraisal of Management*, Harper & Row, New York, 1962.

National Industrial Conference Board, *Corporate Directorship Practices*, Studies in Business Policy No. 90, National Industrial Conference Board, Inc., New York, 1959.

National Industrial Conference Board, *Prevailing Practices Regarding Corporate Directors*, Studies in Administrative Control No. 2, National Industrial Conference Board, Inc., New York, 1939.

Smith, E. E., "Management's Least-used Asset: The Board of Directors," in *The Dynamics of Management*, AMA Management Report No. 14, American Management Association, New York, 1958, pp. 49–60.

Stieglitz, H., and A. Tanger, "When the Chairman Is Chief Executive," *Conference Board Business Management Record*, pp. 7–11, August, 1963.

"The President Looks at His Job," *Management Record*, pp. 7–9, May, 1962.

Thompson, G. C., and F. J. Walsh, Jr., "Keeping Outside Directors Informed," *Conference Board Business Record*, Vol. 18, pp. 29–33, March, 1961.

Thompson, G. C., and F. J. Walsh, Jr., "Directors' Compensation, Fringe Benefits and Retirement: With Tables by Industry," *Conference Board Record*, Vol. 2, pp. 13–24, February, 1965.

Thompson, G. C., and F. J. Walsh, Jr., "Selection of Corporate Directors," *Conference Board Record*, Vol. 2, pp. 8–16, May, 1965.

Towl, A. R., "Outside Directors Under Attack in Form of Proposed Legislation Against Interlocks in Corporate Management," *Harvard Business Review*, Vol. 43, pp. 135–147, September, 1965.

Vance, Stanley C., *Boards of Directors: Structure and Performance*, University of Oregon Press, Eugene, Oregon, 1964.

Watson, J. H., III, *The Corporate Directorship*, Studies in Business Policy No. 63, National Industrial Conference Board, Inc., New York, 1953.

Williams, Lytle G., "The Professional Director: A Needful Member of the Executive Personnel of the Average Corporate Enterprise," *Boston University Business Review*, Vol. 10, pp. 25–38, Summer, 1963.

appendix

TYPICAL EXAMPLES OF POSITION DESCRIPTIONS FOR CHAIRMAN OF THE BOARD AND PRESIDENT*

Borg-Warner Corporation

CHAIRMAN OF THE BOARD AND CHIEF EXECUTIVE OFFICER

Purpose of the Position

To provide leadership to the Board in carrying out its collective responsibility for the management of the property, business, and affairs of the Corporation.

To focus over-all responsibility for the successful administration of the affairs of the Corporation in a single individual.

Duties and Responsibilities

A. Board Functions

As Chief Policy and Planning Officer of the Corporation, the duties and responsibilities of the Chairman of the Board and Chief Executive Officer extend to any and all activities in which the Corporation may engage. These include, but are not limited to, the following:

* Taken by permission from C. L. Bennet, *Defining the Manager's Job* (New York: American Management Association, 1958), pp. 193–200, 202–205, 209–211.

1. He will prepare the agenda for and convene and conduct regular and special meetings of the Board in accordance with corporate and statutory requirements.

2. He will preside at all meetings of the shareholders.

3. He will participate jointly with other members in carrying out the Board's directorial functions, including:

a. Election of officers of the Corporation, determination of their duties, authorities and compensation.

b. Appointment of trustees and agents for the Corporation.

c. Creation and issuance of negotiable or transferable instruments and securities.

d. Approval of the objectives, general policies, principles, practices, and the general organization plan of the Corporation.

e. Authorization of capital expenditures.

f. Authorization for acquisition or disposal of corporate assets.

g. Approval of loans, investments, and other plans to finance the Corporation's operations.

h. Declaration of dividends and establishment of reserves.

i. Establishment of the controls and regulations deemed necessary to protect properly the rights and interests of shareholders and creditors of the Corporation.

j. Control and supervision of the operations and financial affairs of the Corporation through approval of major plans, programs, budgets, and forecasts; review of periodic reports, financial and operating statements, and summary analyses of major operations in relation to authorized programs; and determination of remedial action as required.

k. Performance of all duties imposed by statutory requirements.

l. Revision of corporate By-Laws as may be desirable.

4. He will appoint all members of the committees of the Board of Directors, subject to approval by the Board.

5. He will serve as a member of the Executive Committee, and as ex officio member of all other Board committees.

6. He will present to the Board reports and recommendations from the other officers and committees.

7. He will present any proposed changes in major policies of the Corporation for Board action.

B. Corporate Operations

As Chief Executive Officer of the Corporation, the Chairman of the Board is responsible for all line and staff operations. In addition he will assume specific responsibility for the conduct, operations, and results of the following positions and functions which report directly to him:

The President.
Vice President and General Counsel.
Financial Vice President and Treasurer.
Secretary.
Director, Advertising.
Director, Public Relations.
Assistant to the Chairman, East Coast Representative—
Financial and Shareholder Relations.

1. Business Development

The Chairman will direct the growth program of the Corporation as it relates to the acquisition of new companies, new products, and patents, including participation in such activities as:

    a. Formulation of acquisition policies and plans, subject to approval of the Board.
    b. Evaluation of potentials.
    c. Recommendation of related financial measures required, for consideration by the Finance Committee.
    d. Recommendations to the Board.
    e. Negotiations and commitments, subject to Board approval.
    f. Approve plans proposed by the President and other executives for the integration and operation of acquired companies.

2. Finance

The Chairman will assume responsibility for the financial condition of the Corporation and take adequate measures to satisfy its fiscal needs; and conserve the assets entrusted to his charge.

    a. Insure that each division and department develops and

submits operating budgets and forecasts in keeping with policy requirements.

b. Review, and submit to the Board for approval, the annual consolidated operating budget and forecasts and the proposed capital expenditure program.

c. Establish and adhere to procedures governing the authorization of corporate expenditures.

3. Public Relations and Advertising

The Chairman will direct the public relations and institutional advertising programs of the Corporation, including participation in such activities as:

a. Formulation of public relations policies and plans, subject to approval of the Board when required.

b. The use of various advertising media.

c. Communications to shareholders, employees, industry, and the public.

d. Represent the Corporation in public relations matters.

4. The Chairman will assume over-all direction of the shareholder relations program of the Corporation and will coordinate the shareholder relations activities of the President, Executive Vice President, Vice President and General Counsel, Financial Vice President and Treasurer, Secretary, and East Coast Representative—Financial and Shareholder Relations.

Authority

Within the limits of sound business practice and the further limitations placed upon him by the Articles of Incorporation, the By-Laws of the Corporation, and the policies laid down by the Board of Directors, the Chairman of the Board and Chief Executive Officer will exercise final authority over all corporate policy matters. In addition, he is specifically delegated operating authority to conduct the affairs of the Corporation.

He may delegate to members of the Corporation as much of his authority as may be necessary to effectuate policy formulation and maintain a strong, effective organization without loss of essential control, but he may not delegate his over-all responsibility for results or any portion of his individual accountability.

Relations

The Chairman of the Board and Chief Executive Officer will establish and maintain the following relationships:

A. With the Shareholders of the Corporation

He will be accountable to the shareholders for the proper execution of the duties and responsibilities of the Board and the adequate protection of shareholder rights and interests.

In his capacity as Chief Public Relations Executive, the Chairman will assure that the shareholders are kept adequately informed of the affairs of the Corporation and that sound relationships, understanding, and communications are maintained between management and the owners of the Corporation.

B. With the Board of Directors

He will counsel collectively and individually with the members of the Board, utilizing their capacities to the fullest extent necessary to secure optimum benefits for the Corporation.

In conjunction with the President, the Chairman will keep the Board of Directors informed on the condition of the business and on all the important factors influencing it.

In conjunction with the President, he will review major activities and plans with the Board of Directors to insure that he and the President have the benefit of the Board's thinking and are acting in conformity with the Board's views on corporate policy.

He will refer promptly to the Board of Directors such matters as may require its decision.

C. With the Committees of the Board

As a member of the Executive Committee, the Chairman will participate jointly with the other members in its proceedings.

He will counsel with the Executive Committee, in the intervals between meetings of the Board, on all matters of interest to the

Committee, and will be guided by the decisions of the Committee in the absence of specific directions from the full Board.

He will act as an ex officio member of all Board committees.

D. With the President

The Chairman will advise and assist the President as may be required to assure that the orders and resolutions of the Board and directives of the Executive Committee are carried out.

He will review all important operating matters with the President.

He will keep the President fully informed, and counsel with him on those corporate functions which report directly to the Chairman.

In the event of the disability of the President, the Chairman of the Board will perform the duties of the President.

E. With Other Officers and Executives

The Chairman will coordinate his efforts with those of other officers and executives towards the goals of the Corporation; stand ready at all times to give advice and counsel to them; and call on them for such advice and counsel as he deems advisable.

F. With Corporate Committees

He will act as an ex officio member of all corporate committees and appoint such members of management to such committees as he deems advisable, except those appointments made by the Board.

G. With Persons Outside the Corporation

The Chairman will establish and maintain such outside relationships as he deems advisable in the interest of the Corporation, and will serve as Chief Public Relations Executive of the Corporation in his contacts with industry, other companies, business associations, the community, the government, the press, and the general public.

Standards for Measuring Performance

The Chairman of the Board and Chief Executive Officer is accountable for the fulfillment of the responsibilities, duties, and relationships described herein. The primary measurements of satisfactory performance are as follows:

A. The effectiveness with which the Board of Directors functions in making its optimum contribution to the welfare of the Corporation.
B. The soundness and adequacy of the objectives and policies recommended to the Board of Directors; the effectiveness with which the policies of the Board are executed; and the extent to which the approved objectives of the Corporation are realized.
C. The extent to which the assets of the Corporation have been conserved and strengthened; the soundness of the financial condition of the Corporation; and the extent to which its fiscal needs have been met.
D. The profit results of the Corporation as a whole and of the individual operating divisions.
E. The extent to which the character and quality of the products and services of the Corporation assure leadership position and further the reputation of the Corporation as a whole.
F. The soundness and success of the Corporation's growth program.
G. The extent to which the corporate public relations program achieves public understanding and support for the Corporation and its divisions, and the extent to which the policies and operations of the Corporation are identified with the public interest.
H. The quality, quantity, timeliness, and continuity of the guidance and support rendered to the President and others reporting directly to the Chairman.
I. The cordiality of relations which exist between the Chairman and other persons both within and without the Corporation.
J. The example of leadership, good management, high morale, personal conduct, and effective teamwork evidenced by the Chairman in his contacts with members of the Corporation and others.
K. The extent to which the Corporation carries out its customer, employee, shareholder, industry, government, and public responsibilities.

Koppers Company, Inc.

CHAIRMAN OF THE BOARD OF DIRECTORS

Basic Function

To preside at all meetings of the Board of Directors; to advise and counsel with the President and with other officers of the Company; and to perform such other duties as may be assigned to him by the President and the Board of Directors.

Scope

The duties and responsibilities of this position extend to all activities in which the Company may engage.

Duties and Responsibilities

1. To preside at meetings of stockholders and directors.
2. To participate jointly with other members in the broad direction of Company affairs, by reviewing and deciding upon matters which exert major influence on the manner in which the Company's business is conducted. Such matters include, but are not limited to:

   a. Establishment and revision of By-Laws.
   b. Election of officers of the Company.
   c. Approval of plans and programs.
   d. Authorization of capital expenditures.
   e. Authorization for disposal of assets.
   f. Approval of borrowing and other plans to finance Company operations.
   g. Declaration of dividends on the Company's stocks.
   h. Establishment of whatever controls and regulations may be deemed necessary to proper protection of the rights and interests of stockholders and creditors of the Company.

i. General supervision of the conduct of the Company's business.

3. To advise and counsel with the President and other officers of the Company on major and difficult problems.

4. To establish and maintain good relationships with governmental units, major stockholders, technical and business associations, and with the public and industry in general.

5. To handle major financial, corporate, and legal matters at the request of the President or Board of Directors.

6. To carry out special assignments as may be requested by the President or Board of Directors.

7. To handle special requests for information from directors of the Company.

8. To generally supervise the activities of the Pension Committee and the Retirement Board.

9. To develop broad basic policies for consideration by the Board of Directors.

10. To evaluate, and recommend to the Board of Directors, policies with respect to executive compensation and employee pension and benefit plans.

Organizational Relationships

1. The Chairman, jointly with other members of the Board of Directors, is responsible to his electors, who are the stockholders of the Company, for the proper discharge of the duties and responsibilities of this position.

Limits of Authority

Through consideration and decision on matters of Company policies, programs, and expenditures, and through election of Company officers, each member of the Board of Directors, in conjunction with each other member, exercises full authority over all aspects of Company operations. The specific authorities of this position are covered in the Certificate of Incorporation and in Company By-Laws.

American Enka Corporation

PRESIDENT

I. Major Function

1. The President is the Chief Executive and Administrative Officer of the Company. He is responsible for the proper management of all aspects of the Company's activities so as to insure, over a long term of operations, realization of maximum profits compatible with the best interests of employees, consumers, and stockholders, and to assure the security and growth of invested capital.

2. He is a member of the Board of Directors and the Executive Committee, and in this capacity he participates with the other directors in the responsibility for establishing basic Company policies.

3. It is the President's function to utilize to the maximum degree the Company's material and human resources in administering and carrying out the major policies adopted by the Board of Directors.

4. The President is responsible for the development and maintenance of a competent and adequate organization with respect to both its structure and its personnel. He is responsible for the training and guidance of the members of the organization and for coordinating their activities.

5. He is responsible for acquiring the personnel and developing the methods to insure a thorough, objective, and continuing appraisal of management's effectiveness.

6. He is responsible for conducting himself in such a manner, and encouraging others to do likewise, as will reflect credit on the American Enka Corporation and on the American system of free enterprise.

7. As the Chief Executive and Administrative Officer, the President's performance is measured in terms of accomplishments related to predetermined objectives.

II. Specific Responsibilities and Authority

1. Guides and assists the Board of Directors in the development and formulation of Company policy on both long- and short-term

programs; and presents proposals supported by complete factual information and data.

2. Interprets and administers policies established by the Board of Directors for all the Company's activities.

3. Assumes responsibility for the planning and approval of all long- and short-term programs of all activities in every sphere of the Company's management and operations.

4. May, in order to carry out his functions properly, secure the services of outside agencies or consultants to examine, audit, investigate, or facilitate change in administration, operations, procedures, and methods.

5. Assumes responsibility for the development and/or the approval of performance objectives and measurements of progress.

6. Assumes responsibility for the general supervision and coordination of Company's operations.

7. Approves all budgets, appropriations, reports, and studies designed for transmission to the Board of Directors.

8. Assumes responsibility for the general administration and supervision of employee, customer, stockholder, government, and public relations.

9. Assumes responsibility for inter-corporate relations on all proper matters within the rayon industry.

10. Assumes responsibility for the improvement, development, and maintenance of balanced organization structure and executive personnel.

11. Assumes responsibility for the selection, training, upgrading, and development of executive personnel.

12. Assumes responsibility for the development of improved technical facilities and processes.

13. Assumes responsibility for the introduction and installation of tried and tested principles and techniques of scientific management in all fields of the Company's activities.

14. Assumes responsibility for the general supervision of the activities of all management committees.

15. Assumes the responsibility for the maintenance of a high level of executive and employee morale.

16. Assumes the responsibility for developing, maintaining, and disseminating throughout the Company a basic corporate philosophy designed to insure—on the part of executives and employees alike —the maximum degree of personal satisfaction in the performance of their assigned tasks.

17. Delegates certain of his responsibilities and duties, and reassigns functions and authorities whenever he considers it necessary or desirable; but cannot divest himself of the responsibility for the over-all results.

18. Authorizes expenditures in excess of $5,000 and not exceeding $50,000 with respect to items applicable to the New York, Providence, and Greensboro sales offices or office furniture and equipment at the Enka and Lowland plants.

19. Authorizes expenditures in excess of $10,000 and not exceeding $50,000 with respect to items applicable to the Enka and Lowland plants.

20. Signs checks with other officials in the Corporation, regardless of amount.

21. Authorizes the creation of a new salaried position for the filling of a new or vacant position from outside sources for the Administrative Engineering Department and the Business Analysis and Market Research Department.

22. Authorizes travel of staff department personnel under his immediate supervision.

III. Relationships

1. The President is elected by and is responsible to the Board of Directors and, between meetings of the Board, to the Executive Committee.

2. The Vice President, Treasurer and General Counsel, the Technical Vice President, the Vice President in charge of Sales, the Manager, Administrative Engineering Department, and the Manager, Business Analysis and Market Research Department are responsible to the President.

Koppers Company, Inc.

PRESIDENT

Basic Function

General and active management of the Company's business. General supervision of the manner in which Company business is conducted, and responsibility for carrying out all orders and resolutions of the Board of Directors. As principal executive officer, represents the Company to the general public, other industry, and all fields in which the Company operates.

Scope

The duties and responsibilities of this position extend to all activities in which the Company may engage.

Duties and Responsibilities

1. To direct and generally supervise all Company activities, including but not limited to the development, production, promotion, and sale of its products and services.

2. To be responsible to the Board of Directors for the profitable operation of the Company, a reasonable return to investors, and the safety of the capital funds invested in Company enterprise.

3. To prepare objectives for the Company's future, and to recommend their adoption to the Board of Directors.

4. To prepare plans and programs for the attainment of approved objectives, including proposed expansion into new fields of activity; severance of unprofitable operations; and planned courses of action

for times of economic crisis. To recommend such plans and programs to the Board of Directors.

5. To develop and administer Company policies governing the manner in which its business will be conducted, within the broad framework of policy which may be selected by the Board of Directors.

6. To develop and adopt a sound general organization plan which will insure adequate coverage of all functions. To select and appoint immediate subordinates, and to delegate to each the responsibility and authority for performance of his assigned functions.

7. To supervise all immediate subordinates in their performance of assigned functions and in the manner in which their individual objectives and programs are being pursued. To render advice, assistance, and guidance to subordinates.

8. To coordinate the activities of all units of the organization. In particular, to insure that the operating units receive adequate functional advice, assistance, and service from staff units organized for that purpose.

9. To insure that adequate organization plans, procedures, and controls are employed by all units, to make possible the proper execution of their duties and attainment of their goals.

10. To report the progress of the Company and its components to the Board of Directors, including its performance against programs and objectives for sales, profits, investment, and growth.

11. To promote the reputation of the Company among its investors, employees, and the general public; and to insure that proper and fair courses of employee and public relations are followed at all times.

12. To take action to correct unsatisfactory conditions that may arise in any phase of operations; and to order or direct whatever action may be deemed necessary to accomplish approved objectives.

13. To preside at meetings of the Board of Directors or its Executive Committee in the absence of the Chairman.

14. To refer to the Board of Directors all matters of major importance to the Company's progress and well-being, for purposes of securing advice, guidance, authorization, and/or decision.

Method of Measurement

The measurements of successful performance of the duties and responsibilities of this position will be the operating profits earned (both in dollars and as a percentage of investment); the net earnings to common stock; the relation of these factors to objectives and programs; and the general stature of the Company among the public, competitive enterprises, and other industry.

Organizational Relationships

1. The President is responsible to the Board of Directors for the proper performance of these duties and responsibilities.
2. The following positions are responsible to the President for the performance of the duties and responsibilities of each:

A. *Staff*

Assistants to the President.
Manager, Control Section.
Manager, Washington Office.
Manager, Finance Department.
Manager, Law Department.
Director of Research & Development.
Manager, Marketing Department.
Manager, Production Department.
Manager, Industrial Relations Department.
Manager, Traffic & Transportation Department.
Manager, Procurement Department.

B. *Line*

Executive Vice President.
Regional Representatives.
General Manager, Engineering & Construction Division.
General Manager, Gas & Coke Division.
General Manager, Tar Products Division.
General Manager, Wood Preserving Division.
General Manager, Chemical Division.

General Manager, Metal Products Division.
General Manager, International Division.

3. As member and Chairman of the Operating Committee, the President is responsible for conducting meetings of the committee, and for participating in the review and discussion of such matters as may be presented to the committee.

INDEX

Acquisitions, 30–31, 76–77
Agenda, importance of, 55, 159
Agents of company, board selection of, 75
  liability of, 91–92
Approval authorization chart, 44–49
Assets, disposition of, 29–30
Audit committee, 178–179
Auditors, board selection of, 73–74
  reporting relationship of, 74, 179
Authority, board, 20–21, 44–45
  charter limitations on, 20–21, 86–87
  legal limitations on, 20
    (See also Liability, director)
  scope of, 20–21, 41–43, 45–53
  corporation, legal limitations on, 20
  defining areas of, 55
  executive, 41–45
    (See also Decision areas)

Barnard, Chester I., 27
Board, advisory role of, 42–43
  areas of review, 163–169
  authority of (see Authority, board)
  balanced representation on, 133–134, 230–236
  and chief executive officer, 201–202, 215–217, 227–228

Board, control reports to, 163–169
  criticisms of, 220–222
  effective operation of, 10–11, 55–56, 219–220, 229–230, 246–247
  functions of, 24–31, 33–44, 162–163
    (See also Decision areas, board)
  inside (see Inside board)
  legal role of, 19
  and management appraisal, 214
  and management control, 162–163
  and management process, 10–11
  outside (see Outside board)
  performance appraisal of, 241–242
  responsibilities of, 10–11, 24–31, 33–44, 81–83, 225–226, 247
    (See also Decision areas, board)
  size of, 55–56, 114–122
    and committees, 121–122
    and frequency of meetings, 155–156
    ideal, 55, 119–121
    and stockholder approval, 76
  small company (see Small company board)
  social responsibilities of, 16–17, 224

269